RACISM

Unraveling
The
Fear

Nathan Rutstein

Design by Beth Hinshaw

ISBN: 0-9659945-0-3

Table of Contents

OTHER BOOKS BY THE SAME AUTHOR

"Go Watch TV"
What and How Much Should Children Watch?

He Loved and Served

Spirit in Action

To A Seeker

Corrine True

To Be One:
A Battle Against Racism

Winning Spiritual Battles

Education on Trial

The Invisible Hand

Healing Racism in America:
A Prescription for the Disease

A Way Out of The Trap
An Innovative & Unique Ten-Step Program for Spiritual Growth

Healing Racism:
Education's Role

Acknowledgments

In writing this book I not only needed to satisfy every deep seated concern jabbing at my conscience, I needed help from allies, friends and enlightened race relations field workers.

Bernard Streets' continuous encouragement and support through his genuine willingness to share with me rich historical and sociological sources, was extremely helpful. The long and deep conversations with David DuBois provided me with insights I would have never been able to generate by myself. The keen evaluation of content and structure by Patricia Locke, Elizabeth Knap, Paul Robbins, Kathleen Anderson, Larry Bucknell, Judy Kirmmse—helped considerably.

I'm indebted to my son Tod Rutstein for showing me the way to discuss potentially volatile subjects pertaining to race in a humane manner while maintaining a passionate commitment to overcoming racism.

Elena Mustacova-Possardt's copy editing is deeply appreciated. And I'm extremely grateful to Beth Hinshaw, who not only used her editor's pen wisely, but who designed the book's cover.

Finally, to all those who have labored tirelessly and unselfishly in the scores of *Institutes for the Healing of Racism* in North America and Britain, I want to express my gratitude to you. You have demonstrated to me that there are people in this world who can make a positive difference in the struggle to eliminate racism and unify the human family.

Nathan Rutstein

Preface

This book is a meditation on racism. Certainly not a topic on which people seeking peace of mind would want to meditate. But I have chosen to do just that. For years I have been troubled as to why racism persists in America despite all of the institutional attempts in the past 40 years to wipe it out.

My meditation focuses, in part, on why these attempts have failed. As I analyze what seem to be the reasons for failure, some readers may be challenged by assertions I make. Others may recognize their own hunches which they may have been afraid to share publicly for fear of being branded as troublemakers.

As a consequence, in this book I share views on how racism affects us, our community and our country, most of which, I believe, aren't found in other books. They are personal impressions of racism, thoughts and feelings shaped by lifelong observations that have grown more penetrating in the past eight years, during which time I worked with others on issues of racial unity in North America. During this period I have pondered these observations, which in time, have bloomed into convictions.

One such conviction is my observations on the nature of racism. Racism is more than a prejudice; it is a prejudice that has over the years evolved into an obsession, a **psychological disorder** that affects the perpetrator as well as the intended target, both consciously and unconsciously. And because racism isn't treated as such, even the most powerful institutions have been unable to eliminate it.

While most of this book is devoted to the black-white conflict, it should not be construed as a slight to the other traditional targets of racism in America. What they have endured and still endure troubles me and should trouble every other American. While I have made an attempt to address the plight of the American Indians, Hispanics and Asian Americans, I know that much more needs to be said. But most of my experience in the race relations field has been with African-Americans and whites.

Despite what I have observed over the years, I remain an optimist. I have witnessed and taken part in grassroots movements that are breaking down racial barriers and uniting people who have traditionally distrusted one another. Based on this experience, I am convinced that there is a solution to the racism problem. And those who have experienced what I have experienced share the same view.

While this book offers a solution to a problem that many erudite and well intentioned men and women feel is insoluble, it is important that the reader not comb the book for the solution, by-passing everything else. For in order to apply the solution to the problem, one needs to appreciate the true nature of the problem, how it came into being and how it has affected us, and what we as individuals and our community leadership have done which has prevented us from getting to the root cause of the problem.

I believe all human beings have the capacity to grasp the solution. The challenge is convincing everyone that they possess such a capacity. I wrote this book to help the reader discover their capacity by focusing on what a human being is. Once we have a clear understanding of that as seekers of truth: We will develop an appreciation for the proposed solution, and a genuine urge to apply it personally and to introduce it to our communities.

Chapter One

Deciding To Tell It The Way It Really Is

Deciding to share with you my thoughts on racism in America has not been easy. No one in their right mind wants to subject themselves to ridicule or verbal abuse. As far as I know, I am not possessed by a secret passion for martyrdom. Nor am I trying to carry out a vendetta toward real or imagined enemies, vent repressed anger, or gain notoriety. I am not even looking for a good fight. In fact, I naturally try to avoid conflicts, and, like many people, abhor arguments or any form of confrontation. Yet, I have decided to write this book, even though it has the potential to evoke a considerable amount of protest from conservatives and liberals, from blacks and whites, from Jews and Christians, and even from some friends.

I needed to write this book in order to clear my conscience. No—it is not a matter of confessing sins, or relieving a nagging sense of guilt. It has to do with finally revealing what I feel are the "untouchable" barriers to overcoming the scourge of racism in America. In my book, *Healing Racism in America: A Prescription for the Disease*, I attempt to identify and explain how to overcome the more apparent barriers like institutionalized racism, the distorted view of the origin of race prejudice; and I gently touch on a few of the "untouchable" barriers, which most people are afraid to acknowledge, either in public or to themselves. Though the book has been helpful to many people sincerely trying to heal their own racial wounds and reduce community racial tensions, it purposely avoids addressing in depth the "untouchable" barriers. Ignoring them, I believe, will worsen America's racial condition, placing the nation in serious risk of a paralyzing social stroke, from which it may never recover. It wasn't that I didn't know of the existence of these barriers. Frankly, I didn't have the courage to openly address them.

In my travels, especially after the publication of my book, I have noticed these barriers in every section of the country, in small towns and big cities, in public and private institutions, and so have some others; but no one wants to talk about them in public, even though the "untouchable" barriers are obstructing the efforts of well meaning human rights advocates from making meaningful advances in overcoming racism. With all the money and human energy being expended to improve race relations, the racial conditioning of America seems to be worsening.

I myself have avoided mentioning the "untouchable" barriers in public for nearly four years for fear of alienating friend and foe, possibly hurting people's feelings, and plunging myself into a storm of controversy that would only lead to much unwanted aggravation and grief. However, I realized that there is a desperate need to expose what, I fervently believe, are major deterrents to racial unity; deterrents that many community leaders either don't recognize or refuse to acknowledge for political reasons. In 1996, I made a commitment to tell it the way it really is. And I've received some encouragement. Considering my experience in the race relations field, close colleagues, who see what I see, have urged me to take the plunge, pointing out that there is a fair chance some influential men and women might generate the courage to respond positively, and the process of bringing down the "untouchable" barriers would begin. This is an essential step toward overcoming the scourge of racism in America.

Before proceeding, it is important to point out that some of what I am about to write has been stated before by a few courageous people of color, but discounted by highly credentialed authorities as groundless rhetoric of questionable racial special interest groups, or set aside as the rantings of troublemakers. Unfortunately, the news media has corroborated the authorities' explanations; and the "untouchable" barriers remain untouched.

The "untouchable" barriers of racism

1. The lack of meaningful progress in overcoming racism has led to a growing grassroots separatist movement among blacks.
2. Whites and people of color are in denial.
3. Many whites of good will are unaware of their own racism.
4. Academia has avoided dealing meaningfully with the racism problem.
5. The establishment has refused to acknowledge that America is basically a racist country.

6. People have failed to recognize racism's true nature, it is a psychological disorder.

7. For the most part, North American multiculturalism does more harm than good in overcoming racism.

8. A form of genocide has been directed against America's minorities.

9. The friction between blacks and Jews is a deterrent to achieving community harmony.

10. Formal education has played a role in perpetuating racism.

11. There is disunity in the black community, and whites have exacerbated that condition.

12. Traditional organized religion has played a role in perpetuating American racism.

13. The establishment has refused to accept the reality of the oneness of humankind.

14. Pseudo human rights organizations promote tolerance as a means of promoting their hidden separatist cause.

15. Outspoken critics of the existing racial condition have been demonized.

Some of these barriers are contained in the practices and attitudes that the politically correct pretend don't exist. This will become evident as you read on.

The nation's leadership does not address these barriers for fear of alienating their constituencies and of creating possible social disruption that would result from publicly exposing practices and attitudes which have been around for a long time. As a consequence, considerable energy and money have been funneled into praising the superficial gains in race relations in recent times and in promoting programs designed to numb the potentially volatile blacks. But the containment policy is caving in, and authorities are scrambling for ways to shore it up.

Yes, the racial condition in America is worsening, notwithstanding the Civil Rights victories of the 1960s. It is worsening because the traditional targets of racism, especially blacks, are losing patience, and finding it more and more difficult to contain their rage. Fueling the rage is the fact that more and more blacks are college educated and are more aware of exactly what they are being denied. Most have given up hope of ever living in a race prejudice free America. As a result many blacks are involved in a grassroots separatist movement that isn't being orchestrated by a single charismatic figure, or a particular ideology. This psychological Diaspora isn't the result of a carefully calculated plan. A collective mixture of frustration, bitterness, suspicion, anger and hopelessness is the driving force of this nameless movement. It isn't a sustained propaganda campaign that draws people to the movement. It is purely voluntary. What draws them is desperation, the need to maintain some semblance of emotional stability and sanity in a democratic but fundamentally alien society. The fact that so many well meaning, highly educated whites are baffled by this black rush toward separatism is evidence of their failure to appreciate the gravity of the race problem in America.

Many blacks cite as an example of white unawareness the reaction to the Oklahoma City Murrah Federal Building bombing and the New York City Trade Center blast. Most whites, including leading government officials, were shocked into the recognition that America, like many other countries, has a terrorism problem. Of course, many African-Americans, Latinos, American Indians and Asian-Americans would argue that terrorism has been a part of American history long before the rash of bombings in the 1990s. It was more than the lynchings of blacks that were often sanctioned by local police agencies. Or the activities of the Ku Klux Klan. Wasn't slavery a form of terrorism? And what about the way the American Indians were treated by white individuals, groups and institutions? There were even government sanctioned acts of terror directed against people of color. Wasn't Andrew Jackson's ordering the massacre of several hundred American Indians a terrorist act?(1) And what about the early European settlers' decision to create a nation in a land without consulting its native inhabitants? That was certainly an act of terrorism.

Let's face it—the reason why many whites feel domestic terrorism is a new American problem is because whites were killed and injured in the Oklahoma City and New York City blasts. What men, women and children of color have had to endure at the hands of whites is overlooked by European-Americans because deep down African-Americans, Latinos, Asian-Americans and American Indians aren't viewed as their equals—they simply don't count as much.

It isn't that whites are patently evil, that they lack compassion, or are inherently stupid. It is a matter of being molded by a conditioning process that is nearly 400 years old. The process is actually an element of American culture called racism. Any unbiased historical account of the birth and rise of America will reveal that this cancerous cultural element didn't **evolve** within the society; it was **consciously instituted** when the nation was founded. What evolved was the spread of this social cancer from one generation to another. No section of the country is free of it. And while everyone is affected by it, very few people are willing to talk openly about it for fear of the result.

There are Americans who want to believe that the successes of the 1960s Civil Rights movement eliminated racism. While others concede that the disease still exists, they sense that progress is being made in overcoming racism by citing the fact that General Colin Powell, an African-American, was seriously recruited by some disenchanted Democrats and many Republicans to run for President. But most blacks, including many who circulate among the powerful, who have attained materially, were not impressed with the fuss being made over Powell. They knew that being considered a possible presidential candidate doesn't make a person president. When the time comes to choose a candidate in the next campaign, it won't be a black man, they believe. It doesn't matter that Powell learned how to function successfully in the white conceived and white dominated system. When it comes time to cast their ballot in the next election, I believe, most whites won't forget that Powell is black.

Jackie Jackson, whose husband Jesse has run for president, knows that a black person can never make it to the White House unless there is a grand collective change of heart among whites. "They'll never accept him (Jesse Jackson)," she said in a *New Yorker* interview. "Never. I just don't have the spirit to go through all of the ugliness again... I can't even sing 'We Shall Overcome' anymore, it fills my heart with such pain... We've been taken on the presidential campaigns to every nigger section in America... You must listen to my language and understand what I'm saying: There are no nigger sections in the black community. It is only out there when I leave the privacy of my community. I watched us go through the Democratic campaigns on the nigger side. The press treated us like niggers, and yet before the world I behaved and my husband behaved as if he were a legitimate candidate. Black people understand that, whites never will." (2)

The late Arthur Ashe knew how difficult it was to function as a black in America. Like Powell, he enjoyed considerable popularity among a broad cross section of whites. To them he exemplified the finest virtues of the American ethos, on and off the tennis court, always thoughtful, never boastful, bright, a man of moderate speech and lifestyle, and a wonderful husband and father. Yet, he knew that socially he was never viewed by most whites as an equal to his professional counterparts. He was always seen as that "great black tennis player." Though some may reject my observation, no one can dispute Ashe's feelings about the matter. He wrote about it in his memoirs shortly before he died of AIDS, a disease he contracted through a blood transfusion during heart surgery. In the book, Ashe revealed for the first time in public how racism in his country affected him: "Being African American in America was more difficult for me to endure than having AIDS." (3)

I must admit when I first read Ashe's revelation I found it difficult to believe, for Ashe seemed to have had "it made" in America. When I reread it a number of times, empathy began to well up within me, and I pondered what he had shared from his soul; and this thought came to mind: What must life be like for those blacks who don't enjoy the fame and fortune of an Arthur Ashe?

In reflecting on the Arthur Ashe story, I tried to walk in the shoes of a black person, but I didn't get very far. I couldn't stand the pain. As I was getting into the shoes that naturally fit, a thought I had never shared with anyone flashed through my mind: I don't think I could endure very long being black in America without becoming very angry.

While I failed the test of being black, I have a blood association with blackness. Since one of my daughter-in-laws' father is of African heritage, three of my grandchildren, who fortunately for them, live overseas, would be considered black in America. When my three grandchildren visited my wife and I in 1993, I had an experience with the eldest child which I will never forget.

He was close to five at the time. Both of us were sitting together at the kitchen table, looking through a large bay window, facing our wooded property. He seemed to be fascinated by the squirrels searching the deck for bits of food. But evidently, he had other things on his mind. Without warning, he turned to me, and while running his finger along my forearm, he said almost in a whisper, "Grandpa, why are you a different color than me?"

My first reaction was to grasp his hand. Had I responded right away, I would have broken into tears. To keep from crying, I closed my eyes.

After a moment or two passed, my grandson asked if there was anything wrong with me. To assure him that there was nothing wrong, I had to lie and tell him I was fine. Aware that I had to answer his question, I turned to the child and tried to explain why there are differences. It was one of the toughest explanations I have ever been asked to make.

To this day I'm not sure whether my likening humanity to a garden, and explaining that a flower garden composed of many different colored flowers is far more beautiful than a garden with only white roses, satisfied my grandson's need to know the answer to a question that was very important to him.

One thing I am sure of, however, is that this experience has made me overly protective of my grandson and his two sisters. Should anyone ridicule them because of their complexion, I doubt if I would be able to control my impulse to strike out verbally against the perpetrator, especially if he or she was an adult.

I gained yet another glimpse of what it must be like to be black from an experience I had with a young black woman who had graduated near the top of her high school class in my hometown. Iris had decided to turn down a full scholarship to Harvard University to attend a black college in the South where her parents would have to pay tuition and living expenses.

Dumfounded, I tried to persuade Iris to change her mind, pointing out that in our prestige conscious society a degree from Harvard was like being handed a key to success.

"I can't do it," she said.

"But why?" I countered.

"Mr. Rutstein," she said, "ever since I could remember I would have to psyche myself to go to school so that I could make it in both the white man's world and the black man's world. It is hard enough living in one world these days, let alone two worlds. And frankly, I feel more comfortable in the black world. I wish I didn't have to choose, and simply try to make it in the human world. But in my country, I have discovered, I am forced to make a choice because of my skin color. Trying to live in both worlds takes too much out of me. I no longer want to endure the kind of psychological whipping I have had to endure in the schools I have attended here in town."

This was a compelling testimony of what it must be like to live in a society where, despite your government's official position on race, you are viewed as an inferior, a creature that doesn't fit the accepted image of a real American. God knows blacks have tried in the past to fit that image, creating lotions to lighten their skin and straighten their hair. They have celebrated with gusto America's holidays, fought with pride in America's wars. They have even adopted the white man's superiority-inferiority mindset and applied it within the black community. Lighter skinned blacks were viewed as superior to darker skinned blacks. But despite their efforts to assimilate, deep down they still feel like outcasts. Every time blacks enter a restaurant or a store in the white section of town, they are reminded of that status, always on guard and aware of those stares from the "real" Americans, or from those first or second generation white Americans who are striving to attain that privileged position.

Considering the blacks' condition in America, it is not hard to understand why they created the blues as a musical medium. While whites listen to it to be entertained, blacks view it as more than entertainment; it is also a form of therapy. Through the blues, blacks break out of denial and become reacquainted with the sorrow that flows through their veins. They recall the struggles of the past and present, and at times the blues bloom into a prayer for hope—"One day we will reach The Promised Land."

Though some blacks in the 1960s believed they had reached the threshold of the "Promised Land" through the guidance of Dr. Martin Luther King Junior, most now dismiss that belief as wishful thinking, a mirage. For it is not enough to be able to drink from the same water fountain as a white person does, or eat in the same restaurant that whites frequent. Winning that freedom doesn't eliminate the suspicion and anxiety in a black person's heart as he waits in line to drink from the integrated fountain; nor does it remove the sense of superiority of the white man who waits on the same line. Although nothing is said, a lot is felt. Tragically, too many presumably responsible white and black men and women, holding important positions in the community, are afraid to address those feelings, and avoid probing into what has led to their development and how to shed them.

The reluctance to engage in the exploration is motivated by more than a fear of upsetting the social tranquillity in the community. There is usually a more intimate fear: Becoming acquainted with one's true feelings on race. As a consequence, many well meaning whites engage in human rights enterprises that promote tolerance and respect for all cultures. They enthusiastically participate in diversity workshops, parades and race unity picnics and display their beliefs through bumper stickers, T-shirts and shiny metal buttons. They become avid promoters of multiculturalism, and learn to master the etiquette of political correctness. The more involved they become in anti-racism activities, the more convinced they are that they are free of race prejudice. When a group of such people is formed, their delusion is reinforced as each member praises the others for the righteous cause they are involved in, while beneath the benevolence, the infection of racism continues to fester. Multiply that condition by tens of millions and you gain some understanding of how formidable the job of eradicating racism in America is. In reality, a tightly constructed web of denial blankets the entire nation. And sadly, most white Americans, especially those who wield the greatest power, are unaware of this denial as being the major obstacle to overcoming racism in their country.

The deep roots of the barriers

In some respects, many contemporary liberal whites remind me of the white abolitionists prior to the Civil War who actively opposed southern slavery but ignored the plight of the northern blacks in their struggle to achieve social equality. The great black abolitionist, Frederick Douglass, was aware of their duplicity, calling them "sham abolitionists." In fact, he was the brunt of their paternalism and subtle race prejudice. When they insisted he use the slave dialect in his speeches and criticized him for starting his own newspaper, Douglass realized that most white abolitionists had difficulty seeing a black rise to their social level.(4)

Just as with many 20th century liberal whites, the motives of most white abolitionists were hardly malicious. In fact, some sacrificed a great deal in their battle against slavery. The trouble is—they were in denial, unable to accept the fact that they felt superior to blacks. To them, the fact that they were fighting the pro-slavery forces was proof of their freedom of race prejudice. A similar position was taken by many well meaning whites involved in the civil rights movement in the 1960s, as well as by many contemporary promoters of human rights causes.

Some might ask, why do you want to focus on those whites who are trying to do good? Because they are the most educated, possess most of the nation's wealth, are the most powerful and are the social trendsetters. Get these folks to break out of denial; then, and only then, will others follow suit and meaningful progress be made in rescuing America from the poison pool of racism. Channeling all of our energy and funds into campaigns to subdue the influence of the openly bigoted groups like the Ku Klux Klan and the Aryans simply diverts attention from the more critical challenge of helping the more moderate Americans break out of their denial and begin the process of healing their racism. After all, the hate groups represent only a small fraction of the population. Armed with meager resources and an outlandish reputation, their ranks will continue to dwindle. Sure, they can terrorize their sworn enemies and blow up a building or two. But those well-meaning whites who are in denial are more dangerous, because there are many more of them—all over the country—possessing a lot more legitimate influence in most communities than members of the Klan. They are the well meaning doctors, teachers, college deans and professors, engineers, lawyers, merchants, the clergy, and politicians who shape and carry out community policy. Unbeknownst to them, they, and their denial, are like an invisible, odorless, poisonous gas that cripples, little by little, people of color every day. Those blacks, Latinos, American Indians and Asian Americans who work with whites can attest to that. It is the well-meaning white's patronizing attitude and condescending manner that continually remind people of color of their lower slot in America's social hierarchy, of their skin color, of their past, and of their inability to be accepted as real Americans no matter what they do. In her *Newsweek* "My Turn" column, Angela Bouwsma, an African-American, reveals what it is like for a black person to interact with well-intentioned whites who are in denial:

> That kind of racism is subtle and insidious, not something that can be photographed, like a corpse swinging from a tree or a burning cross. It's a racism that smiles at you, shakes your hand, wishes you luck. But its effects are clear and measurable.(5)

What is desperately needed is a nationwide, honest acknowledgment of our racial condition. We must finally face the painful fact that ours is a racist society. To achieve that understanding, it is essential that all Americans become aware of how racism came into being in their country. For this reason we cannot ignore what has happened in the past. The excuse that the sins of our forefathers shouldn't be held against us is invalid, for what was done in the past helped to set the social tone and the thinking of the present. Though we no longer condone slavery and the genocidal campaigns directed against American Indians and blacks, our thinking, feelings and beliefs have been influenced by the thinking, feelings and beliefs of those honored figures of the 1600s, 1700s and 1800s who created and molded what has become the most powerful nation in the world. After all, they were our national role models who were glorified and glamorized in our school textbooks, films and legends. Their cherished views, including those on race, were passed on from one generation to another, as the gospel truth.

Though courageous, idealistic and self-sacrificing, the Founding Fathers held warped views on race. They believed that whites, especially Anglo Saxon men, were inherently superior to all others; that blacks, Asians and American Indians weren't capable of functioning effectively in a democracy because they were subhuman by "nature" and incapable of becoming truly "civilized" through "nature." Because of this belief, Congress enacted the Naturalization

Act of 1790, which restricted American citizenship to whites only.(6) The Founding Fathers' ideal of the so-called real American was what most Americans consciously or unconsciously uphold today. It is not an African-American person, nor a Latino, American Indian or Chinese and Japanese American; they are still struggling to be accepted as equals in the mainstream of America despite the recent production of children's' books sprinkled with characters of color, and the public service television ads that call for racial and cultural tolerance.

This became very clear to me in mid-November of 1993 in Norfolk, Virginia. After a national teleconference on racism in which I participated, several news reporters approached me. Among them was a Chinese-American woman who stayed long after the other reporters had left. During our heart-to-heart discussion she shared that though her great grandparents had fled China to settle in the United States, white and even black strangers often ask her what country she is from. It started, she said, when she entered kindergarten. Her teacher was the first one to pose the question. I am sure no fourth generation white American has to face that kind of slight day after day. Before leaving the TV studio, the young Chinese-American reporter said, "I know that as long as I live in my country I will never feel certain that I am a part of it."

The Real Americans

I learned from my father, who had fled Russia in 1920, what kind of a person qualifies as a real American. He never pointed one out. The message was conveyed through body language and attitude change while in the presence of certain people. For example, I will never forget the day he broke one of his cardinal rules: Never buy anything from a door-to-door salesman. I was around seven years old when a tall, blond, blue-eyed young man dressed in a light blue suit, white shirt and golden tie knocked on the door of our South Bronx apartment. My father's eyes lit up when the man, in impeccable English, explained why the book he was selling was worth having. I doubt my father understood much of what the man was saying. What impressed him was that a real American had taken the time to talk to him, a poorly educated immigrant from Russia. To impress the salesman, my father tried hard to hide his accent when he asked for the book's price. I am sure the man couldn't care less that my father failed miserably in talking like a real American. Without hesitation my father paid the man five dollars for a book he would never read.

Though most white immigrants never reach real American status, their children and certainly their grandchildren have an opportunity to be a member of that highly prized level of society by changing their name and studying and mastering the behavioral pattern and lifestyle of what constitutes a real American. Once initiated into that privileged circle they develop a subtle pride of being among the "chosen ones." It becomes very important to belong to the right churches, schools and clubs. Whatever charity work they do is driven by a "white man's burden" attitude that was flaunted proudly by the British during the peak of their empire-building days. The idea was that whites, who are believed to be naturally endowed with superior intelligence and strength have an obligation to care for the naturally weaker and less intelligent people of color. Although it is no longer politically correct to openly proclaim the Manifest Destiny policy that was popular in nineteenth century America, most real Americans still believe in that policy, which stated that because of America's economic and political superiority it had the right to rule all of North America. Americans' obsession with being "number one" in today's world is an outgrowth of the Manifest Destiny spirit.

One of the reasons it is no longer respectable to openly advocate a Manifest Destiny policy is because fair-minded historians have revealed the crass injustices carried out in the name of that policy—an example is the Mexican-American war that resulted in the US seizing 900,000 square miles of the Mexican nation. Imagine, had that war not taken place, Texas, California, Arizona, New Mexico, Utah, Nevada and parts of Colorado and Kansas would be provinces in today's Mexico. The origin of this war is extremely important to know for those who cherish the truth.

Some real Americans took advantage of Mexico's liberal settlement policy in the mid 1800s, setting up farms and businesses in an area of Mexican territory known as Texas. When the Americans brought in slaves, the Mexican government balked, because it had abolished slavery in 1830. When American settlers refused to heed the order to free their slaves, Mexican troops were dispatched to make sure that the Americans obeyed the law of their nation.(7) In Washington, the US government, no doubt troubled by the fact that brown Mexican men were applying force against white American men, felt obliged to intervene militarily, not only to rescue their brethren, but more importantly to seize as much territory as possible. It was during this war that some real American patriots proclaimed openly and proudly that America's victory was a case of Manifest Destiny, a policy driven by a sense of racial superiority. A report in the *Congressional Globe* of February 11,1847 reflected most white Americans' sentiment about the Mexican-American War: "...We must march from Texas straight to the Pacific Ocean, and be bounded only by its roaring wave... It is the destiny of the white race, it is the destiny of the Anglo-Saxon race..."(8) For decades the white conquerors violated the native population's human rights, which included murder, rape and the pillaging and seizure of personal property.

During World War II, the "real American" syndrome was a factor in how the descendants of America's enemies living in the US would be treated by their government. Shortly after Japan's attack on Pearl Harbor, the hatred toward the Japanese was so intense nationwide that a US congressman proclaimed openly: "I'm for catching every Japanese in America, Alaska and Hawaii now and putting them into concentration camps... Damn them! Let's get rid of them."(9) Sensing the mood in the country, President Franklin Delano Roosevelt had US troops round up all of the 110,000 Japanese-Americans on the West coast and shipped them to internment camps, where they remained through the duration of the war. Once freed they discovered that their farms, businesses and homes had been confiscated. It is interesting to note that not one Japanese-American ever was cited for espionage or collaborating with the Empire of Japan. Yet, literally hundreds of German-Americans aided and abetted Nazi Germany.

People of color weren't surprised that what was done to the Japanese-Americans wasn't done to the German-Americans or Italian-Americans. After all, Americans of German and Italian extraction were white and therefore members in the "real American" club. Since Anglo Saxon roots stem from what is Germany today, German-Americans quite naturally fit the preferred physical image. The fact that they shared a similar religion, enjoyed the same kind of music and that both had a deep appreciation for order and discipline, made it a lot easier to be admitted into the club. It didn't matter that thousands of German-Americans packed New York's Madison Square Garden in the 1930s to participate in Nazi Bund rallies that extolled the virtues of Adolph Hitler. During that time, almost every New Yorker knew that the Yorkville section of their city was a hotbed of pro-Nazi sentiment, a potential nest for German spies. Yet the German-Americans were never shipped to internment camps.

It wasn't only losing the war in Vietnam that disturbed most real Americans. It was losing to "backward Asiatics" that was hard to accept. Sure, there were blacks, Latinos and American Indians among the US military force, but they were the sweating armed sloggers in the rice paddies carrying out the orders of the real Americans who were masterminding America's involvement in Vietnam from air-conditioned executive suites in Washington DC. Presidents John F. Kennedy and Lyndon Johnson were real Americans, as were Secretary of State Dean Rusk and Secretary of Defense Robert McNamara and Generals Creighton Abrams and William Westmoreland. Though most whites today wouldn't openly admit it, in their hearts they still feel that the Vietnamese are "gooks." And the reluctance to share that deep-seated feeling doesn't only stem from the fear of being accused of a hate crime or being considered a bigot—it may very well stem from a sense of shame. The fact that whites don't know how to rid themselves of these deep-seated feelings is a tragedy the existing religious, social and political institutions aren't addressing. Unless these deep-seated feelings are addressed, no meaningful progress will be made in overcoming racism.

What makes this challenge even greater is a personal belief that at first glance may seem implausible to the reader. But this belief is more than a hunch; it is based on nine years of intensive and, at times, heart-wrenching experience in the race relations field. I have observed carefully the interactions of whites with people of color. Behind many a white facade of politeness stirs a conviction that they are inherently superior to the blacks, Indians, Hispanics and Asians living in America. In fact, I believe that many well established whites unconsciously replace the word "American" with the word "human being" when using the term "real American."

In reality, America is not a social melting pot, and it never was. It is a land whose states are united, but whose people aren't. In most cities, there are still Italian, Polish, German, Swedish, Jewish, Chinese and Korean, and African-American neighborhoods with their own churches, schools and cultural centers providing programs that continually reinforce pride in their ethnic heritage. Unfortunately, some of the acquired pride evolves into feelings of superiority which often breeds prejudice, sometimes setting off physical clashes between ethnic groups.

Even in those neighborhoods that are mixed, attending the same schools and frequenting the same restaurants doesn't eliminate the suspicions and prejudices acquired at home, in church, from relatives, close friends, and from the social patterns created by respected figures of the past. To avoid trouble, people try to create an atmosphere of toleration, where no wholehearted attempt is made to break down the invisible barriers that keep people apart.

No attempt is made to eliminate the negative feelings that people harbor toward other ethnic groups; no attempt is made to truly unite everyone. What is devised is an apparatus that tries to create and maintain an atmosphere of peaceful coexistence or "polite aloofness" in the community. The hope is that respect for each other will result from such an enterprise. But genuine respect isn't easily achieved. Oh, there's a lot of phony respect shown toward blacks by well-meaning whites. But what these whites don't understand is that you cannot show blacks respect if you feel superior to them. No amount of generosity or proficiency in political correctness can conceal the feeling of superiority. To respect a black, a white must truly feel the black is his equal as a human being. When that happens, a black usually reciprocates in kind.

Respect isn't achieved by simply learning each others' dances, participating in each other's festivals, eating each other's food and observing each other's holidays. Nothing that superficial. In fact, festering beneath this thin and fragile veneer of desperate social accommodation are the real feelings of the members of the different ethnic groups toward each other. And you can understand why people of good conscience would want to hide those feelings through some of the inter-community activities already mentioned. But hiding them doesn't get rid of them: What results is a community that is outwardly integrated and inwardly segregated. Generally, blacks don't confide in whites and whites don't confide in blacks. Outside of work or school, blacks and whites live in separate worlds, where their misconceptions of each other are magnified and there is no chance for meaningful dialogue. This social schizophrenia, which is prevalent throughout the United States, is sapping the nation's vitality and thwarting its spiritual growth.

The traditional targets of racism, who are growing in number, are continually harmed by the unconscious attitudes and behavior of well-meaning whites in denial. The deep racial wounds, especially among blacks, Latinos and American Indians, are so painful that most of their energy is directed at dulling the pain. As a consequence, the contribution of many to the social and economic development of their community is minimal, often becoming a drain on the treasury. Unaware of their potentialities and their intrinsic goodness, these human beings have grown obsessed with the need to strike out at those who are causing their pain. This growing element in the nation's population is a factor in the rise of violence in America. Sadly, the response of our national leadership is to build new prisons and expand the old ones, a course driven by fear, not enlightenment.

Chapter Two

Unveiling The Web Of Denial

As I see it, the top priority in overcoming racism is the dismantling of the web of denial that blankets America, not an easy task when you consider how extensive and well established the web is. But it must be done if the nation is to realize its potential as a just democracy. Let's face it, America cannot be considered "the land of the free" when large segments of its population have yet to attain their full freedom. The web is standing in the way.

According to University of Florida Sociologist, Joe Feagin, who has researched race relations in America for thirty years:

> We whites are in denial. Our top political leaders, scholars and commentators all tell themselves and the general public racism is dead or dying, and it's a great white lie. Racism is very much alive as studies demonstrate.(1)

Prevailing attitudes

In my travels as a race relations consultant over the past seven years, I have discovered that some places are more difficult to penetrate than others. I have found, for example, that the more sophisticated the community, the more deeply entrenched is denial, and the more artfully it is concealed. The most difficult places are the elitist universities, and the towns they are located in like Cambridge, Princeton, Ithaca, Hanover and Palo Alto. Why? Because they are populated by highly accomplished critical thinkers, who thrive in an atmosphere of skepticism and pessimism, and relish debunking concepts that threaten their heavily invested belief system, or that spring from paradigms they are unfamiliar with. Convinced that there can be no solutions to something as complex and volatile as racism, they have become skillful at adapting to the existing racial conditioning in the most comfortable way possible; and that is done by focusing most of their attention and energy on their academic discipline and surrounding themselves with those who harbor a similar outlook, and are likely to stroke their egos. As a consequence they advocate a form of toleration based on the principle of "let everyone be allowed to do their own thing," an attitude that fosters intellectual apartheid. Deep down, I believe, they feel the race problem is insoluble because prominent thinkers at universities like theirs have been unable to come up with a solution. This form of benign arrogance and subtle snobbery is a safe way to stay clear of a problem that can upset a psychological comfort zone which has taken years to construct.

Amherst College, one of America's leading liberal arts colleges, is a repository of such attitudes. Of course, most of those associated with the college would disagree vehemently, citing its progressive diversity admissions policy, its distinguished minority alumni, and its efforts to expose its student body to a wide variety of minority lecturers and performing artists. There is no doubt that if Amherst College were being graded for its political correctness it would be awarded an A+.

However, several unsuccessful attempts have been made by various people to get Amherst College to change its name. The college is named after Lord Jeffrey Amherst, a racist mass murderer, and it is for that reason that many want to change the name. Since nobody today would name a college after Adolph Hitler, those for changing the college's name feel it's disgusting for an institution of higher learning to continue bearing the name of a racist mass murderer. Is the college's refusal a reflection of its true position on racism? Some believe it is. In reply to this, college apologists say, "What's in a name? We are simply honoring tradition." In reality, this is not true.

As an English general serving in New England in the mid-1700s, Jeffrey Amherst distinguished himself by becoming a pioneer in biological warfare. In a gesture of "good will" he distributed hundreds of blankets to freezing Indians along the Connecticut River Valley one bitter winter. What the Indians didn't know was that the general had the blankets infected with smallpox. Hundreds of Indian men, women and children perished. European settlers hailed Amherst's military tactic as a great victory over the "native heathens." Amherst's contributions in North America were so highly regarded that the British crown made him a Lord and Governor General of British North America.(2)

It is not as if the people who run Amherst College are unaware of the general's infamous deeds. While they are aware of them, they don't dwell on them. In fact, they have even hidden them from the public. For example, during the peak of the civil rights movement in the 1960s, the college's Jeffrey Amherst dinner plates disappeared overnight. Suddenly Amherst College students were no longer eating off plates with their frieze showing a white English military hero, presumably Jeffrey Amherst, attacking American Indians.(3)

There are some traditions revolving around the memory of Jeffrey Amherst that the college refuses to scrap, for fear of alienating the alumni, a major source of preserving the college's hefty endowment. One of these traditions is the college's fight song which glorifies the school's namesake. Usually after touchdowns at football games and during campus parties faithful alumni and student will enthusiastically sing:

> *Oh, Lord Jeffrey Amherst was the man who gave his name*
> *To our college on the hill;*
> *And the story of his loyalty and bravery and fame*
> *Abides here among us still —*
> *Abides here among us still.*
> *You may talk about your Johnnies and your*
> *Elis and the rest,*
> *For they are names that can never dim,*
> *But give us our only Jeffrey, he's the noblest and the best,*
> *To the end we will stand fast for him.*(4)

The town of Amherst where the college is located is one of the most liberal and politically correct towns of its size, and it, like the college, has steadfastly refused to consider changing its name. I have serious doubts as to whether the college and the town are truly committed to playing a meaningful role in ending racism. There are no doubts, however, about their "political correctness." Maybe to some a name change may appear inconsequential, even ludicrous. But think beyond the mere changing of a name for a moment and focus on the reason and intent for doing so. If both sincerely decided that they no longer wanted to be associated with the name of a person whose claim of distinction was that of a genocidal racist, because this is incompatible with their beliefs, just imagine the psychological impact of such a message on the public, and what it would say about the administration of both entities with regard to racism. Think back a few years ago. When the Russians learned of the atrocities committed by Stalin, they changed the name of Stalingrad back to its original name, Volgograd. This was generally considered an act of integrity, and it was by no means inconsequential.

Highly respected and well-meaning whites, in such prestigious places, must come to grips with social pretenses and denial, if we are to make meaningful progress in overcoming racism. Once that is done they will recognize the need to become involved in a racial healing process. Only when a significant number of men and women make such a commitment will the majority of elitists have a change of heart and make some effort to break out of the hard shell of denial.

Overcoming the delusion of being unaffected by racism

The first step to healing for well-meaning whites is overcoming their delusion that they aren't affected by racism. When that is achieved, they can get on with healing their own infection of race prejudice. Of course, to do that means disturbing one's comfort zone and undergoing a period of internal transformation, which can be a painful process. The most painful aspect of this process is letting go of one's feeling of superiority toward minorities. For some, the loss is so great that they experience a period of grieving. After all, losing something you have lived with all of your life, something you have relied on to prop up your ego, is tough to take. On the other hand, if pursued regularly, the process can lead to a sense of liberation. No longer expending energy to hide a lie, you find yourself basking in the refreshing atmosphere of the truth. You feel clean inside. You feel unburdened. And others, especially blacks, even militant blacks, are drawn to you. They are drawn to you because the invisible antennae they have been forced to develop to check out which whites are safe to deal with registers "okay" when you appear. You feel welcomed and are able to develop an open and honest relationship with a black person, no longer having to make safe, innocuous small talk; no longer fearful of saying or doing the wrong thing. You can be your true self.

I know what that's like. Not that I had been able to avoid being infected by racism. That's impossible for any white American brought up in America, and I obviously fall into that category. It is just that I have been able to break out of denial and become involved in the healing process, and thus enjoy some of the benefits that one derives from such an experience. Because I feel freer, I can see and hear things I could never see and hear in the past, especially in interacting with people of color. I can now acknowledge the reality of another person's need; I'm now able to sense the pain of some of those oppressed.

Normally, a white person isn't invited to speak to an all black audience these days unless he's the President of the United States escorted by a legion of Secret Service men, or a potential underwriter of a black-oriented project. So, I was surprised when I was asked to address the congregation of a mosque made up primarily of African Americans; most of them were recent converts to Islam. A lay leader, who had heard me speak, felt his fellow Muslims would benefit from my message. Frankly, I didn't see how. I wasn't a Muslim; I was still struggling with healing my own infection of racism, and with a name like Rutstein I felt I would be greeted by a great deal of hostility.

I was wrong. I received a standing ovation—and hugs from young and old, some attired in West African outfits. Baffled by the loving reception, I asked the person who had invited me if he could account for the way I was received by his co-religionists. He said when a white person is sincere, genuine, honest and shares openly his struggle in healing his infection of racism, "our compassion comes to the fore." His observation was correct, because wherever I speak most blacks receive me warmly, and an open dialogue develops where we learn from each other on levels of both the mind and the heart. My acceptance by blacks isn't based on my trying hard to bash whites in order to curry favor with blacks. In fact, I don't shrink from mentioning how some blacks obstruct the cause of racial unity. What is helpful is my emphasis on the principle of the oneness of humankind. I try hard to explain how blacks and whites and everyone else on our planet are related to each other. When I reveal the realities underlying that principle, most blacks I encounter act naturally, and I am at ease. We come together like family members who hadn't seen each other for a very long time. That belated recognition of a family member is an experience I will never grow tired of—mainly, because it feels right.

Believe me—I wasn't born with a natural appeal to black people. I can remember the time when blacks never went out of their way to befriend me or even speak to me. I suppose to them I was just another white face in the crowd who enjoyed privileges they would never enjoy in America. Before discovering my infection of racism, I never gave any serious thought to how I related to blacks. It was not an issue for me, because I believed I was one of those white Americans who was free of race prejudice. After all, I had always been an active advocate of human rights, even as a child. Why, I was so liberal that when Jackie Robinson broke into major league baseball, I wept. Of course, I was always on the right side of the Civil Rights struggle in the 1960s. Like other well-meaning whites, I was appalled at the sight on TV of police dogs attacking black children on their way to church, and I too was mesmerized by Dr. Martin Luther King's "I Have a Dream" speech, and outraged by his assassination.

The discovery of my own infection of racism

While being an outspoken promoter of social justice, and an avowed defender of the oppressed, I was hiding from myself and others the poison of race prejudice festering in my heart. There were those rare shameful moments when I would catch a glimpse of the poison.

After months of serious soul searching, precipitated by a racial encounter, I was able to recall some of those painful moments. One stands out: It occurred while driving on a two lane highway. Trying not to be late for an important appointment, I needed to be going at least ten miles faster than the 40 miles per hour the driver ahead was driving. Furious, I blew the horn and pressed my face against the windshield to see who was at the wheel of the car ahead of me. When I realized it was an old black man, the words "move nigger" flashed through my mind, and bursts of anger and disgust shot through my heart. The shock that I could think and feel that way made me forget about the appointment. I could distinguish between what is right and wrong, and it was wrong to think and feel that way. Yet I had no control over those thoughts and feelings. I was horrified. The word "nigger" which passed through my mind had never passed my lips. And those feelings that invaded my heart mystified me. Where did that ugly stuff come from? I wondered. When no answers were forthcoming, I began to feel sorry for myself. That part of consciousness that always comes to my rescue when I'm in trouble let loose a stream of rationalizations. How unfair, I thought. I didn't choose to think and feel that way about blacks. I was always liberal in my social beliefs. I was always solicitous of my black classmates. I always went out of my way to assist a troubled black person. More and more past experiences featuring my human rights work and what I had believed were positive relationships with blacks rushed into my mind. At the time I didn't realize that my shame had set off the cascade of evidence supporting the belief that I was not a racist. Convinced that I wasn't, I forgot about the "move nigger" incident. I had repressed the experience and gone into denial, and didn't know it. Years later, after considerable self-evaluation, I discovered the anatomy of racial denial. It is a carefully concealed mental maneuver that springs from a sense of shame. This, I believe, is a condition born out of an unconscious need for redemption. Though denial per se is a very human reflex, and not an evil deed, it keeps us from knowing the truth on a conscious level. When the majority of a community is actively avoiding knowing the truth about their real feelings concerning a serious social problem like racism, no effort on their part can produce meaningful progress in solving the problem. God knows, we have tried: Civil Rights legislation, affirmative action, multiculturalism, school busing. But racism persists. It persists because all sorts of ways have been created by whites to avoid ripping away the scab to get to the mounting poison beneath. Band-Aids don't work. Yet we keep applying them, thinking that by not seeing the messy wound it would somehow disappear. Avoiding the truth can be a painful and energy sapping exercise. Yet whites in denial keep doing it. When it comes to improving our racial conditioning, whites find ways to avoid taking to heart the biblical adage, "The truth shall make you free."

How did I break out of the shell of denial? It took a traumatic racial encounter. Not that there weren't other racial encounters before that unforgettable experience. But they were manageable. During a stressful racial encounter, the monster of racism would reappear. Ashamed, I would shove it back into the unconscious and go on trying to impress everyone around me that I was committed to social justice by openly supporting liberal causes and expressing my outrage at hate crimes reported on TV and in the newspapers.

That traumatic racial encounter materialized like a time-bomb reaching its explosion point. When it happened, I was rendered spiritless, even speechless for a while, my self-esteem terribly damaged. I began to question whether I was worthy of possessing values I cherished, values I thought had set me apart from racists and those with parochial views. I felt hypocritical, a characteristic I had always found so contemptible in others. At the time the pain was too intense for me to appreciate what I was going to gain from the experience. I wanted to hide; I was unable to think of even the possibility of recovery.

After I graduated from DePauw University in Greencastle, Indiana, Bill, a close friend and classmate, invited me to spend the summer in Chicago, his hometown. My initial response was to turn down the invitation, for I had grown weary of the conservatism of the Midwest. I wanted to spend some time on the more progressive East Coast. When I returned to New York, however, I found myself drawn to Chicago. There was no rational explanation for the feeling. During a weak moment, I gave in to the unexplainable urge and bought a one-way railroad ticket to Chicago. The first thing I did when I got there was call my friend, relishing the thought of surprising him. But it was he who surprised me. Intuitively, he had anticipated my arrival, and had subleased a furnished three-room apartment on Chicago's near North Side, which borders on Lake Michigan and is famous for its eating places, jazz clubs and cosmopolitan atmosphere. Not only was I impressed with the location of the apartment, I liked the idea of sharing the flat with a friend of Bill's. After all, how could I turn down an opportunity to split rent, food and utilities costs. Besides, I respected Bill's judgment of character.

A couple hours later I was ringing the bell to the apartment where I would be spending the next three months. Bill had another surprise for me. The tall, broad shouldered man standing next to him, who was introduced to me as my prospective roommate, was black—and very dark. I had never thought that my roommate would be black. It never entered my mind that such a thing could happen, because, in reality, blacks were part of a different world—not mine. Could it be that my obsession with promoting the blacks' cause was my way of getting back at an unjust government? I wondered. While I always championed the blacks' struggle for social justice, my help was always given from a distance. By distance is meant never getting heart-to-heart close to a black person, never sharing my intimate feelings with one, never spending the night at a black's home, talking about things other than race. The prospect of living with Pete frightened me. My latent racism surfaced and for the first time in my life I was unable to shove it back. At that moment I wasn't thinking about how those feelings had developed within me. I wanted to run from the room and never return, to wring Bill's neck for getting me into this predicament. The dumb son-of-a-bitch, I thought, he should have warned me that Pete was black.

Bill stood between us, smiling, all innocence and spirituality, unaware of the fire raging within me. I'm certain Bill wasn't aware of how I felt, for he was the kind of person who only saw the good in others.

Fortunately, I wasn't completely out of control. In fact, I pretended to be thrilled with sharing the apartment with Pete. While smiling and extending my hand of friendship to him, I was thinking of ways of getting out of the living arrangement. Though at the time I felt confident I was doing a good job concealing my true feelings, I later realized that Pete probably saw right through my desperate charade, for he had been conditioned to deal with folks like me.

Though deciding not to flee was one of the most difficult decisions in my life, it proved to be an opportunity to gain some insight on how racism affects us. Of course, I didn't know that at the time. It became apparent during the three months I lived with Pete. I gained valuable insights about myself, my upbringing and how racism infects and wounds people.

The first week was the most painful. There were moments when the impulse to leave was acute. The reasons that my family and friends put forward as to why I should have remained in New York seemed more and more sensible. Being in Chicago was only causing me grief. And working in a butter factory wasn't my idea of a good job for a university graduate. I was sure I could have done much better back home.

I don't know why I decided to remain in Chicago. There was no rational explanation for it. But I stayed, trying to untangle myself from a web of intense feelings. At first there was a desire to protect myself from Pete. I tried to think of ways to avoid him: perhaps, I thought, by working the night shift while he worked days. But that wasn't easy: as a bus driver Pete was continually changing shifts. Spending weekends at Bill's place wasn't possible because he didn't have the space. I had to face the situation—or leave.

It was a battle I never thought I would have to fight. Not me, the staunch liberal. I stayed, trying to sort out feelings I had never before consciously had. Although I was frightened, I was annoyed with myself for being afraid. Rationally, I knew it was wrong to feel the way I did about Pete. But it wasn't Pete per se that disturbed me—it was having to live with a black. Another concern, a deep concern, was the realization that this feeling was a fact, a reality about myself. For as long as I could remember I had committed myself to working for world unity. I wasn't a bigot. I was the guy who always protested my friends' use of racial epithets and racial jokes. What hurt most was knowing that my feeling about Pete wasn't right, and I couldn't do anything about it. It was as if that terrible feeling had been pressed into my being.

The prospect of resolving the inner dichotomy seemed bleak. Seeking advice was out of the question: I was too proud to admit to anyone my true feelings about blacks.

I guess it was pride—and the hope that somehow I would experience a miraculous change of attitude—that kept me from leaving the apartment. Perhaps being stubborn helped, too.

I tried not to think about my predicament, hoping it would resolve itself, but that failed. Pete's new 3 PM to 11 PM shift under mined my scheme of self-deception. During the first week I would go to bed at 10 PM and not fall asleep until he was asleep, sometimes as late as 3 AM. The shortage of sleep took its toll on me physically as well as emotionally. I began dozing off during the day, infuriating my work supervisor. With only 15 dollars left, I couldn't afford to be fired: it cost 40 dollars just for a one-way railroad ticket to New York City.

I couldn't sleep because I was scared, afraid that Pete might come home drunk or bring home a bunch of drug addicts from the black ghetto where he grew up. When those thoughts seized me, a sense of shame gripped me as well. How could I think such terrible thoughts?, I wondered. Yet I did. They sprang from the core of my being. A sense of futility swept over me, for I didn't know what to do to rid myself of those thoughts. They were much stronger than the rational defenses I tried to raise. In the past I had always been able to emerge from a crisis unscathed, but this one was overwhelming me.

During those sleepless nights I groped for answers. While I could distinguish between right and wrong, I was unable to correct what I knew was wrong. A part of me knew that my fears regarding Pete were unfounded, especially since he always came home alone and sober. Nevertheless there was that damned inner voice: "What about the next time?"

Those long, hot nights produced other revelations. I grew angry at Pete for staying out so late and preventing me from sleeping. What could he be doing at that crazy hour? I wondered. While mentally castigating Pete, I realized that I felt superior to him, more intelligent, more socially aware. It didn't matter that I couldn't prove it, that it wasn't true. I acted as if it were a matter of fact, a natural law, that a black was inferior to a white. Normally, I would not have allowed myself to feel that way. I never would have admitted harboring such a thought. But then again I had never been so close to a black before.

I really felt I knew what was best for Pete. It didn't matter that he was four years older than I. He could have been 75 and it wouldn't have altered my view. I didn't dare complain about his coming home late, for that would have upset the image I was trying to project. I didn't want to think that I was like most other whites he knew. I wanted him to feel that I was a liberated person, someone free of prejudice, truly his brother. I wanted him to feel that way about me because I knew that was the right way to be.

But Pete wasn't fooled, something I learned later on. Out of necessity, the persecuted develop a sensitivity of how to cope with subtle and overt hostility, and they recognize sincerity. He never said anything about my true feelings toward him. Through the years he had learned how to make the best of most situations—and there had been worse situations in his life than sharing an apartment with me.

I didn't know then that Pete sensed my fear. I was too preoccupied with trying to face up to what I had learned about myself while giving the impression that everything was fine. That was a torture I hope I never have to endure again. At least a bodily disease can be treated with medicine. But I was wrestling with something invisible. There was no pill to take to dissolve the poison of prejudice in my heart, nor was there a surgical procedure to cut it out of me.

The pressure intensified as I groped for ways to change my situation. Running away, I knew, wouldn't help because you really can't run away from an attitude. Dealing with racism is one thing, but dealing with the fact that I was so different from what I had thought I was was horrifying. I had been so secure, and suddenly I found myself confused and gripped by the kind of pain I had never felt before. My pain was fueled by a deep sense of shame.

A part of me didn't want to believe what I had discovered. I grew defensive and rationalized that I wasn't ready to endure the pain that was necessary to eradicate my racism. I should be expending my energy on developing my career.

Fortunately, I didn't succumb to that powerful urge. And I have Pete to thank for that. Every time I saw him I was struck by the need to pursue my struggle.

Chapter Three

Discovering The Fundamental Fallacy Of Racism

Though my three month experience with Pete didn't cure my infection of racism, I made some progress in curing it. I found myself out of the shell of denial, facing the truth, which in the beginning was difficult to do. There were moments when I wanted to crawl back into the shell, for I didn't know where to turn for help. Most of my friends were either in deep denial or openly prejudiced. Governmental agencies appeared to be equally veiled from the reality of the nation's race issue. I was in unfamiliar psychological territory, seized by a strange combination of emotions—much fear and some hope. There seemed to be a chance of one day freeing myself of my prejudice; but I was fearful of what I would have to endure to reach my goal. What would have helped was an *Institute for the Healing of Racism*, but they didn't exist then. (More on the Institutes in a later chapter.)

What saved me from reverting were those sleepless nights the first week I lived with Pete. While there were some fearful and painful moments, there was plenty of time to dig into my past to learn how I became infected. Every now and then I would waver, but recalling what I had learned during that tortuous time encouraged me to continue the healing process. I came to realize what a burden I would have to live with the rest of my life if I didn't follow through with this process; what energy I would have to expend to maintain an image that I knew was based on lies and deception. I could see why many people prefer the state of denial. They don't have to face doing something about what they discovered about themselves, and end up refusing to believe what they discovered. But I knew what I had discovered; as a consequence, I had broken out of the shell of denial.

I was like a bird who had spent all of its life in a cage, and was suddenly allowed to fly free. I flew into my childhood to recall how I became infected. That helped me to gain some idea of how the infection of racism spreads.

What I learned during those sleepless nights in Chicago was that the day I was born in America, I, like everyone else, was destined to be infected or wounded by race prejudice, because it permeates every section of the country, every county and town. It is a powerful part of the nation's collective consciousness.

The fact that I didn't choose to be infected helped to soothe the pain somewhat. I wasn't evil after all! Knowing that, however, didn't relieve me of the responsibility to heal my sickness.

What I did learn through a journey into my past was that there were a number of places in my circumscribed world where the germ of racism was nourished and energized. On the surface, they were the most unlikely places, places I normally associated with security, joy and fun. Take the movies, for example. I loved Tarzan and cowboy and Indian films. Of course I always rooted for Tarzan to defeat the "black natives" who were depicted as savages and subhumans, and cheered on the cowboys as they mowed down the "wild and uncivilized" Indians. At the time I never considered how those films impacted on black and Indian children. The only blacks that set foot on our property were garbage collectors who to me resembled the natives in the Tarzan movies. Little did I know at the time that at eight years of age I had already formed an understanding of where blacks belonged in the American caste system.

Sadly, my childhood home was a breeding ground of racism. Not that my parents regularly uttered disparaging remarks about blacks and Indians. They were devoted liberal Democrats who viewed President Franklin Delano Roosevelt as the savior of the poor. And we were poor. However, I was able to dig out of an environment where blacks were mentioned as a threat to our way of life. Though rare, these events were so stressful and emotionally packed that they had an everlasting effect on me, and I suspect on my sister as well.

When a black family expressed interest in buying a house on our block, my parents felt threatened. I remember how our family gathered in the front sunporch, watching the nicely dressed black couple approach and enter the house across the street. My father spoke openly about his concerns regarding the prospects of blacks living in the neighborhood. "It'll become a slum," he said. "Our house won't be worth a nickel."

When my mother challenged him, he grew angry, and said, "You don't understand. I don't have anything against them, but I know what they can do to a neighborhood. The streets won't be safe. There will be drunkenness and drugs."

My mother was convinced, and we remained on the sunporch for what seemed a long time, leaving only when the black couple drove away in their shiny new car. I hated seeing my father and mother so upset.

When my father learned a few weeks later that a white family had bought the house across the street, he said it was a time to celebrate and took us to a fancy ice cream parlor where I ordered a double dip chocolate cone.

As I lay in bed staring into the darkness, waiting for Pete to come home, I tried to understand how an incident like that had helped to shape my real attitude towards blacks. Seeing my father so agitated must have bothered me. After all he was my father whom I loved, and who was, in a sense, my god. In my childish eyes, he could do no wrong. Therefore he had to be right about black people. Because they had upset my father and threatened the stability of my family, blacks became a natural enemy of mine, though I never stated that openly or in private. It was a secret I even kept from my conscious self. As I matured, that notion was buried under layers of shame and artfully constructed rationalizations, which helped to develop in me a belief that I was a natural ally of blacks and other oppressed people. This was a classical case of head and heart being out of synch.

I wasn't sure I had the stamina and patience to remove from my heart those unspeakable feelings towards blacks. I turned to prayer for assistance. In my mid-twenties, a sense of assurance swept over me regarding the necessity to engage in an endless struggle if need be, to release the poison of prejudice from my heart. I felt led out of the clutches of self pity, and I began to gain a clearer focus of where I stood in my struggle. Knowing my true condition was a step in the right direction. The adage, "The Truth shall make you free," was no longer a nice sounding platitude. I felt a new energy in me. I became committed to freeing myself of my negative racial feelings. Having gained some insight on how racism entered my life, I began to understand the anatomy of race prejudice. A definition unfolded before my inner eye: Race prejudice is an unquestioned emotional attachment to a falsehood that is assumed to be the truth. In other words, prejudice is an emotional commitment to ignorance. What was I ignorant of when I formed my real views of people of color? I knew absolutely nothing about Africans and Indians who were depicted as savages and subhumans on the movie screen. When those strange looking creatures tried to harm my movie heroes, I became incensed, angry; an urge to eliminate the enemy seized me. And when the "good guys" won, I not only felt relieved; I felt that the blacks and Indians got what they deserved. Those feelings did not leave me when I was handed my university diploma.

My struggle included a number of challenges. One of them was to substitute ignorance with knowledge, especially about those ethnic groups that I never really accepted as being part of my world. In my ongoing search, I eventually realized that those groups that were so strange and posed a threat to all that I admired were part of cultures that contributed significantly to the development of my country. I never knew before that the American form of government was based largely on the political pattern practiced by the Iroquois League; that many of the views enshrined in the U.S. Constitution were borrowed from the Iroquois Constitution called the *Great Law of Peace*.(1) Nor was I aware that if it wasn't for the Indians, whites would have never feasted on french fries or hash browns. It was the Indians who developed the potato, hundreds of varieties to be exact. In fact, American Indian horticulturists developed 3/5's of the food the world consumes today.(2) No history textbook I read in school ever revealed that Africans were using iron when Europeans were in the Stone Age;(3) that Africans were producing carbon steel before the birth of Christ; the process was introduced to Europe nineteen hundred years later. The African steel was so fine that surgical instruments were manufactured, allowing black physicians to operate on the human eye.(4) Imhotep, a black Egyptian physician practiced medicine 2,000 years before the birth of Hippocrates, whom Europeans call the "father of medicine."(5) I didn't learn in my history courses that in ancient Timbuktu, the site of the African University of Sankore, more profit was made from the book trade than from any other line of business.(6) Nor did our teachers tell us that much of the wisdom shared with the world by the Greeks originated in Egypt, an African country.

And no teacher ever shared with our classes some of the scientific contributions made between the 1780s and 1940s by some African-Americans to the development of America. For example, I learned that:

The mathematician and surveyor, Benjamin Bannecker, built the first clock in America and laid out the city of Washington, D.C.;

Norbert Rillieux revolutionized the sugar refining industry;

Lewis Temple invented the toggle harpoon;

Jan Matzeligen invented the machine for the mass production of shoes;

Elijah McCoy developed self-lubricating systems for locomotives and steamer engines, as well as for air brakes;

Among Granville T. Woods' many inventions were railway telegraphy, the overhead conductory system for electrical railways and the "third rail" for subway systems;

Lewis Latimer developed a process for making electric lamp elements that made his lamp run much longer than those of Thomas Edison. He supervised the installation of electric light systems in New York City, Philadelphia, Montreal and London;

Garrett A. Morgan invented the gas mask and the traffic light;

Frederick McKinley Jones adapted silent projection to the "talkies";

Dr. George Washington Carver developed 325 products from peanuts, 118 products from the sweet potato, 75 products from pecans, hundreds from cornstalks, clays and cotton;

Dr. Ernest E. Just was the first to discover that the cell's nucleus was not the only determinant of heredity;

Dr. Percy L. Julian developed synthetic cortisone and other important therapeutic drugs for arthritis, glaucoma, birth miscarriages, male hormonal disorders, and cancer;

Dr. Floyd A. Hall developed new ways to sterilize foods, spices and medical supplies;

Dr. Daniel Hale Williams performed the first open-heart surgery;

Dr. William A. Hinton was a world authority on venereal disease;

Dr. Louis T. Wright was the first to experiment with aureomycin, an antibiotic, on humans;

Millions of people are alive today because of Dr. Charles R. Drew's development of blood plasma for transfusions.

The reason I share this incomplete list is to dramatize the heinous omissions of African-American contributions to our country.

While all of this information and a lot more opened up my mind, what impressed me most in my findings was the fact that Tarzan, the African natives, the cowboys and Indians and everyone else on the planet were all related, at least 50th cousins.(7) That's right! The Hasidic Jew in Jerusalem, the Inuit in Alaska, the Chinese, the Italians, the Russians, the Nigerians, the Micronesians, the Puerto Ricans, the Lakota Sioux Indians, the white Anglo-Saxon industrialist from Greenwich, Connecticut, the Pope, all the kings and queens in the world are cousins.

According to some of the most prominent geneticists (Haldane, Dobzhansky and Huxley), you don't have to be a genius to figure this out. Simple arithmetic will do. Double the number of your ancestors for each generation. As you compose backward (consistently multiplying them by two) your personal pedigree would cover humankind before the thirtieth generation (this calculation takes into consideration that we have shared relatives that wouldn't be counted more than once.) In other words, you are related to some Africans, Chinese, Arabs, Malays, Mexicans, American Indians, and Europeans who lived in the 13th century. Go back further to the eighth century and your ancestors would include all the Africans, Chinese, Malays, Latinos, American Indians, Europeans and everyone else on Earth at the time.(8)

I discovered the principle of the oneness of humankind, and investigated the realities underlying that principle. The scientific evidence that all five and a half billion human beings, despite geographical location, skin color or hair texture were members of the same family—was overwhelming. Cultural anthropologists have given up on the idea that there is any scientific criteria to divide the human species into races. They now believe that in reality there is only one race, the human race and one human color with many different shades. As a protest to the use of the term "race," anthropologist Ashley Montague coined the phrase "ethnic group."

Some of the world's leading experts in genetics, anthropology, endocrinology and psychology gathered in Austria in June of 1995 to assess the scientific validity of the concept of race. In summarizing their scholarly dialogues, anthropologist Lionel Tiger wrote:

> The fact is that all contemporary population genetics and molecular biology underscores that the nineteenth century notion of races as discrete and different entities is false. There is only gradual genetic diversity between groups. We all merge smoothly into each other. Nearly all the physically observable differences reflect very limited local adaptations to climate and other specific environmental conditions.(9)

World renowned geneticist Luca Cavalli-Sforza states in his book, *The Great Human Diaspora*, that the "pure race" theory that many ultra right-wingers subscribe to is absurd. All of us are mixed. In fact, he points out:

> The idea of race in the human species serves no purpose. The structure of human populations is extremely complex and changes from area to area; there are always nuances deriving from continuous migration across and

within borders of every nation, which make clear distinction impossible.(10)

By examining DNA evidence, most scientists embrace the idea that all modern humans originated in equatorial Africa about 200,000 years ago. Our primitive ancestors' genes were programmed to produce dark skin. Their pigment protected them from the tropical sun's ultraviolet rays, which can cause skin cancer. By a flip of the genetic dice, some of the migrants to what we now call Europe had a variant gene that gave them lighter skin. These men and women tended to get more vitamins, live longer and have more children, who in turn passed the trait on to their descendants. The trend continued for generations, eventually producing fair-skinned northern Europeans. According to University of Florida anthropologist John Moore, "Skin-color genes are turned off and on very quickly in evolution. People can go from black to white or white to black in 10,000 years."(11)

Interbreeding between different ethnic groups is the greatest proof that they are members of the same species—or family. A black Ghanaian and white Swede can produce a child; a human and a gorilla cannot. Two different species cannot produce a fertile offspring.

Sure there are differences among humans, just as there are differences within plant species or animal species. Though members of the same species or family, every human has his or her own individuality. No two people have the same fingerprints. The principle of unity and diversity operates on all levels of nature. One of the best examples of this principle is the structure of the human body. Though the heart, lungs, pancreas, liver, stomach and kidneys have different functions, they must operate harmoniously if a human being is to manifest good physical health. They are the essential parts that help to make up the whole. Wouldn't life be boring if all humans thought alike, felt alike, ate the same foods, dressed alike and lived in the same kind of houses? Why, we would have to surrender our humanness and function as robots made of protoplasm. While diversity beautifies humanity, it has a practical side. For example, people living in hot, sunny climates produce melanin, which darkens their skin; and the dark skin functions as a shield against the skin cancer-producing rays of the tropical sun. But while diversity has aesthetic and practical values, our differences are trivial in a biological sense. In fact, geneticists estimate that the variations of genetic makeup regarding what is commonly known as racial differences occupy only about 0.01 percent of our genes.(12) Also, Yale University researchers studied the DNA of men representing every major population in the world. They discovered that all of the men shared exactly the same pattern for a portion of the Y chromosome indicating that they came from the same father. These findings add to the evidence that all humans share the same basic genetic blueprint. Population differences and ethnic characteristics, though they appear large, are really superficial variations.(13) The important point is that people living in Africa, the Arctic, Asia, Europe, the Pacific, North and South America are one—and yet superficially different. This is just another paradoxical piece in the puzzle called reality.

While learning about the oneness of humankind through books and lectures is important, it alone cannot dry up the venom of race prejudice in our hearts. More knowledge is required, knowledge that comes from regular heartfelt interaction between blacks and whites, between Asians and blacks, between whites and Indians, between Latinos and whites. Meaningful dialogue is absolutely necessary. When that takes place, what was learned through reading takes on greater meaning; it becomes a part of us. Knowledge is transformed into understanding. And with understanding we become a force for unity in our home, neighborhood, community, workplace or school. In other words, wherever we find ourselves, we become a catalyst for bringing people together, regardless of skin color, religion or nationality.

Through friendship, blacks and whites are in a better position to share with each other feelings they would never reveal to someone of a different ethnic group they don't really know. Trust is usually a byproduct of friendship. And where there is trust both parties are willing to open up to each other. Whatever bonding already exists between the two is strengthened. That's what happened between Pete and myself. After a month of living together, we shared feelings we had never revealed to our parents. It was no longer a relationship between a person preoccupied with his blackness and a person preoccupied with his whiteness. It was a relationship between Pete and me. Not that Pete was no longer aware that I was white or that I was no longer aware that Pete was black. It's just that this fact was simply secondary.

I remember one night while washing dishes, we got into a discussion about why he disliked his Aunt Ophelia's Jamaican friend, Duane. What he shared with me that evening would have never been revealed if we only had a casual acquaintanceship. When Pete shared what was festering in his soul, my heart drew closer to his heart.

I was puzzled as to why Pete disliked Duane. Surely, I thought, Pete had to agree with many of Duane's views—they seemed to make so much sense, especially for a black living in America.

After much prodding on my part, Pete reluctantly explained why he was annoyed with Duane. "The man is arrogant," he said, handing me a dry dish to stack.

"But the guy cares for you," I said. "He told me so."

"Maybe it's a personality conflict. But I never could take anyone who had all of the answers."

"I think with Duane it's a case of having some strong convictions. What's wrong with that?"

"Nothing. But I want no part of anyone who demands that I adopt his convictions."

"I see. You reject his trying to turn you into a Marxist."

"It's not that so much as his air of superiority. When I'm with him I feel like shit. It's hard enough taking that stuff from my white boss at work."

Pete folded the dishrag, placed it on the rim of the sink and sat down at the table. "Look, I don't hate the man; I just hate being with him, especially when he badmouths American blacks." Pete swept the salt shaker off the table and into his hand. "Every time he does that I feel like he's plunging a knife into my heart."

I hadn't realized that antipathy existed between black West Indians and African-Americans. But Pete wasn't finished. "They come from Jamaica and Trinidad, cocky as hell, always critical of us for not taking advantage of the opportunities in America to get ahead.

"It hurts me to see them come here and excel in school and business and seize leadership positions in our community. The trouble is that their attitude towards us fuels the bigots' view of American blacks. With their fancy accents and English-style education, they can get into places I can't, even though I was born in this country and they're foreigners.

"Duane has no feeling for what our system has done to us. It doesn't matter that he can name every American president, that he has a better understanding of how my government operates. He isn't the product of a society that brainwashes you into believing that you are inferior because of your skin color and where you were born."

"I don't understand," I interrupted. "You mean that you feel blacks are inferior to whites?"

"Yes—deep down I feel that way. And there doesn't seem to be a damn thing I can do about it."

"How do you feel inferior?" I asked. "Because you don't give me the impression of being that way."

"How?" he said, raising his voice and slamming the salt shaker onto the table. "When I'm about to enter a train, and I notice the engineer is black, I begin to worry about an accident. I never feel that way when a white man is in the driver's seat."

That was a revelation to me. Not only because he felt that way, but because he was baring his soul. It was so uncharacteristic of him. He seemed to be a reserved person. But then it seemed like he wasn't only thinking about himself as he spoke. It was as if he was speaking for the thousands, maybe millions, of other blacks who felt the same way.

"Ever since I could remember I have had to live with fear. While I tried to drive it from my mind, it was always there, deep inside me, as if it was a natural part of me. There were times when I wondered whether fear and my soul were one and the same.

"Even in safe places like South Side Chicago the fear was still there. There was the fear of not being able to survive, the fear of not being able to find a job, or if I found one, not being able to perform well—or hold onto it.

"My worst fear was not being able to pursue a desire because of my skin color. That hurt because that, more than anything else, prevented me from fulfilling myself as a human being. I wanted to be a doctor, but I didn't know what to do or who to turn to to realize my dream. Even Ophelia, who I knew loved me, discouraged me by urging me to settle for less.

"I have to believe that she wanted me to do what I really wanted to do; but having more experience of the reality of our country, she wished to protect me from being crushed. I know Ophelia. She wasn't about to shoot craps with my life. She cared for me too much to do that. She knew I didn't have much chance making it. She was protecting me from insults and rejection I would have to endure if I tried for it." Pete paused, then added, "Now I understand, as Ophelia does, that for us, surviving is more important than attaining.

"In the white world, my fear is more intense. It was always like that, even as a child. First my mother, who was a live-in maid and cook for a wealthy white family, warned me about the hostility I'd face in the neighborhood we were living in.

"She was right. Even in kindergarten I learned that I was different. Different not like a violet is from a rose—more like a weed is to a flower. And I was always the weed.

"All my teachers were white. So were my heroes—Superman and the Lone Ranger. Even Tarzan who beat up on blacks. The only mention of blacks in school was in the fourth grade when some references were made to slavery. I'll never forget the pictures of slaves in my textbook. They were the only colored faces in the book. One picture was of blacks hunched over, picking cotton with the white master on a horse overseeing them. From my teachers I got the impression that my ancestors were a bunch of savages and cannibals. I think it was in school that I learned how inferior I was to all of the other students."

Pete grabbed the salt shaker again and squeezed it hard. "There were nights when I went to bed hoping I would be white when I woke up the next day, and that my mother would be white, no longer working as a maid, and that my friends in school would invite me to their houses, and they would come to mine to play. No white kid ever invited me to his house.

"When my mother died suddenly of a stroke, I ended up at Ophelia's, my mother's oldest sister. That was a traumatic experience. For ten years my mother had been the only black in my life. I was thrown into a strange world. I was a black but to the kids on the block I didn't act like one. All the kids, even in school, spoke a kind of English I wasn't accustomed to. It took time and a lot of ridicule before I could fit in. But the transformation was made, because it had to be made.

"I still feel uneasy among whites. I feel like a stranger no matter how nice they treat me. I feel apart from the scene because somehow some reference is usually made to my blackness. When that happens I feel a spotlight is on me, with everyone staring at me. Often someone will tell me how great Ralph Bunche is even though I have no interest in politics. When that happens I hear what is really being said: 'Man, you'll always be a nigger.' No matter what I do, I will always be a nigger, even if I become a doctor."

Chapter Four

The Depth Of American Racism

I learned a lot from my experience with Pete. Not that I had completely healed my infection of racism. On the other hand, I had gained insights that had eluded me all my life. Living with Pete, I discovered things I could have never learned from psychology and sociology textbooks. By being close to Pete, I was able to hear him with my heart as well as with my ear. What I heard was a human being crying out for acceptance as a full fledged human being. That disturbed me because that should not be, not in this enlightened age. My immediate impulse was to acknowledge his unspoken appeal. I tried hard to embrace him as a fellow human being. The fact that I had to try—troubled me. What my head could accept, my heart couldn't, at least not all the way. How I wish there had been no reservations. Yet, they were there; but it wasn't all bad. The fact that I knew they were there, and that I had a responsibility to eliminate them—was progress. Prior to meeting Pete, I had been unaware of what I had repressed.

My reaching out to Pete, though restrained somewhat by reservations, wasn't born out of pity, but rather empathy and a genuine desire to show him the respect he yearned for—and deserved. Our closeness allowed me to appreciate his pain, at least in part. My awareness of blacks had expanded beyond what I had read in magazines and what I saw flash across TV screens. For the first time in my life it included a black man in the flesh who was struggling for a right that had been denied him because of his skin color.

It felt good to know that Pete found in me a white person he could really talk to, share his true feelings with, and not have to pretend and try to impress, or conceal and con. With me, he didn't have to engage in survival exercises that were so emotionally draining that the thought of having to interact with a white man often made Pete feel sick to his stomach. Knowing this, I tried to put myself in his place, wondering what I would do if I had to endure the indignities he had to face every day. It didn't take me long to realize how fortunate I was being white in America.

When I finally realized how all-encompassing racism was in America, my first inclination was to abandon the idea of doing something to eliminate the social scourge. Why, it is so big, so complex, I thought, only a collective psychological transformation of a people clinging proudly and possessively to the "American way," can wipe out the epidemic. Was I being unpatriotic, even subversive, in thinking that racism was embodied in the "American way?" I wondered. Yet, I knew it was so, mostly by intuition, but also from the little real American history I knew.

Not recognizing that racism is part of the "American way" fortifies the web of denial that encompasses America. Of course I can understand why whites are reluctant to challenge this assumption. They are content with the official story of the origin and development of the great American democracy. Created by our original political, religious, academic and business leaders and perpetuated by their successors and our school systems throughout the decades, the story has evolved into a sacred belief too precious to question. The trouble is—the story was shaped by white men. The black, Indian, Asian and Latino versions were never considered. For example, take the period between 1900 and 1924, hailed by the historian establishment as perhaps the most progressive period in American history. Major reforms were enacted like the Pure Food and Drug Act; the Meat Inspection Act; the Federal Reserve Act, which created the Federal Reserve Commission; the Federal Trade Commission; the Interstate Commerce Commission. The railroads were regulated and the sixteenth and seventeenth amendments to the Constitution were adopted, establishing a federal income tax and taking the power of electing the senators of the state from the state legislature and placing it in the hands of the people of the state.(1)

To blacks the so-called progressive era was a nightmare. It was during this time that more black people were lynched than at any other time in American history. The Ku Klux Klan's popularity was soaring in the North as well as in the South. In Dixie, the federal government's promise of giving the freed slave forty acres and a mule wasn't kept, and as a result many rural blacks resorted to sharecropping, a more sophisticated form of slavery. The poll tax kept most blacks from voting, which had been guaranteed by the 15th amendment to the Constitution. In the north, those blacks that fled the south found themselves immersed in poverty in segregated slums; the children who were able to go to school attended segregated schools. Labor unions barred blacks, who found it almost impossible to find jobs except as servants or unskilled laborers. There were murderous race riots against blacks in a number of northern cities.(2) It was during this period that most blacks realized that the American Dream was not meant for them.

Though slavery had been abolished, racism was as virulent as ever—and still is. It didn't matter that the 14th and 15th amendments to the Constitution had been adopted. For about 100 years the federal government did little to enforce them, allowing various forms of Jim Crowism* to operate as an established social law of the land. And it didn't matter whether a liberal or conservative was in the White House. The will to enforce those amendments didn't exist because racism was and still remains a powerful part of the "American Way." The underlying and unspoken reason for the lack of action on the part of the national leadership was that there was more important business to attend to than guaranteeing people of color their civil rights. This attitude was based on the belief that minorities, especially blacks, were inherently inferior. And by being inferior, blacks didn't deserve the kind of attention that the "superior (white)" constituencies called for.

Let's face it, it took more than a sustained, well organized civil rights protest in the 1960s to move Congress and President Lyndon Baines Johnson to enforce the 14th and 15th amendments by passing the Civil Rights acts of the 1960s. It was the rioting in American cities across the country; seeing whole neighborhoods engulfed in flames, the disenfranchised and disadvantaged looting stores; federal troops battling Molotov-cocktail-throwing youths in American streets—those scenes, and those scenes alone, shook the leadership of America. Out of fear, they forged laws that were meant to cool off the raging tempers of a people they believed deep down weren't worthy of the respect they had fought for so long. When property-damaging-rioting erupted in more than 120 American cities, including the nation's capital, the government introduced its affirmative action policy for minorities and women. I doubt that there would have been any civil rights legislation had there not been such widespread rioting by blacks over a five-year

---

* Jim Crowism was a form of racial discrimination, which came into being after the freeing of the slaves. The U.S. Supreme Court Plessy vs. Ferguson decision, which in effect legalized the separation of blacks and whites in public places, helped to legitimize Jim Crowism, especially in the South.

period. The fear among whites, who witnessed the rioting on television, was generated by the chilling thought of the rebellious blacks carrying their campaign of destruction into white neighborhoods. If there were a foolproof way of preventing blacks from doing to white communities what they were doing to their own communities, many whites would have stood by as approving spectators hoping the rioters would do a thorough job.

The black-on-black violence reported graphically by the news media reinforced many whites' suspicions that blacks were more animal than human. They therefore adopted the attitude that the rioting in the ghettos was justified, because they reasoned: The fewer blacks around, the less of a race problem there would be, and the United States could get on with solidifying its "number one" position in the world. This hidden ethnic cleansing attitude is a reality among many whites in every section of the nation. To whites, black violent behavior is like a bolt of lightening, blinding them from seeing what really triggers the violence. Scared, they are quick to judge and support efforts to assure that ghetto violence doesn't extend into white communities. They become strong advocates of "law and order" policies.

The high incidence of black-on-black violence is a reality not because of the false assumption that blacks have a natural proclivity for violence or the fantasy that within them is a powerful "rage" gene. And it's not a case of blacks searching out other blacks to assault. It's just that they spend more time with blacks, and when the rage they live with all the time explodes, it is usually in black neighborhoods. Living with this rage, anger and the pressure of trying to survive in an alien society are contributing factors to the high incidence of high blood pressure among blacks, along with many other serious problems.

Black violence is often an act of desperation, springing from a deep internal cry to be free; to be something they are not allowed to be; it is also an expression of self-hatred and a repressed hatred of everything that is black. Sociologists call the latter *internalized racism*. Being human, African-Americans want to grow socially, intellectually and spiritually, but are plagued by certain impediments that keep them from being completely free; the biggest one is being black in a racist, white-dominated society. Realizing that it is impossible to change their skin color, attempts are made to glorify and glamorize blackness. While this chipping away process has made some headway, the lingering aversion to blackness that most blacks try hard to conceal—remains, continuing to cause doubts about their worthiness.

Blacks are trapped. And it is not by choice. Though they sense who is to blame, they lack the power to alter the situation. What whites need to know is what it is like being in the trap. When that occurs, they grow empathetic to a black person's plight in America and supportive of such policies as affirmative action.

Trying to break out of a condition of subjugation is a natural human reflex. Didn't many of the European settlers in colonial America, whose descendants today are real Americans, try to break out of a condition of subjugation when they revolted against the British Crown? While we consider those who revolte to be patriots, the British authorities at the time considered them terrorists. In 1863 Irish immigrants in New York City carried out one of the worst riots in American history. It lasted three days; at least 100 people were killed (The exact figures have never been given); the Irish marched through the streets, destroying buildings, factories, streetcar lines, and many homes of the rich, and they shot, hanged or burned almost every black in sight. They torched the only black orphanage in the city. What sparked the riot? They blamed the blacks for the Civil War, which led to the military draft, something they did not want to participate in. Then there was the discrimination they experienced whenever they ventured outside of their ghetto; the abject poverty; their inferior schooling; having to compete with blacks for the few available unskilled jobs; and the Conscription Act of 1863 was infuriating to the Irish poor. The Act allowed the rich to avoid military service by paying the government $300 or by buying a human substitute.(3) You can imagine what real Americans during that period thought of the Irish after their bloody rampage in New York! Undoubtedly, it was much like what most whites, including 2nd and 3rd generation Irish-Americans thought when they witnessed via TV the black rebellion in South Central Los Angeles in 1992.

When confronted by prejudice and persecution, even a people who traditionally have been passive will resort to violence. Immediately after World War II, Jewish leaders pressured international agencies and prominent figures to help them create a homeland in Palestine, the place their ancestors once ruled. Holocaust survivors needed some place to settle. Jewish leaders remembered that during the war America refused to take most European Jews seeking political asylum. They weren't about to beg the US to open its doors. They wanted a land they could call their own, one that would assure their security.

When opposition to the Jewish request was raised in Europe and the Middle East, Jews organized terrorist groups. They bombed

British army barracks in Palestine as well as a hotel, killing scores of innocent men and women. They assassinated a British diplomat and a United Nations official.(4)

The Jewish Warsaw Ghetto uprising during World War II was another example of what a desperate people will do when trapped by an oppressor who is bent on exterminating them.

By providing these few examples, I'm not trying to convince the reader that social justice and freedom can be won only through violence. It is simply that desperate people regardless of skin color, religion, or ethnic origin will resort to violence when their physical and psychological survival is at stake. Though the form of revolt is different, the spark that ignites the revolt stems from a similar emotion—the desire to be free, to be treated justly, and as equals.

In large measure, black violence in America is an attempt to break out of a trap they did not create.

Chapter Five

America Was Created For Whites

The trap is the result of racism which is a powerful part of the American way. In order for the entrapped to obtain complete freedom, it is essential for all of us to understand how the collective psychological structure of racism has developed and how it has been maintained in America for nearly 400 years. To effectively dismantle any well-established structure, it is necessary to know how it was constructed in the first place. Proceeding without that knowledge could lead to disastrous results.

The first European settlers in North America believed that as Christians they were superior to those who didn't share their religious beliefs. As a result, the people who greeted them, the American Indians, were immediately viewed as pagans, ignorant of the most sacred truth. Because the Indians were much darker than the Europeans and their ways seemed so strange, the settlers considered the natives—savages. It didn't take long before the settlers convinced themselves that the Indians were subhuman creatures, unworthy of the respect humans normally give to one another. Thus, the settlers felt justified in breaking pacts made with the Indians, or in seizing their lands. To the settlers, getting rid of Indians on a section of land was like getting rid of animals inhabiting the area they craved. High and low among the settlers felt that way, including the clergy. When Dr. Cotton Mather, the esteemed Puritan theologian, received word of Puritan troops annihilating a Pequot Indian village, he announced to his congregation: "It was supposed that no less than 600 Pequot souls were brought down to hell that day."(1)

The early European settlers' view of the Africans brought to North America as slaves was not much different than their view of Indians. Most colonial clergy, Catholic and Protestant, as well as educators and merchants and politicians, believed that blacks were inherently inferior to whites. In all of the original 13 colonies there was the prevailing belief among whites that the Caucasian race was not only superior to the African races, but that Africans were part of a lower species, something between the ape and the human. As a consequence they could at least tolerate the enslavement of blacks. Those who promoted slavery as a legitimate institution profited from it in a big way. As free labor, blacks helped to make many whites, including powerful men like George Washington, Thomas Jefferson and James Madison—wealthy. In fact, Madison once boasted to a British visitor that he could make $257 on every black slave in a year, and spend only $12 or $13 on his keep.(2) The whites' belief in the blacks' inherent inferiority was reflected in the drafting of the US Constitution. In that sacred document, the founding fathers stated that a slave, in effect, was three-fifths human.(3) To justify that classification, James Madison wrote in Essay 54 of *The Federalist Papers* that a slave had the dual quality of being property and a person. In defining the slave as property, Madison wrote: "In being compelled to labor not for himself, but for a master; in being vendible by one master to another master; and in being subject at all times to be restrained in his liberty, and chastised in his body, by the capricious will of another, the slave may appear to be degraded from the human rank, and classed with those irrational animals, which fall under the legal denomination of property..."(4) Thomas Jefferson must have felt the same way when he proclaimed that blacks were a form of orangutan.(5)

With that view, wealthy northern merchants and southern plantation-owners could argue that slavery was not in conflict with the professed ideals of the American revolution. Slaves, they claimed, were property much like cattle, sheep and pigs. While there was a small group like the Quakers who called for the abolition of slavery, their petitions were either summarily rejected or ignored. The dominant view in white America was that blacks were animals, devoid of human reactions and emotions. With that understanding, the slave owner had no qualms about breaking up a black family, selling the father to a white man in Kentucky, a daughter to a plantation in Maryland, a son to a mill operator in Alabama and keeping the wife and mother, who was sometimes forced into being the master's secret mistress. Killing a black man wasn't considered murder; it was likened to butchering a steer.

This attitude didn't disappear as the nation matured. On the contrary, it was reinforced. The American economy, in large measure, was dependent on slavery. The burgeoning textile industry in New England relied on the cotton planted and picked by slaves in the South. With the invention of the cotton gin, cotton and textile production soared. Because both northern merchants and southern plantation-owners feared that the abolition of slavery would cause their economic demise, they became fierce advocates of the prevailing notion that blacks were subhuman, citing the three-fifths clause in the Constitution to prove their point. They actively promoted that view in speeches, books and articles. Perhaps the most articulate and persuasive spokesman was the South Carolina senator John. C. Calhoun, whose powerful intellect and oratory swayed many minds. Many American politicians of the time embraced Calhoun's rationale that slavery was one of the best ways to maintain equality and unity among whites, something that was essential to preserving national solidarity and preserving a healthy economy. Calhoun exploited the poor white man's hope of improving his quality of life and his fear of losing whatever status he already had. Calhoun proclaimed that every poor white had the potential of bettering his lot, even growing rich, and that he remained ahead of the black on America's ladder to success. To preserve his status, the poor white became an advocate of slavery and a firm believer in the inherent inferiority of the black.(6)

Fueling the prevailing white view of blacks were the findings of the so-called scientific studies of slaves. Based on the theory that the size of one's head determines creativity and intellectual capacity, scientists such as Dr. Josiah C. Nott concluded that blacks were little above the level of apes.(7) The French philosopher, Count de Gobineau, endorsed this view. His book, *The Inequality of the Human Race*, was published in Philadelphia and circulated among American intellectuals. The Frenchman claimed: "Some of his (the black's) senses have an acuteness unknown to the other races, the sense of taste and that of smell, for instance... But it is precisely this development of the animal faculties that stamps the Negro with the mark of inferiority."(8)

This kind of thinking was popularized by magazines like the *Texas Almanac*. In 1857 it featured an article stating: "... the African is an inferior being, with wool instead of hair on his head—with lungs, feet, joints, lips, nose, and cranium so distinct as to indicate a different and inferior being."(9)

America's view of blacks just prior to the Civil War was summed up in the US Supreme Court's Dread Scott decision. Chief Justice Roger Taney declared that blacks "are not included, and were not intended to be included, in the word 'citizen' in the Constitution... being a subordinate and inferior class of beings."(10)

White abolitionists, meanwhile, clamored for an end to slavery. Not that most of them were free of the belief that blacks were inherently inferior to whites; they were opposed to any thinking creatures being held in bondage. While their appeals were passionate, and many of them sacrificed much for their cause, their cry didn't change the average white person's basic opinion of the black. Most white Americans viewed the abolitionists as wild-eyed radicals. Even President Abraham Lincoln considered them a nuisance. Though he freed the slaves, he remained a believer in the inherent inferiority of blacks, thinking they could not function effectively in a democratic society. He was also opposed to interracial marriage.(11)

After the Civil War most whites showed little compassion for the more than three million freed slaves who had been set loose to live in a world they had not been prepared for. Whites in both the North and the South quickly came to the conclusion that their fundamental feelings about blacks were justified when they saw the ex-slaves—who had never been schooled on how to live in a democracy—awkwardly trying to adapt to the white man's world. It gave whites cause to believe that blacks were incapable of living in a civilized society.

The passage by Congress of the Fourteenth Amendment to the Constitution, which eliminated the "three-fifths" clause, failed to uproot it, however, from the hearts of most whites. The pattern of racial thinking had been set.

America's bloodiest war hadn't really freed black people; it had simply lengthened the chain around their neck. What happened after the Civil War was proof of that. Despite a sincere effort on the part of some northern liberal churchmen to prepare the ex-slaves for life in a free society (the schooling was always in segregated conditions), two kinds of Americans emerged: white people still harboring the strong feeling that blacks are inherently inferior to whites, and a mass of alienated, frustrated and restricted African-Americans.

About ten years after the war northerners who were once sympathetic to the blacks' plight turned their attention to other causes. Swept up by the spirit of "rugged individualism" as exemplified by John D. Rockefeller and J.P. Morgan, they sought to create their own fortunes. Many headed west, ignoring the atrocities being heaped upon blacks in the South.

Even the White House and Congress turned their backs on what was happening to the ex-slaves. Secret organizations such as the Ku Klux Klan terrorized those blacks who dared to exercise their rights as citizens. In 1924, the KKK's membership grew to four and a half million, operating in the North as well as in the South.(12) The few whites who sided with the blacks' cause also came under attack. The Confederacy was reborn in the South, with Jim Crowism replacing slavery. The thousands of blacks who migrated to the North fared little better than those who remained back home. In both the North and the South blacks were put in their place—which was far from the advantages enjoyed by whites, but close enough to see what they were being deprived of.

In the 1880s, influential white thinkers revealed publicly that even if given equal opportunity, people of African heritage were incapable of measuring up to white standards of achievement. The renowned British philosopher David Hume was one of those thinkers: "I am apt to suspect the negroes and in general all other species (for there are four or five different kinds) to be naturally inferior to the whites. There never were a civilized nation of any other complexion than white, nor even any individual eminent either in action or speculation. No ingenious manufacturers among them, no arts, or sciences."(13)

Racism will never be eliminated in America until its white citizens overcome their deep-seated belief that blacks are inherently inferior to whites. Simply put, it is a matter of accepting blacks as full fledged human beings. While many whites claim they already do, their behavior usually doesn't reflect what they say.

Though it can be done, it isn't easy to eradicate a 400-year-old pattern of thinking and feeling that is part of a culture you admire and respect and believe is the best in the world. In some respects, reluctance to deal with the truth stems from a fear of diminishing a way of life you cherish and trust. Many people of good will—black, Latino, Asian, American Indian and white—find it too painful to deal with the racial injustices of the past and are fearful to resurrect them. Most people want to forget about the past and start anew, hoping a sudden social metamorphosis will occur. But the past is a part of us, influencing, to a degree, our thinking and behavior. In reality, rejection of the past doesn't remove what we have been exposed to as children and youth. As a consequence none of us have been able to escape being infected or affected by racism while being brought up in America. The smog of racism insidiously blankets our nation penetrating us all, just as the fine particles of environmental smog penetrates deeply into our lungs' air sacs, causing—unbeknownst to us—tissue damage.

Let's reflect for a moment on how the past has affected our racial conditioning. The superior attitude of the European settlers toward people of color was reinforced in their homes, schools, churches, and political rallies their families attended. The dominant attitude toward people of color was passed on from one generation to another until it became ingrained in white America's psyche and institutionalized as a powerful part of the American way. Imagine—in the past two centuries American children listening to their teachers describe in segregated classrooms the romanticized version of how America came into being and flourished, never really explaining what blacks, Indians, Asians and Latinos had to endure during America's climb to greatness. It was the establishment's way of saying that people of color didn't really matter, for they were destined to be the props and tools needed to make America great. And it wasn't only white children who were influenced by this highly valued legend. It was drilled into the cerebrums and hearts of children of color as well, planting in them seeds of inferiority that today still inhibit their development.

The white Pilgrims, the white pioneers who forged westward, the vision and bravery of the white founding fathers, our children were told, turned a wilderness into the mightiest nation in the world. When the white clergy supported from the pulpit what the teachers taught in school, many of us viewed that as God sanctioning the white racial belief system. And even when the clergy wasn't directly boosting the white racial belief system, the parishioners received the message anyway. All they had to do was scan the pews and not see a black face in the congregation. They knew where the blacks were on Sunday morning—in the black churches on the other side of the tracks, where the poor, the uncouth and the less intelligent belonged. Since that was the accepted prevailing collective attitude among the dominant population, most people of color reluctantly adjusted to that condition for so long that it crystallized into a social pattern.

You would have thought that the great influx of immigrants from the 1840s to the 1920s would have diluted the poisonous atmosphere of racism that encompassed America. After all, many of them had been targets of discrimination in the lands they came from.

But that wasn't the case; in fact, they strengthened the poisonous atmosphere of racism. Not because they were passionate bigots. Being seasoned survivors, the immigrants bought into American racism. In their desire to adapt to a land that offered economic opportunities that weren't available in the "old country," they tried to adopt the prevailing social attitude of the powerful in their adopted country. And the powerful were the real Americans who were white and who believed that blacks, American Indians, Asians and Latinos were inherently inferior. Deep down the white immigrants sensed that to be an acceptable American you had to harbor and manifest race prejudice, for that was the real American way.

Though my parents, who were white immigrants, bought into American racism, I didn't feel resentment towards them; they weren't malicious people. They worked hard to make their family comfortable. Much of what they earned was invested in their house. Not that being protective of one's possessions is an excuse for racist behavior. I simply didn't feel that their ignorance warranted my punishing them. Though my parents and I quarreled often, especially during my youth, I always knew that they loved me and had my best interests at heart. I was grateful for the sacrifices my parents made so that I would have every opportunity to succeed. They were good people who often helped others in trouble. I'll never forget the day an old pensioner stopped us on the street to tell me what a kind father I had. My father, who was a plumber, had refused payment for fixing the woman's leaking bathroom pipe.

Yet I wondered: how could my parents, who had fled Russia because it wasn't safe for Jews, possess the feelings they had towards blacks? It didn't make sense. You would think that they would have been sympathetic to a people who had suffered for so long. After all, my mother and father had been persecuted, had narrowly escaped being killed by marauding bandits whose idea of a good time was torturing a Jew. And there were the periodic government-inspired pogroms in which Cossacks sacked Jewish homes, whisking away their young women.

The stories of their plight made an everlasting impact on me, undoubtedly awakening my deep concern for the oppressed.

There was always a sense of terror in my father's voice when he would recall the times he and his family huddled in their vegetable cellar, praying that the Cossacks wouldn't find them. How he wished he had been able to prevent the intruders from plundering his family's home. One thing they never seized was the brass candelabra that his mother used for the Sabbath candle ceremony. It was the only possession she would take into the hiding place.

As a twelve-year-old, my father witnessed in horror a band of drunken soldiers arguing over who would be the first to rape his sister. Only the wrath of a Russian Orthodox priest, who was passing by and heard the commotion, kept the Cossacks from carrying out their intent.

My father's family—his mother, sister, younger brother and cousin—finally abandoned their small farm. With their meager savings and some basic belongings stuffed into their wagon, they pushed across Ukraine, heading for America.

Even after my parents reached the United States, sad news from the "old world" followed them. In the fall of 1941 my mother's sister and brother-in-law, who had remained in Russia, were burned at the stake by the Nazis after being rounded up with all the other Jews in town. I remember vividly how my mother reacted to the letter from her nephew that bore the bad news.

Recalling how much my parents endured because of their being Jewish only reinforced my quandary over their attitude towards blacks. They should have been the first to support the blacks' appeal for equal status, I thought. Why did my parents allow themselves to be victimized by racism?

I now realize they had little chance of avoiding the disease of racism. Knowing how hard they had tried to adopt the ways of their new homeland, they had become aware of its laws and customs, even the unofficial ones like racism. To be a good American, they felt, you had to do what the majority did. Being astute survivors, they sensed quickly what the right attitude was and what to do to fit in, to be accepted. Though they never talked about it, they demonstrated by their actions that they knew that interacting socially with blacks was unacceptable if they wished to succeed in the land they believed with all their heart and soul was the most free in the world.

There was another reason, too, for their attitude. It was something they would have never mentioned, not even to their closest friends. They gained satisfaction from knowing that Jews were no longer the most despised in the land, as they had been back in Russia. To them it was a sign of "getting ahead." Also, they benefited economically by coming to America. Being white, they found themselves on the fifth rung from the bottom of the socio-economic ladder. Below them were the blacks, Latinos, Asians and American Indians.

American racism isn't confined to its borders. It exists overseas wherever a significant number of Americans are living. This became apparent to me during a pleasant outing at the American embassy in Pakistan in 1995. It was Christmas time, and my wife and I were visiting our son and his family. Our son Dale is an official with UNICEF, based in Islamabad. When he asked if we would like to attend a Christmas party given by the American embassy for all of the American children living in Islamabad, we accepted the invitation, because we wanted to participate in the fun our three grandchildren would experience.

And it was a lot of fun. About 100 children met Santa Claus, were given gifts by him, and most had an opportunity to sit on his lap. There were lots of American treats like hot dogs, roasted marshmallows, ice cream, kool-aid and cookies. The embassy compound green had become a carnival of happy children. All sorts of games were offered and the children, including our grandkids, tried them all.

While it was nice seeing our grandchildren having a happy time, it troubled me that there were no African-American children at the party. And it wasn't a case of there being no African-American children in Islamabad. They were there, and they had received invitations to attend the party. But their parents refused to go, I later learned, because they are made to feel uncomfortable in white organized social functions. As a consequence, American blacks tended to socialize among themselves in Islamabad.

But the absence of African-American children wasn't the only thing that disturbed me at the embassy's Christmas party. It was what went on at the most popular treat—the camel ride. Almost every child lined up to ride on an authentic camel. With the help of the brown-skinned Pakistani camel trainer, and an assist from their parents, two children at a time climbed onto the double humped animal. The trainer led the camel around a court yard for about three minutes, had the camel kneel to let the children off, and picked up another batch of kids. This routine went on for nearly two hours.

What struck me was the attitude of the children and their parents toward the camel trainer. I didn't notice any of the Americans thank him for his services. He was taken for granted, as if he were a machine, a non-human entity being used to satisfy the desires of a group of people who thought of themselves as superior to him. I'm sure the American parents and children went home that afternoon glad that they had attended the Christmas party, and full of wonderful memories, never giving a thought about the camel driver, where he came from, how he learned his craft, whether he had a family. It was a case of a human being not treated as a human being by fellow human beings on a holiday that is meant to celebrate the birth Christians believe is the savior of all humankind. Witnessing what went on at the most popular treat at the embassy's Christmas party for children made me feel ashamed of being an American.

Chapter Six

Coming To Terms With The Nature Of Racism

It is understandable why most people reject the idea of racism being a disease. They resent attempts at turning what they consider a social problem into something they think it is not. They also resent being called sick when they don't feel sick. After all, they point out, no reputable medical association lists racism as a disease.

But, then again, history is replete with examples of the majority's perception being flawed. Not long ago the medical establishment didn't consider alcoholism a disease. Now it does. And there was a time in the past when the most erudite felt the world was flat and the center of the universe. And they supported their belief through mathematics and logic. But we know now that they were wrong.

A group of mental health professionals led by Dr. Chester Pierce and Dr. Price Cobbs put together a position paper in 1967, explaining why they thought racism should be treated as a disease. After the paper was presented to a U.S. Senate subcommittee studying the mental health of America's children, no action was taken by the legislative body. It was "too hot to handle," according to the subcommittee's chairman, former Senator Fred Harris of Oklahoma. Harris, by the way, was one of the senators who agreed with the paper's rationale.

Unfortunately, those in power today are following the wrong path in their quest to find a solution to racism. In fact, one could argue they haven't found a path. What they follow is a mirage. America's present racial condition is evidence of that. Had we treated racism as what it truly is—a disease—we would not be faced with the hatred and suspicion that exists between most of the elements in the national racial construct. Instead of healing, we're hiding from the problem. Afraid to delve into it, even talk about it, and hoping that somehow it will disappear. The longer we refuse to accept the reality of racism's true nature, the wider the chasm between people of color and whites will grow—and the more their suspicion and misconceptions of each other will intensify—A formula, I feel, for impending disaster.

Racism: a psychological disorder

Racism is a psychological disorder that can trigger psychosomatic effects in people in the form of heart problems, hypertension and kidney failure. The high incidence of high blood pressure among African-Americans is due, in large measure, to the stress and distress of being black in America. To appreciate how racism affects the American population, Dr. John Woodall, a psychiatrist at Harvard's Medical School, draws a parallel between the national racial condition and the functioning of the human body.

Certain principles seem to always be present in healthy living systems whether these systems are in nature, the human body, or in society. Deviations from these principles tend to result in the disorder and disease of the system. One of the ways racism can be considered a disease is in the context of deviations from these universal principles.

First, is the principle that health represents a reciprocal interplay between parts of a system and the whole. In the body, for instance, when we are healthy, all of the systems are harmonized and work in perfect unison. Our lungs provide sufficient oxygen to fuel each cell of the body. The heart circulates adequate blood for all the body's needs, our digestive tract absorbs nutrients and eliminates waste efficiently and our liver disposes of toxins and performs its unnumbered metabolic functions with wonderful proficiency. Our endocrine system regulates the various body rhythms to deal with all manner of environmental stresses, metabolic and reproductive needs. The immune and repair systems fight anything that would disturb this marvelous balance. All of this regulated by a nervous system infinite in its complexity.

Anyone alive knows that this harmony of function does not describe the relations between races and peoples in the world, let alone America's ethnic subgroups. Not only is there no harmony among the component parts of the body politic, there is barely a concept of a body politic. This is especially true when it comes to racial identity. The division along racial lines is so ingrained, so much a part of our assumptions that we can not honestly visualize any other type of America. Consequently, a state of paralysis has marked the social dialogue about race...

In a healthy system, there is a reciprocal relationship between each part and the whole. The healthy function of one system has a strengthening effect on the whole. In turn, the harmonious functioning of the whole body has a directing and nurturing effect on each system. The oxygen exchange of the lungs, for example, becomes important only when we see the vital role it plays in the life of each cell of the body. The oxygen can't get to the cells without the pumping action of the heart, which is regulated by complex neural and hormonal feed-back loops, through the medium of healthy blood in healthy vessels, and in a narrow acid-base equilibrium supported by the kidneys and the entire metabolic rhythm of the body! We appreciate the role of one organ only when we see it in the context of the whole body as life shows itself to be an intricate web of balanced interconnectedness.

This balance between parts and the whole is referred to as the principle of unity in diversity. In this case unity is not intended to mean uniformity in function or ability. In living systems unity does not mean sameness or uniformity. Rather, unity describes a dynamic reciprocal process between all the parts in relation to the whole. Unity implies and requires both diversity of component parts and a dynamic interplay between them and the whole. This diversity and dynamism are both required elements of the idea of unity. For our purposes unity will be defined in this organic way as seen in nature.

Then the opposite holds true for the context of the racial dialogue in America. We use stilted notions of racial identity that betray the opposite of an appreciation of diversity. Also, the dynamism between society as a whole and its component racial elements is painfully lacking. Uniformity, not unity, marks the current state of the racial dialogue in America. Uniformity lacks these two principles of diversity and dynamism and is therefore the opposite of unity.

This principle of unity in diversity has tremendous organizational power in the natural world. The nuances of this principle offer essential insights into the requirements for, and the nature of, life itself. The degree of a living system's compliance with its requirements determines the degree of that system's health or disease. Racism represents the exact opposite of this principle of life, and is the archetype of social disease for this reason. For America to become socially healthy a dispassionate and careful study of the subtleties of the principle of unity in diversity must be made. Balancing these requirements in society is the task before us as we set the context for healing the disease of racism.(1)

It doesn't take a Ph.D. to see that America's social system is way out of balance. On the one hand, whites suffer from an inherent sense of superiority toward blacks, coupled, in most instances, by a hidden fear of losing their privileges to those they have been conditioned to view as inferior. In the black community there's a deep-rooted suspicion of the majority population, stemming from an ingrained sense of alienation. Among the Asians, Hispanics and American Indians there is a constant struggle for acceptance as equals. Overcoming a deep sense of not belonging to the inner circle of "real Americans" is an obstacle that makes striving for equality painful. As a consequence, the wounded American body-politic limps fearfully toward an uncertain future.

Among whites there are different levels of manifesting their sense of superiority. There are those who flaunt it; there are those who admit feeling that way but restrain from outwardly expressing it; and there are those who want to believe that they are free of it—but are not.

Regardless of what their racial attitude is, from a reality standpoint their unquestioned presumption of inherent superiority is baseless. As has been pointed out already, there cannot be any superior race because there is only one race—the human race. That so many whites refuse to accept scientific fact only compounds their shaky state of mind. Since mental health is determined by our proximity to reality, those of us who consciously or unconsciously cling to the fallacious belief in white superiority are partially disconnected from reality. Therefore, we have a mental health problem. We allow a warped view of an aspect of reality to rule our feelings toward a black person, Asian, American Indian or Latino. By refusing to correct the view, our collective condition becomes more deeply entrenched. Many grow progressively fearful when encountering the object of their prejudice.

To illustrate how twisted white thinking has been toward America's minorities, consider the way American writers, folk artists and filmmakers portrayed the white-Indian conflict. The Indians were depicted as savages, preying upon innocent whites, torturing them, killing them, destroying their villages, torching their land; while, for the most part, the opposite was true. Every Buffalo Bill Show featured a segment of a simulated Indian attack on a white community, in which the whites always ended up victorious. And the crowd loved it.(2) The popular western dime novel reinforced the deranged notion that the white settlers were the innocent victims of the Indian-white conflict in America. After being subjected to decades of such propaganda, many of today's whites have difficulty ridding themselves of negative feelings about minorities even though they are based on falsehoods. Getting rid of an emotional attachment to a falsehood that's been internalized as the truth—isn't easy.

This kind of twisted thinking about minorities has infiltrated the unconscious mind of many whites of good will. They are overcome by shame whenever negative racial feelings slip into their conscious mind. Usually, those feelings appear during unplanned stressful racial encounters, like my "move nigger" episode. Driven by shame, I repressed the ugly thought and feeling of hatred that welled up in my heart toward the elderly black man in the car ahead of me. Resorting to repressing shameful feelings is like carrying a cancer that needs to be removed. The fact that those feelings are a part of you can't help but affect the development of your attitudes and behavior. It just makes sense that what's festering in the unconscious needs to be drawn to the conscious where what troubles you can be examined thoroughly and realistic steps taken to overcome what you have been trying to hide from yourself and the world. Otherwise, well meaning whites will continue to expend considerable energy in pretending to be free of race prejudice. And they are not going to fool the traditional targets of racism, who, out of necessity, have learned to distinguish between white pretense and white genuineness. Moreover, it is worth remembering the admonition of Socrates that "the unexamined life is not worth living."(3)

There is a simple test that well intentioned whites can take to determine whether they are infected by racism. The Third Webster's International dictionary defines disease as a lack of ease; discomfort, distress, and trouble. There is no question that racism has

caused a lack of ease, discomfort for the individual and community, distress and trouble. When whites are in the company of
blacks and feel ill at ease, distressed, uncomfortable or troubled,
they are sensing the symptoms of the disease of racism. Usually
those who don't recognize racism as a disease will not associate
those negative feelings as symptoms, and because they are
ashamed of those feelings they will try to find or invent ways to rid
themselves of them. The easiest way to accomplish that is by avoiding situations involving blacks. If they are committed to promoting human rights, they will do it in safe places, where there are
only fleeting interactions with blacks or Latinos. And when they
do that they unwittingly strengthen the unofficial system of apartheid in their country.

On the other hand, those few whites who accept racism as a
disease and experience negative feelings in the presence of blacks
will view the symptoms as a sign to seek help.

In the same way that medical researchers need to know the
cause of physical maladies before they can devise appropriate remedies, the cause of the infection of racism in whites must be found
before healing can take place. The closer researchers get to the
source, the more effective is the treatment. When they are certain
they have found the cause, a vaccine is often developed, which in
time eliminates the disease.

I believe we have discovered the cause of the infection of racism that plagues whites. It was touched on in an earlier chapter. In
this chapter we'll take a closer look at it.

The history of the disease of racism among European settlers

Today's whites have inherited a psychological obsession that
began to form when the first European settlers arrived in America.
Their intellectual, emotional and spiritual reaction to the Indians
that greeted them, and the Africans they enslaved, make up the obsession's core. To illustrate what the early white settlers' opinions
were regarding blacks and Indians, it is important to know the
views of their leaders who influenced everyone else's thinking. The
leaders' twisted views of people of color reflected not only an ignorance of who qualifies as human, but a bit of dementia as well.

Influencing the European settlers' attitude and behavior toward red and black people in America were decrees issued by leading European Christian leaders. In 1452, for example, Pope
Nicholas V decreed in a papal bull entitled Romanus Pontifex that
Portugal's King Alfonso had the right to "invade, search out, cap-

ture, vanquish and subdue all Saracens and pagans whatsoever and all the land and possessions of these heathens be taken away and reduced to perpetual slavery."(4) The papal decree was viewed by some European entrepreneurs as a license to engage in slave trade; it also empowered the Catholic clergy in the Americas to enslave Indians and become involved in the black slave trade, as a means of funding the church's work in the "new world." No doubt the English settlers' attitude toward the Indians and blacks brought over from Africa was influenced by Britain's King Henry VII's 1496 decree to explorer John Cabot to, "conquer, occupy and possess the lands of heathens and infidels."(5)

When Governor John Winthrop of the Massachusetts Bay Colony learned that small pox, a disease brought to America by Europeans, was sweeping through Indian villages and killing hundreds of them, he attributed the epidemic to an act of God. It was God's way, he believed, of removing obstacles to achieving His rightful believers' destiny—and that was, to conquer and rule the land occupied by the Indians, who Winthrop believed were savages and pagans. Leading 17th century European thinkers promoted the theory that American Indians were a separate lower species, that they did not spring from the Biblical Adam and Eve.(6) The Puritan clergy felt the same way. In one of Reverend Cotton Mather's sermons, he thundered: "We know not when and how these Indians first became inhabitants of the mighty continent, yet we may guess that the Devil decoyed these miserable savages hither, in hope that the gospel of the Lord Jesus Christ would never come to destroy or disturb his absolute empire over them."(7) Mather and his fellow clergymen felt the same way about the kidnapped Africans. The Puritan church's official reason for sanctioning slavery was to civilize a savage people who didn't know, as the English did, who God was. Theologians like Mather combed the Bible, searching for passages that would justify on religious grounds the enslavement of blacks. They pointed to the Book of Genesis, to the curse of Ham in particular, purporting to mean that he who was black was forever branded as outside the pale of humanity—that his destiny was to serve the needs and wishes of the "superior" whites. In a way, Puritan thinking in regards to undesirables like Indians and blacks is reminiscent of Hitler's deranged thinking about Jews and gypsies.

The common European settlers adopted the racist views of their political and religious leaders. The settlers' schools reflected these views, which were passed on from grade to grade, from colony to colony, and from generation to generation. By the time the

United States of America came into being, a collective educational attitude had been set regarding the status of people of color in the new nation. The attitude reflected the thinking and feelings of Colonial America. Even the Founding Fathers manifested this attitude. Benjamin Franklin, perhaps the most sophisticated and enlightened Founding Father, promoted the idea of using rum as a way "to extirpate (annihilate) these savages (American Indians) in order to make room for the cultivators of the earth."(8) Thomas Jefferson, who drafted the Declaration of Independence, had his caught runaway slaves flogged. And he looked upon slave-breeding, as one would look upon the breeding of dogs and horses. Though in principle he was opposed to slavery, he believed blacks were inherently inferior to whites and had no place in a country like the United States as citizens. His solution to the black-white conflict was to round up all blacks and dump them either in Africa or a black dominated island in the Caribbean.(9) Jefferson's deportation views of African-Americans were also shared by James Madison, who drafted the Bill of Rights, as well as James Monroe, Andrew Jackson, Henry Clay, Daniel Webster, Francis Scott Key and Abraham Lincoln. By sharing their racial views publicly, they reinforced the prevailing anti-black views of most whites in the North and South. And those views were inculcated in the nation's educational institutions.

It wasn't only what the teachers and textbooks did and didn't state about race that reinforced the whites' psychological obsession concerning people of color.

The fact that white students had no association with black and Indian children in the classroom from the early 1600s to the 1900s was a message that didn't need any explaining. Its meaning was very clear to everyone: "Superior" whites and "inferior" people of color don't mix socially, and even school was out of bounds. While the mixing was discouraged, all students were exposed, in the main, to the same white created brainwashing, a version of history that made whites look like heroes and the rest as ruthless obstacles to fulfilling America's mission. People of color didn't count. Everyone learned, for example, that a European, Hernando De-Soto, discovered the Mississippi River. All students embraced the information as the truth, as did the teachers who shared it. They believed this falsehood as the truth, because the likes of Winthrop, Mather, Jefferson, Madison, Franklin and Washington viewed those who lived along the Mississippi, and used it as a trading artery long before the whites appeared, as a lower order of beings—not qualified to be considered fully human. Thus teachers were justified in proclaiming a European discovered the Mississippi River.

For three centuries all Americans were exposed to this type of thinking, leading to the creation of a persistent national pathology. We have been locked into a cycle of blind imitation, where everyone practiced the racial beliefs held by the first white settlers and the Founding Fathers. It was drilled into us repeatedly from one generation to another. Those heartfelt beliefs, based on a twisted view of reality, took such strong hold on the population, that not even the abolitionist movement, the Civil War, the end of Jim Crowism, the 1960s civil rights laws, or school busing have been able to change those deeply ingrained warped beliefs. What has changed is how those heartfelt beliefs are expressed. Today, whites are more diplomatic than they were prior to the 1960s. Two worlds still exist in America. The world of the "superior" whites and the world of the "inferior" people of color. There is still little genuine mixing in school and church, and interracial friendships based on equality is a rarity.

The challenge for whites to recognize their racial obsession

The psychological obsession is so deeply rooted in the soul of America that it has continually grown despite some superficial attempts to dull the pain that racism sets off. The obsession's powerful core was wrapped, at first, by layers of superiority, conviction, pride, grandiosity, and narcissism, and after the 1960s, layers of denial. Because of those layers, the core is well protected, making real healing difficult. The greatest difficulty is for whites to accept the fact that the obsession is part of them. But a few have, like author Bradford Miller. In his book, *Returning to Seneca Falls*, Miller reveals what he has discovered since breaking out of the hard shell of denial. It is an up-close account of how the obsession has affected him; and I might add, many others like him, who are afraid to come forward.

> After I left graduate school and began working temporary jobs in small towns while trying to write and publish poetry and find a job teaching English, I felt the heartworm of racism. The older I became and the more clearly I was defined in the context of American society, the more difficult I found encountering black people with the same sense of openhearted warmth as I would greet most white strangers whose path I might cross. I

suppose that increasingly I began to walk like a white man, talk like a white man, and read and think like one.

As hard as I tried to apply my own understanding of the danger of narcissism as it laced white American society, I found myself succumbing from time to time to the opinion that black people lived in drug-infested, crime-riddled streets, scammed the welfare system, were unmotivated to work, and were dangerous.

Sometimes if I encountered a black person, or read about black people in the news, I would be aware of irrational, racist thoughts emerging from the front of my brain. Back in my more spiritual and sagacious brain, I would analyze this data, try to figure out the source of this racism, and attempt to annihilate it. This is something I continue to do with white Americans' singular narcissistic loyalty to their mirrored artificial image. And in my spiritual brain, I still cling to the ideal that we are all human beings on this planet, marvelously diverse, and that we must overcome racism if we want to bring our society to fruition.

While this ideal is immovable, set deep in my being like a bridge piling, I still feel some degree of culture shock when I see a black face, even though I know it is a racist stereotype. I still spontaneously fear black neighborhoods as past the point of no return, with discourteous, unsupervised kids running the streets, and gang-infested schools. Most importantly, I feel uncomfortably vulnerable to black people. I feel like a hateful target of what I believe is their rage against white men in particular. I feel helplessly book smart, endowed with obscene amounts of leisure time, shamefully immune to their suffering. And while I can intellectually understand how things got that way, I have very feeble tools with which to change the status quo. And there is the whisper in my breast that says let the black people save themselves — they don't want me or need me anyway.(10)

There are so-called emancipated white folks who don't believe that blacks are inherently inferior to whites; and do not grow fearful when they see a black man walking towards them on the sidewalk late at night. And they even support wholeheartedly black political initiatives to win true equality in America. Yet their fixation about race seems to be a permanent part of them, so deeply entrenched in their consciousness that no self-induced exercise is capable of wiping it out. It is a form of torture, as Wendy Darling describes in a column she wrote for the *Collegian*, the daily University of Massachusetts newspaper:

> I consider myself a racist because I discriminate on the basis of race. I notice it. I think about it. I get confused about it. I see a person and there it is: race. The skin color is there. I see it. And then things happen inside my mind that I can't explain, things I am forced to label as racist.

> I'm standing on North Pleasant Street in Amherst waiting to get a bus back to the University of Massachusetts. Standing next to me is a black man. I see him. And then it begins.

> If he is well-dressed, I think to myself, "God, he must have had to work hard for that." And I mean really work, well beyond the actual labor, but actual work against the great white current, racial politics, maybe even poverty, depending on his situation. Or maybe he looks like an Amherst College student. "Wow," I think, "I wonder what it feels like to be at an elite school like that when there are so few people who look like you, so few role models."

> Maybe the man looks like he's from UMass. "Well, then, he must think I'm a prissy little white girl," I think. Me with my transparent, snowy white skin, short red hair, black trench coat. Could this guy relate to me? Or does he resent me? Does he think I'm like the rest?

> I hate myself at times like this. Why can't I just see this man and have that be it? If it was a white man, none of these processes would occur. If he was well-dressed, I'd say, "Oh, just another businessman. Big deal." Or if he was an Amherst College student: "Yup, another of those handsome scholars." For a UMass student, I probably wouldn't even register except to say: "Another one."

> But it's not a white man, it's a black man, and as a result, I am hit with all these stupid thoughts relating to his race. This man, through no fault of his own, has handed me a hefty load of mental baggage just by standing there, the civil rights struggle, employment discrimina-

tion, urban poverty, institutional racism, on and on and on.

And forced with this load, all I can really do is smile and try to turn my thoughts to something else. Burying my guilty conscience (forged by years living in this race-crazy society), I try to return to the island of security and homogeneity I keep hidden within myself... (11)

Most whites are so close to the posture they have constructed concerning their racial conditioning that they are unaware of how racism affects them. Unlike Darling and Miller, many don't want to know, because they are afraid of what they might learn about themselves. This condition is keenly described by Bernard Streets, an accomplished scientist; and a serious student of American racism. Streets has explored racism from a special vantage point because he can easily pass as a white, although he views himself a black man in our race classification conscious society. He has the opportunity to get close to whites and probe into how racism impacts well intentioned whites.

Racism has the remarkable ability to bring out negative tendencies in fundamentally good white people to the point of obscuring their positive and caring inclinations, their senses of compassion, understanding, fairplay, and justice. Rationalization is an important tool for the racist and a means by which to justify one's feelings and/or actions toward someone of color. For centuries, whites have proclaimed themselves to be the "primary race" and have offered biblical "evidence" to support the notion that God so ordained the white race as the one to maintain dominance and power, and thereby be preeminent over all others. Well, that same source of biblical evidence also mentioned "brotherhood," God as being the creator of all people, and the gospel of loving one's neighbor. Now, enters the aspect of "guilt." How to reconcile all of this? Corruption, perversion, and debasement set in, and over time rationalization, ignorance and fear lend more persuasion over "guilt"; and one, then, begins to find something inherently "wrong" with these folks of color; and, so, a list of character defects, perceived as natural inclinations, is drawn and passed on to one's progeny as the "truth."

One effect of racism in America has been that whites, as the dominant, controlling power, in creating our national identity have defined "American" as white. As such, deep down, many whites do not perceive people of color as American. Holding onto a widely-shared, yet very narrow sense of history, they view "American" as one of European or white ancestry. This even excludes the native Americans who lived in the Americas long before Columbus' arrival. Thus, race "has been a social construction that has set apart racial minorities from European immigrant groups."(12) From this philosophy and the practice of exclusion and discrimination throughout the years, it is easy to see how white people could develop feelings of superiority and dislike, distrust, and fear of America's minority people of color.

Fear! Fear of the dark masses plagues many whites, and this fear leads to all sorts of psychological and physical disorders. Fear of people of color tends to make some whites think and act unjustly. In these times, many whites are cognizant of their "minority" status among the world populations and are becoming uncomfortable; they are fearful of losing dominance, privilege, and the advantage. And, why not? If one's dominance over others has been accomplished in a certain way, one might fearfully expect those others would use the same means to "get even" once they got the opportunity. Hence, there is "suspicion." In the United States, it has been predicted that by the middle of the 21st century, whites will be a "minority." This fear is partly manifested, I believe, in the growth of militant white groups, such as the White Aryan Nation, and numerous "militia" groups which allegedly were formed in protest to "big" government, but who in reality fear government's attempts in promoting civil rights, entitlements and restitution for people of color. The avowed, militant white racist is confronted with extreme anxiety because he cannot deal humanely with reality. As for the passive white racist, the same dilemma is present except, in my opinion, he rationalizes to the point that if he ignores it, the situation will correct itself or simply go away.

The person who does not, or does not want to, acknowledge her or his own racism, as well as that of the overall society, will not be able to get beyond guilt and fear to any kind of action that is directed toward justice. They will continually fall prey to verbal abuse from others and self-incrimination. They become unable to find and deal with real causes and ultimate solutions.

Some white people do not understand why black people often feel enraged; some are intimidated by "black power," and their racism stifles their own development of inner strength and self-worth. When there is a lack of inner strength and self-worth, whites feel threatened and, therefore, do not support or even recognize the value and importance of black empowerment. Racism blocks the pathway to the develop-ment of understanding and the practice of fairplay and openness.

Racism compromises whites' sense of justice and affects their feeling of power, in that they want to maintain it in order to keep a dominant position in the overall scheme of things. In no way can complete justice prevail when one group has all the power and uses it for advantage and domination. The irony is that white power, for most whites, is an illusion, because the real power in the United States is held by a very few people, big industry, and institutions. Thus, the majority of whites, too, are locked into a system as victims and are used by powerful whites to maintain the system.

Racism has created a unique burden for the white man. He has been told in so many ways over the years that he is the 'premier' man. So, whenever he is bested by a man of color in sports, politics, business, socially, etc., his racism often leads to intense frustration and the develop-ment of an inferiority complex. Take basketball, for example.

A few years ago, I was on a business trip, and sitting next to me was a late middle-aged man who was the president of a medium-sized company. We were talking about sports, and all of a sudden he became very adamant in expressing his displeasure that professional sports, par-ticularly basketball, had "too many" blacks on the vari-ous teams. He did not know that I was black, obviously, and he railed on that it was unfair to white athletes, that it was gross overrepresentation of blacks relative to their percentage in the total population, and so on. Now, here was an educated man of means, prestige and position; yet, somehow he was afraid, angry, irrational, and feeling insecure. Racism had infected him. I asked him if his main purpose as president and CEO of his company was to maximize profits and increase shareholder equity. He answered, "Yes." Then, he stated that he was proud that he had hired outstanding people to assure this. I mentioned to him that, to my recollection, none of the professional teams were owned by blacks; it was whites who not only owned the teams but did the recruiting and hiring of players—that I was certain that they made those hiring decisions in much the same way that he did, and for the same reasons. He began to smile a little. I then said, "Let's pretend that you were just given the Los Angeles Lakers basketball team (this was when they were one of the dominant forces in the league), would you get rid of most of the black players such as Kareem Abdul-Jabbar, Magic Johnson, and James Worthy and replace them with white players?" By this time, he was laughing loudly. I said, "Probably not, because you, like the other team owners, would want to maximize profits and increase shareholder equity. You would want to have the people who you believed were the best to accomplish this, and if they just happened to be black, you would hire them." He did not reply, just nodded, and changed the subject.

Dr. Anita Remignanti, a psychologist who has probed the nature of racism, likens racism to a deep seated anxiety, fueled by confusion and a set of distortions believed to be the truth:

Racism is the systematic denigration of a group of people, based on confusion and distortions. Racism is based on the thinking error that whites are superior and people of color are inferior. This inaccurate view put forth in racist thinking implies there are clear divisions between "races" of people. In reality, there are no separate races; human beings have never been bred like dogs to get pure breeds or races. A more accurate observation of humankind portrays people as individuals with characteristics more or less similar to others. All human beings are inherently and undeniably more similar than they are different. Racist thinking comes from confusion and fear

just as anxiety does. Take a look at the steps in thinking
that go wrong in racism just as they do in anxiety:

Distorted Thinking on Racism
1. I am scared that people of color are similar to me.
2. I am going to make any differences between us look much
bigger than they are. This will help to convince me that I am
different and better.
3. I want to band together with others who are worried about
similarities between whites and people of color, and we can
all encourage each other to exaggerate the differences.
4. If I am viewed as similar to people of color, then I will have
their bad traits, too, and that is why I have to accentuate differences.
5. I feel I belong to a separate and superior race.

Racism has been around for a long time, probably as
long as people have been around. Psychologists have
studied racism and found that there is some inherently
human predisposition to cast people as same or different
from the self. When people take this discrimination too
far they begin to view 'sameness' as good and 'differences' as bad. Racism rears its ugly head as 'sameness' becomes an excuse to form an in-group and 'differences'
means an out-group. These distinctions are dangerous
because they involve distortions and misperceptions.
For millennia, groups of people have segregated other
people into in-groups and out-groups.

Why is racism like anxiety? The main reason is that both
are based on distortions of reality which are symptoms
of mental illness... Racism is a misperception and a mis-
interpretation of the characteristics and traits of a group
of people, based on confused thinking and emotional
reasoning. Racism, based upon confusion and mis-
interpretation of reality is, like anxiety, a serious mental
illness. It is a more virulent illness than anxiety because
it destroys the lives, hopes and potentialities of millions
of people in one fell swoop.(13)

Impact of the disease on people of color in America
The white's anxiety over race has affected America's people of
color, too. And it stands to reason. Since whites have always controlled the political, economic, social and religious power, the peo-

ple of color have had to abide by the official and unofficial guidelines for living set by their rulers or else face pain worse than what they had learned to adjust to in order to simply survive.

While people of color and whites have been victims of a grand, natural government sanctioned brainwashing, each group has been affected differently. While whites have been pumped up into believing they are superior to the rest, a deep-seated suspicion plagues people of color, and blacks in particular. This suspicion ranges from personal doubts, dealing with one's ability to compete with whites, to lacking trust in anything to do with whites. And some blacks still question, silently, of course, whether they are less developed humans than whites. In spite of the fact that in reality that is not the case, the feeling still persists, obviously the product of blacks having lived in a racist society all of their lives.

Black suspicion has led to a full blown paranoia in the African-American community, which whites have noticed. Their reaction reflects the white's political position on race matters. The liberal white, who is usually in denial, turns a deaf ear to anything negative about blacks, and pretends there is no black paranoia. He takes that position, even though the nonpublic part of him wonders nervously. On the other hand, those of a conservative bent point to black paranoia as evidence of African-Americans' craziness, of their lack of mental and emotional stability, of their inability to function effectively in a civilized society, of their inherent inferiority. Most other whites pay little or no conscious attention to black paranoia and go on with their business, making sure to avoid interactions with blacks as much as possible.

Black paranoia is real, and most blacks don't hide it. All sorts of rumors and conspiracy theories circulate in black communities and are being embraced as the gospel truth. Talk of government plots to exterminate all blacks is among the most persistent rumors. The plots, they claim, are carefully camouflaged. For example, in most black neighborhoods black men are boycotting the Church Restaurants because, they claim, their fried chicken is laced with a chemical that renders black males sexually impotent. Many black AIDS patients refuse to take the AZT drug, claiming it is the white man's way of quickening their demise. Snapple Iced Tea doesn't sell well in black neighborhoods, because the residents believe the label on the bottle features slave ships, which they view as an affront. Despite company claims that what is mistaken as slave ships is actually a rendering of the Boston Tea Party incident, many blacks, including college educated men and women, insist on holding to their opinions.(14)

Though much of what blacks presently fear is unfounded, and at first glance may appear crazy to most white social observers, what should be addressed is what causes this kind of paranoia. Just as the whites' obsession is a sickness, so is the blacks' deep seated paranoia. What has heightened the paranoia in recent years is a growing awareness of how whites created and maintained racism, and what underhanded practices were employed by a white dominated government to keep people of color in their "proper place." This new awareness is the result of more blacks attending college since the 1960s—and a sustained burst of black scholarship in the race relations field.

More blacks than ever before know the "Great Emancipator" Abraham Lincoln wasn't their savior as our history books portrayed him; that he wanted to get rid of nearly four million freed slaves by carving out a colony in the jungles of Central America and dumping them there. Nor was the government's promise of giving each former slave family forty acres and a mule ever kept. They have also learned in recent years of government sponsored medical experiments, where black men were used as human guinea pigs;(15) much like what Nazi physicians did with concentration camp inmates during World War II. They now know that the US Supreme Court's Plessy vs. Fergusson's Separate but Equal decision in 1896 helped to establish a system whereby blacks were conditioned to function as second class citizens. And they are sure that the F.B.I.'s hounding of Dr. Martin Luther King Jr. led to his assassination. The fact that the U.S. government broke every treaty it made with the American Indians reinforced the blacks' distrust of whites and the nation's leadership.

And Corporate America is highly suspect. For example, the revelation of senior Texaco officials deriding their African-American employees as "black jelly beans" and worse, didn't surprise many blacks within or outside of the company. The Texaco bunch simply got caught. As a consequence many blacks view corporate gifts to groups like the NAACP as a smokescreen tactic designed to keep the public from knowing the executives' true feelings toward America's minorities.

Their distrust is so ingrained that a paralysis of motivation emerges in the black community, which, in time, becomes demoralized, because it doesn't know where to turn for help. It doesn't trust the white dominated forces on the outside; nor does it trust the community's ability to help itself. Blacks lack the will to try to improve their lot, because they have been conditioned to be more sure of their dependence and incompetence then their inherent strengths. The conditioning has been so thorough that even among those few blacks who "make it" in the white man's world, there are some who are still haunted by doubts of being able to succeed. They wonder if they would have been able to make it without an assist from affirmative action.

"The disabling of the natural cycle of personality development is the dynamic that racism plays upon," Dr. Woodall points out. "And this outcome is one of the chief legacies of the disease of racism.

> A society that conveys to children of color in unnumbered ways that they are inherently inferior stacks the deck against the child as it would any child. The years of overt and subtle messages conveying the inferiority of blacks weighs heavily in the balance. By adolescence, it is not necessarily clear at all to a black child that they possess inherent strengths that are of value to a larger society. As they would for anyone, these messages hinder the mature expansion of the child's identity. There are at least two consequences that act as intractable symptoms of racism. The first affects the individual identity in that the person becomes trapped in their sense of personal inadequacy by the paralysis of their motivation. The second, is that it becomes infinitely harder for the individual to identify beyond the identity group of their race. The result of these two is an ingrained sense of despair reflected in the fact that twice as many blacks as whites commit suicide, there are more blacks in prison than in college, and the epidemic of violence in the black community.(16)

The deep-rooted suspicion among people of color has given rise to disorders like post-traumatic stress disorder (PTSD). Ashamed of their people's past and their present lowly condition, they turn to alcohol and drugs to avoid thinking about their origins and existing plight. And the alcohol and drugs often lead to violent behavior. Alaskan sociologists attribute the high incidence of alcoholism among the Yup'ik people of Northern Alaska to post traumatic stress disorder. The Yup'iks want to block out what the white missionaries and teachers did to their parents, grandparents and great-grandparents—who were told that they had to scrap their religion, customs and language because they were the work of Satan.(17)

Harold Napoleon, a Yup'ik social activist, who had been plagued by PTSD since childhood and has witnessed what has happened to those close to him who suffer from PTSD—writes from personal experience:

> The person who suppresses that which is unbearable to the conscious mind is trying to ignore it, trying to pretend it isn't there. In time, and without treatment, it will destroy the person, just as any illness left untreated will in time cripple and kill the body.(18)

Napoleon views PTSD as a disease "born out of evil or of events perceived as evil by the person. And the nature of evil is such that it infects even the innocent, dirtying their minds and souls. Because it is infectious, it requires cleansing of the soul." As a solution, he suggests the establishment of "talking circles," where the afflicted can discover and share what has been repressed.(19)

What's frightening is that more and more black children living in inner city neighborhoods are becoming PTSD victims. Instinctively they try to block out the violence they experience almost daily, because it hurts too much to try to remember. And keeping children indoors most of the time doesn't always protect children from the stress that street violence produces. There seems to be no escape from the mayhem outside. Children can hear the gunshots and cries of help. To them, watching from the window is like watching TV. As a result, many of these inner city children's fears are as real as those who are allowed to roam the streets. Too poor to move away, they live with their fears daily, becoming victims of PTSD. Some of these children spend more time sleeping under their beds than on them. Many youngsters have difficulty sleeping, suffer from nightmares, depression, fatigue and a short attention span that inhibits classroom behavior. Others, especially teenagers with repressed bad memories become desensitized to violence and grief. The latter was displayed in a Philadelphia courtroom in 1992. When a black teenager was sentenced to death for shooting another boy for his sneakers, he turned to the victim's family and taunted them, saying: "It still ain't going to bring him back."(20) What matters most to such desensitized youth is being able to instill fear in others. It provides them with a sense of importance that they don't experience in school or at home.

Having to live with the race issue all the time is a symptom of the sickness of racism that haunts many blacks. In his book, *Makes Me Wanna Holler*, Washington Post journalist Nathan McCall explains to a complaining white friend why he can't stop thinking about being black:

> You can sit around and intellectualize about race when you want to, and when you get tired of it you can set it aside and go surfing or hang gliding and forget about it. But I can't. Race affects every facet of my life, man. I can't get past race because white folks won't let me get past it. They remind me of it everywhere I go. Every time I step in an elevator and a white woman bunches up in the corner like she thinks I wanna rape her, I'm forced to think about it. Every time I walk into stores, the suspicious looks in white shopkeepers' eyes makes me think about it. Every time I walk past whites sitting in their cars, I hear the door locks clicking and I think about it. I can't get away from it, man. I stay so mad all the time because I'm forced to spend so much time and energy reacting to race. I hate it. It wearies me. But there's no escape, man. No escape.(21)

But many black young men, who haven't "made it" in our society, have found a form of escape—suicide. To most whites, however, it is more like homicide. Why is a black-on-black gangland killing a form of suicide? Because the person pulling the trigger knows that in time he's going to pay for it with his life. If not through revenge, then by the law's criminal system. Why not swallow a bottle of sleeping pills? It isn't as manly as taking a bullet to the heart, or dying defiantly in your oppressor's electric chair. It is his way of preserving his dignity. To the black youth who kills, the act of homicide is a suicide note that explains why he has resorted to such drastic action: he's tired of being rejected by the existing systems; he's tired of being viewed a failure; he's unable to shed his chronic state of hopelessness; he's depressed over the violation of his sense of justice; he has lost faith in his family, his school, his church and his country to help him find a way out.

The white superiority obsession that afflicts whites, the suspicion that plagues blacks, and the alienation felt by other people of color are the leading symptoms of a social sickness that is destroying America. Like a person with undiagnosed walking pneumonia, America keeps functioning, less dynamic, and confused over the source of its declining strength. And this process of disintegration will continue until Americans, especially those wielding the reigns of power, awaken to the fact that racism is killing their country and that to prevent its demise there needs to be a nationwide acknowledgment of what racism really is, followed by a sustained campaign of healing, reaching into every village, town and city in America. Sincere cooperation from the nation's schools, churches, synagogues, and governmental institutions is required.

I'm not the only one who feels drastic measures are required to eliminate the epidemic of racism in America and elsewhere. Many others do as well, including scientists like Luca Cavalli-Sforza:

> Racism is a chronic disease that one cannot hope to suppress rapidly or easily. But the frequency of terrorist racist actions, whether organized by government, secret or not-so-secret societies, and gang warfare has become so high that countries should take strong measures to prevent them.(22)

Just as smallpox didn't evaporate without medical intervention, racism isn't going to disappear without an intervention based on an accurate diagnosis of its pathology. Without proper intervention it will continue to spread—for like most diseases, racism is infectious. It is picked up at home from parents and relatives who are unaware of passing their prejudices onto the children. It is picked up from friends, even church members, and in the way churches organize themselves. And the infection is reinforced everyday, at the workplace, at school and at the playground. Television news is particularly poisonous and looms large in the lives of children and adults alike. Sure, programs like multiculturalism are produced to eliminate racism, but because they don't recognize its nature, they concentrate in overcoming its symptoms, much like aspirin is used to make flu less painful.

The trouble is—when you place all of your faith in a remedy that doesn't get to the core of the disease, then much valuable human energy and time is diverted from healing the disease, and the disease continues to spread.

Chapter Seven

The Hapless Attempts To Overcome The Disease Of Racism

The fact that decent people in America could be infected by racism—mystified me. One has to wonder what makes the infection so powerful. After considerable soul searching, study and heart-to-heart discussions with blacks and whites and American Indians, I began to realize the psychological complexity of racism. It isn't a fad; it isn't an ideology, and it is more than a simple prejudice. It is an irrational fixed idea or feeling, over which a person has little control. In other words, it's an obsession; an obsession rooted and nourished in the white American psyche for nearly 400 years; enough time to become institutionalized and take on conscious and unconscious forms, and do a lot of damage along the way. The bigot is conscious of his racist feelings, and unabashed about sharing how he feels about a certain ethnic group; while many of those in denial try so hard to conceal their racist feelings they are able to convince themselves that they are free of them. How this obsession developed has already been explained in the previous chapter. Now I'd like to focus on how this obsession is manifested.

It is manifested through compulsive behavior. In other words, it is manifested through irresistible impulses to perform irrational acts toward a people believed to be inherently inferior. Such acts as burning a cross on a person's lawn, parading around in hoods and robes, engaging in racial graffiti campaigns and telling racial jokes are obviously irrational acts. But there are the less obvious, private acts like what I experienced when I grew furious at the old black driver ahead of me; and there's the patronizing attitude or the condescending manner of a white person in denial. While they aren't flagrant acts, they convey a message of disrespect, of benign superiority to people of color, which reinforces their suspicion of whites. While on the surface these acts don't seem irrational—they are when you realize where they stem from. They spring from the emotional base of a human being, a place where fixed ideas and feelings dwell and often fester. Among these festering fixed ideas and feelings are those regarding race, which originated centuries ago with people we never knew, and were passed on to us usually unintentionally by people and institutions we respect and love. We, in turn, unintentionally pass them on to our innocent children through unaware irrational racial acts committed in a normal setting like our homes, the church, our neighborhood street. The passing-on can be very subtle.

For example, a psychotherapist friend of mine relates how one of her white male patients discovered the source of his negative feelings toward blacks, this, despite being brought up in a liberal home with parents who claimed to be color blind when it came to race. After weeks of probing into his childhood, he recalled an incident that took place when he was five or six, that turned out to be the source of those anti-black feelings he was ashamed of. While walking down a street, hand in hand with his mother, they noticed three black teenagers approaching. When the youth got fairly close, the child remembered his mother squeezing his hand and moving out of the way. From that day forward, he tried to avoid blacks. It was as if his mother's squeezing of his hand drilled into his six year old consciousness an alarm system that would go off every time he saw a black, setting off a powerful learned instinct within him to avoid the person that he was programmed to fear. This case and many similar ones have never been listed in the hate crimes docket in city hall. While they are not as dramatic as those cases where parents regularly and openly downgrade different ethnic groups, they are just as lethal. These are some of the steady and unconscious ways the cycle of racism has been perpetuated in North America for the past 400 years.

Those of us of good will are so ashamed of these feelings about race we consciously block them out. We are ashamed because we know they aren't based on reason and fact; and we don't know how to get rid of them. As a consequence they keep surfacing from our hiding place during stressful racial encounters. Yes, decent people in America engage in irrational acts of racism practically every day without consciously knowing it. But the traditional targets of racism know it, because they are on the receiving end every day.

Since these acts occur everywhere in America, it is safe to declare that America is gripped by a coast-to-coast, border-to-border obsessive neurosis about race. The trouble is that most whites either refuse to accept the idea that racism is a psychological disorder, or they are unaware that it is. As a result, they develop programs that address the symptoms and not the cause of the condition. And it doesn't matter how sincere or creative they are, their efforts don't make any significant changes in people's attitude and behavior. In fact, they end up alienating many of those they try to help. Why? Because the alienated know the programs fail to focus on the root cause of the condition. They view as artificial the aura of peace and goodwill the programs attempt to create. It doesn't take long for those people of color involved in the programs to drop out, usually more disillusioned, frustrated, and angrier than when they joined. And the creators of the programs are dumbfounded as to why people of color quit.

That's just what happened to a New York City based anti-racism campaign known as *Racism—Just Undo It*. Its creators were all dedicated human rights advocates, essentially good people, who genuinely wanted to play a meaningful role in eradicating racism. Most of them were established professionals in broadcasting, in advertising and public relations; all were of good character and spiritually-oriented. Fueled by lots of enthusiasm, they created what they believed was a catchy slogan and proceeded to promote the slogan through a media campaign. Slick billboards appeared in buses and subway trains. There were TV and radio public service spots. *Racism—Just Undo It* T-shirts and sweatshirts were produced. So were posters and big and little buttons. They set up booths at diversity rallies to make available their anti-racism materials. Local governmental and independent public affairs agencies that don't have a clue how to eliminate racism hailed the group's work. With that kind of public support, the group launched a national campaign.

I became aware of the group's "success" at a wedding in metropolitan New York. One of the creators of the group, an energetic young man whom I had known for a few years, sat next to me. We were both part of the ceremony. Before the bride and groom appeared, he turned to me with great pride and asked if I had heard about his group's *Racism—Just Undo It* campaign, and what I thought of it. Sensing his good intentions, I didn't want to hurt the young man's feelings or deflate his enthusiasm. So I responded to his question with my own question: "Tell me, how do you undo it?"

"Well," he said, a bit flustered, "we haven't dealt with that yet."

Though his response didn't surprise me, it did sadden me. Here was a wonderful young man, as I'm sure his colleagues were, engaged in an altruistic enterprise that will widen the gap between whites and people of color. Certainly this was not their intent.

Though catchy, the slogan demonstrates an ignorance of what racism is. It isn't the kind of problem that can be solved by trying to internalize some magical phrase. Eliminating an obsession isn't easy. It takes time, patience, persistence, and most of all a genuine willingness to engage in the healing process, which can be painful at times. Any reputable psychologist will attest to that. So will a recovering alcoholic or drug addict. Most people of color fighting racism on a community level, whom I know, are insulted by the slogan *Racism Just Undo It*, and pass it off as another "do gooder" scheme to help whites relieve their guilt. These blacks know how deep-rooted and convoluted racism is in America and what kind of a struggle is required in overcoming it. As a result, they equate the slogan with the foolish "Just Say No" to drugs campaign launched by former President Ronald Reagan's administration in the 1980s—which had no positive impact in curbing drug use among its target audience—teenagers. In fact, teenage drug use reached an all-time high in the mid-1990s.

The point is—telling someone to undo what has taken years to develop doesn't work, even if the recipient of the message sincerely tries to do what he's told to do. He will eventually give up the strain of trying, and will divert his energy to avoiding serious racial encounters and mastering political correctness techniques in order to survive in a growing multicultural society. He will eventually give up, because the irrational fixed ideas and feelings about race are a part of him, and the slogan isn't. What is needed to become free of race prejudice is an awareness of the nature of your affliction, and an understanding of why it must be healed. Of course what is also needed is a way to heal, and the support of others who are either undergoing what you are involved in or who have already healed. In other words, healing comes from within, with the encouragement of others who you have learned to trust, because their struggle is similar to yours.

While a poignant appeal by an individual or an institution can motivate someone to want to change one's attitude and behavior regarding a complicated social disorder like racism, it takes a sustained emotion-centered follow-up program that fully understands the nature of the problem in order to achieve the change. Again, fully understanding the nature of the problem is the key. Unfortunately, there is an extremely popular anti-racism approach in North America—multiculturalism—which doesn't recognize the nature of the problem it is attempting to solve. As a consequence, its efforts are proving to be counterproductive, despite the good will and enthusiasm of its practitioners. It is not enough to learn about the history of other cultures and become acquainted with their customs, songs, dances, favorite foods and traditions. That information can't draw out from your unconscious a long standing repressed obsession regarding those ethnic groups you have studied—and eliminate it. In a way, that's like painting over the rust and barnacles of a ship and convincing yourself that those impediments are gone. The only way to get rid of the rust and barnacles is to acknowledge their existence, understand how they developed and engage in a sustained effort to remove them. Otherwise the deterioration of the ship will continue unabated.

In the meantime, millions, maybe billions of dollars, are being poured into nationwide campaigns to promote multiculturalism in schools, universities, corporations, governmental agencies, police departments, professional societies, churches, synagogues and mosques. Billboards on the side of major highways promote multicultural themes; TV and radio public service spots produced by leading advertising agencies trumpet the need for ethnic tolerance, a goal of multiculturalism; leading entertainers and sports figures publicly proclaim their support of these campaigns, which have turned into a crusade. It has become so popular that business interests, sensing a rich market, are turning out books, manuals, slide programs, videos, audio cassettes, and films designed to help multiculuralists communicate their message more effectively. It has spawned a new industry. Race relations consulting firms have sprung up throughout the nation, offering their services to corporations and public institutions that want to create and maintain a strong multicultural image that would attract federal business and produce the kind of social climate in the work place that won't provoke minority employees to file discrimination suits against them. Sadly, greed has turned many of these consultants—black and white—into race relations hustlers willing to compromise their beliefs and principles in order to obtain lucrative contracts. For example, someone I know, who has been active in civil rights work over the years, and respected by friend and foe as a fighter for social justice, confided in me that though he knows multiculturalism can't eliminate racism, he's peddling the philosophy because it is an easy way to make lots of money. He reminded me that "You've got to strike while the iron is hot."

To produce the desired coating of pacification and toleration in a corporation or school that is rife with racism, many multicultural practitioners avoid using the term racism. Raise the word, they claim, and whites won't participate in your training sessions. Of course what isn't dealt with is the question: Why are so many whites afraid of the word? Well, in many cases it is a matter of cowardice. By trying to find the answer, you might discover things about yourself you don't want to know, causing much pain and shame; two feelings most modern western-oriented men and women try to avoid like the plague. Producers of painkillers and mind altering drugs are profiting mightily from this American phobia. Sadly, by not uncovering hidden feelings, people miss an opportunity to begin the recovery process, and opt instead for the seemingly safer route—multiculturalism, which concentrates in promoting tolerance of people's differences. So "diversity" has become the acceptable term. As a result diversity workshops are in vogue, emphasizing the importance of creating an atmosphere of tolerance of each other's cultures. Not that tolerance can't be a positive step in the development of a truly harmonious community. When tolerance doesn't lead to love and unity, when it becomes an end in itself, it becomes a fragile condition, bordering on pretense and artificiality. All it does is curtail overt prejudicial behavior. The intense fixed feeling from which the behavior springs remains in a subdued state. However, an irrational remark or rumor can easily reactivate prejudicial behavior.

Participants in most diversity workshops learn intercultural manners; how to react to cultural slights, what words and gestures to avoid in dealing with different cultures; they learn to appreciate the good aspects of different cultures, purposely avoiding the bad aspects. And there are bad aspects! They also learn conflict resolution techniques, to be used to settle disputes between ethnic groups. The sufferings that cultures had to endure because of a lack of tolerance in society are stressed, particularly World War II's Holocaust and American slavery, as well as the oppressive treatment Asians, Latinos and American Indians received from white individuals and institutions. The history of persecutions of different ethnic groups is stressed in order to generate within workshop participants a commitment to do everything in their power to prevent the recurrence of genocidal campaigns directed against any people. This is of particular interest to ethnic groups like the Jewish and Armenian communities that have been the target of severe oppression throughout the centuries.

Armed with this new knowledge, and the enthusiasm of a convert, most white multiculturalists develop a false sense of confidence, believing they are prepared to combat racism and play a meaningful role in creating a society free of racial and ethnic prejudice. Most are so convinced of their cause that they bristle at the suggestion of the fundamental flaws of multiculturalism.

North American multiculturalism gives the impression that culture is a fixed social entity. And it is not. A culture is dynamic, continually changing. In time, cultural characteristics change because of a whole host of reasons: climatic alterations, a shift in economic emphasis, political revolutions, foreign conquests, the introduction of new technologies, migrations—to name a few. Changes take place because change is a law of life. Some cultures' changes are more apparent than others. For example, the British culture has undergone some dramatic changes in recent years. With the influx of millions of immigrants from former colonies—Pakistan, India, The West Indies, Kenya, Ghana, Nigeria, Uganda and Malaysia—British life is a lot different than the Victorian image most people outside of Britain still have of that land. The music, attitudes, behavior, philosophies, customs, and foods of the new arrivals are blending with the established counterparts. The fact that Britain joined the European Union is another factor. So was the building of the tunnel that links the European mainland with Britain. A new British culture is in the making, which would be unrecognizable to those middle-to-high class tea-sipping, stiff upper lipped Britons who lived prior to World War II.

Certainly we all benefit from learning about different cultures. It helps to broaden our outlook. But when only the differences are stressed, as most multicultural programs do, you reinforce the lingering suspicion that ethnic groups are so different that they are not meant to mix on a regular basis, and certainly to not intermarry. This kind of emphasis can lead the impressionable, young and old, to suspect that the Chinese, Swedes, Nigerians, Lakotas, Latinos, and Malays are different species.

I contend that this impression is not merely the result of sloppy programming design. There are reasons to believe that some influential proponents of multiculturalism purposely stress cultural differences in their slick, heavily financed programs, as a means of preserving the "purity" of their own culture and preventing its extinction. Hundreds of institutions, who purchase these programs, are so desperate in seeking ways to avoid a racial eruption in their schools, or places of work, that they are unable to detect the real slant of the programs. As a result, fear is exploited in order to spread the wrong message, with considerable success.

The advocates of cultural purity, operating within the purview of multiculturalism, seem to be achieving their goal of institutionalizing cultural separatism. And this is cleverly done, by

billboarding terms like toleration and respect in their literature and
public pronouncements, terms we associate with goodness, human rights, justice and equality: They are terms most people of
good will are attracted to and feel comfortable with. Taking advantage of the prevailing fears associated with interracial encounters,
and the desire for community social tranquillity, the sophisticated
purveyors of cultural separatism have defined toleration and respect as a condition where every culture is allowed to do their own
thing without any positive or negative interference from outsiders.
To uphold the image of being human rights advocates, they engage
in charity work for the economically disadvantaged of other ethnic
groups; they participate in an intercultural festival once or twice a
year. But regular intercultural fraternizing is frowned upon. On almost every university campus, in every school in a so-called integrated neighborhood, black and white students avoid any
meaningful, sustained social interaction with each other. This is
most evident in the schools' dining halls and cafeterias, on the
school grounds, and the nearby ice cream and soda shops. There,
one observes a sophisticated form of apartheid in America that
most people are willing to accept if that's what's needed to assure
community safety and peace.

It isn't surprising that those multicultural programs whose
real intent is to establish cultural separatism never urge people of
different ethnic groups to love each other. The word love is missing
from their texts because love can lead to unity, the serious mixing
and banding together of ethnic groups. As a result you rarely see
the word unity in their materials. What is vigorously emphasized
instead—often through dazzling presentations—is an appreciation
for each ethnic groups' differences. Perhaps the greatest evidence
of their success is that love and unity aren't mentioned as goals in
present day race relations conferences, speeches and literature. The
leading race relations pundits avoid using those terms. I think it
was Dr. Martin Luther King Jr. who was the last American human
rights light to proclaim passionately in public the need for all people to learn to love one another so that true unity could be realized
in America.

Sadly, the preoccupation with differences has not only kept
us from dealing with the obsessional neurosis that plagues America; it is also preventing us from comprehending an aspect of reality that has eluded humanity for too long—the principle of the
oneness of humankind. Should the vast majority of the planet's
population internalize this principle, this scientific reality, there
would be no need for books like this. Racism would become a social

fossil, a bad memory, and many of the other social problems that plague us today would no longer exist.

Those multiculturalists who aren't driven by a hidden agenda of cultural separatism, and who are earnestly working to eliminate racism, are usually energized by their activities. The more activity they are involved in, the more enthusiastic they become. Their whirling carousel of social activism becomes a way of life, providing them with what seems to be a substantive purpose and meaning, something they can't get anywhere else, not even from their churches or synagogues. Participating in numerous workshops for a variety of organizations, attending race unity picnics, intercultural activities, marching in human rights parades, joining groups like the National Association for the Advancement of Colored People—all of that activity creates a false sense of progress for well meaning whites. What makes it false? The absence of confronting the obsessional neurosis called racism that plagues them and everyone else. In a way, they are like enthusiastic archers trying to hit a target blindfolded.

One of the reasons why very few blacks are involved in multicultural programs is because the programs are doing nothing to improve their quality of life or remove the negative social stigma they inherited by being born black in America. Many blacks, friends and people I have met in my travels, have expressed disappointment with multiculturalism. They view it as an arena for white guilt removal, and an organized, well intentioned movement headed in a direction that is taking their participants further and further away from the real solution to a problem people of color have had to endure all of their lives. To most blacks, even those who are getting rich from it, multiculturalism is another white man's exercise in futility in trying to end racism. The overriding message blacks receive from all of the multicultural programming hoopla is to place no hope in any white-generated race relations enterprise.

While most blacks reject multiculturalism as a viable means of ending racism, whites point with pride to the rash of television programs and films that feature positive multicultural themes like blacks and whites working together. Such films as *Pulp Fiction, Die Hard with a Vengeance, Lethal Weapon 1,2,3*, and *White Men Can't Jump* come to mind. What these productions do is lull white moviegoers and TV viewers into believing that meaningful race relations progress is being made. Of course, this infuriates blacks, because they know what the true picture is—after all, they are the featured players in it.

Beneath Hollywood's glitz and gleam is the shameful and painful reality that is the result of racism, a condition that multiculturalism unwittingly reinforces by steering its efforts away from the root cause of the social malady it is committed to eliminating. And this, in part, is the reality that satisfied white moviegoers don't see and don't want to see, or refuse to see: Black infants die in America at twice the rate of white infants. One out of every two black children lives below the poverty line (as compared with one out of seven white children). Nearly four times as many black families exist below the poverty line as white families. More than 50 percent of African American families have incomes below $25,000. Among black youths under age twenty, death by murder occurs nearly ten times as often as among whites. Over 60 percent of births to black mothers occur out of wedlock, more than four times the rate for white mothers. The net worth of the typical white household is ten times that of the typical black household. In many states, five to ten times as many blacks as whites ages eighteen to thirty are in prison.(1)

Statistically, the condition of the American Indian community is just as bad. For example, the average life expectancy of the American Indian is just 47 years (the national average is 78). American Indians have the highest poverty rate of any ethnic group in America—nearly 31%. The national rate is just a little over 13 percent. They suffer unemployment rates ranging from six to ten times the national average. The unemployment rate for all Indians living on reservations was 45% in 1991: Some tribes have unemployment rates as high as 80%. Of those who found work, only 28% earn more than $7,000 a year.(2)

You would think those statistics would be reason enough for most whites to support governmental initiatives to improve the quality of life of the majority of people of color, who, because of racism, are struggling socially and economically in America. But that is not the case. Proof is the inclination of many whites to view affirmative action as reverse racism. Such an attitude borders on hypocrisy. Affirmative action is not a new American preferential policy. Many whites in the past and present have benefited from various governmental preferential policies. It is, however, new for people of color. There was no outcry of "foul play" when the late President Franklin Delano Roosevelt inaugurated preferential social and economic policies for mostly whites during the Great Depression. The New Deal was a massive affirmative action approach to a national crisis.

Yes! Affirmative action is not a new governmental preferential policy; it has been going on for a while. Examples of that are the GI Bill for World War II veterans; the federal price supports given to farmers, including giant agri-businesses; the government's tax break for homeowners; as well as the $160 billion bailout for a select body of mismanaged banks. As writer Paul Rockwell points out:

> Tax breaks for homeowners may not be wrong. That's not the issue. What is wrong is the smug psychology of some middle class whites who take advantage of all kinds of breaks for themselves while denying affirmative action for the most oppressed areas of society.(3)

Chapter Eight

Racial Genocide In America

There is much more to the pitiful picture of the real African-American and American Indian conditions. One aspect is the racial genocide in America, in the past and present. I know most white Americans would denounce such a charge as absurd. At one time I reacted the same way, brushing off the claims of genocide as delusional. How could America be accused of genocide, I thought. The nation has produced no Hitler or Stalin. When such claims were made in my presence, the Statue of Liberty would come to mind. So would the signing of the Constitution, and the freeing of the slaves and the legions of immigrants passing through Ellis Island, coming to a land where freedom reigns. It wasn't that I didn't feel sorry for the people of color who made those claims. But deep down I felt I knew better; and was quick to analyze why such outrageous claims were expressed. Living in poverty and as second class citizens for too long, I reasoned, had warped their sensibilities, allowing for paranoia to set in. I never shared my analysis with blacks for I didn't want to offend them, lest I be accused of being prejudiced.

But I was wrong. There has been and still is genocide being carried out in America. Not in the fashion of Nazi Germany. Today, there is no master plan guiding certain elements of the government on how to exterminate undesirable ethnic groups. The genocidal efforts, for the most part, are subtle, so subtle that most of those who are carrying it out are unaware that they are playing a role in this odious practice. What drives the campaign is the racial obsessional neurosis that afflicts, to some degree, all whites regardless of political or religious affiliation. This synergistic process operates, for the most part, on an unconscious level. It has been going on for so long that it is on automatic pilot, switched on centuries ago.

Genocide in America is more psychological than physical. The extermination policy, which is a 400-year-old closet covenant crafted by the first European settlers—whom we were taught to honor—and passed on from generation to generation as a sacred truth, isn't designed to physically eliminate people of color. It is a procedure to put perceived inferiors in their proper place, to keep them from interfering with the perceived superiors achieving their inalienable right to "life, liberty and the pursuit of happiness."

To achieve this condition, means were devised to convince the establishment's acknowledged "inferiors" of their inherent inferiority. Through various brainwashing techniques, like the slave catechism, which will be spelled out later in the book, the idea of inferiority was successfully planted and cultivated in the minds of people of color. In time, the white-crafted notion became a national norm, and most blacks, Latinos, Asians, and American Indians voluntarily stayed in what was designated by the dominate culture as their "proper place." And this not only pertained to residence, but employment as well. People of color were to function as the worker ants of American society. For example, thousands of Chinese men were imported to America to build its railroads in the mid to late 1800s. They worked 12 hours a day, 7 days a week at pitiful wages ($31 a month); and in whatever free time they had they were often the objects of continuous violence, perpetuated by the whites. The Chinese working in the mines were continuously harassed. In 1885, whites attacked 500 miners in Rock Springs, Wyoming, massacring 28 of them. The Chinese living in the larger cities in the 1880s didn't fare much better. In Los Angeles, whites rioted against them, killing 23. In Seattle, hundreds of Chinese were rounded up and placed on a ship headed for China. The anti-Chinese fervor got so bad, that California's State legislature passed a law, prohibiting the hiring of Chinese.(1)

People of color weren't considered mentally qualified to handle responsible jobs. This was true even during World War II when there was a crucial need for workers in the defense industries. When the president of the North American Aviation Company was pressed as to why he wouldn't hire blacks, he replied, "While we are in complete sympathy with the Negro, it is against company policy to hire them as aircraft workers or mechanic... regardless of their training... There will be some jobs as janitors for Negroes."(2)

Ending up in reservations or ghettoes, people of color were cut off from mainstream America, creating subcultures that were foreign to most "real Americans"—so foreign and strange that whites felt justified in disqualifying people of color from entering the privileged circle reserved for "real Americans." Superiority and inferiority were determined by how well ethnic groups internal-

ized the ethos created by those who held the political and economic power. Trying to accomplish that in a ghetto was almost
impossible. Even Arthur Ashe, who seemed to fit into the circle,
had to live with the thought that he couldn't belong to it because
of his skin color, that he could never measure up to the real American standard, that in the final analysis he was an outcast in his
country, and nothing he could do could change his social status.
This invisible barrier is the desired outgrowth of the perpetrators of
the genocidal efforts in America.

What it is like to be an outcast was described to me by Sherlock Graham-Haines, a black man who had graduated from Williams College and holds a Masters Degree from Harvard University:

> While at Harvard, I developed a friendship with a mem-
> ber of the Rockefeller family who was living in Cam-
> bridge. One evening, as I was descending the front stoop
> of my friend's house, I froze in terror when I noticed a po-
> lice car with a white policeman in it, approaching very
> slowly. Though I had done nothing wrong, I was seized
> by a sense of guilt, as if I had done something illegal. It
> didn't matter that I had simply visited a friend and
> played a game of chess. I felt guilty. I had no control over
> that feeling, which I get every time I'm around a large
> number of whites. Being a graduate student at Harvard,
> and a friend of a member of a highly respected American
> family, could not remove that terrible feeling from me.

> I was in a place blacks are not supposed to be, especially
> at night. Will the policemen arrest me, beat me? Those
> questions struck fear in my heart. Should I run? I won-
> dered. "Play it cool," an inner voice cried out. "Running
> would only heighten the cops' suspicion." I gritted my
> teeth and proceeded to my vehicle, never once glancing
> at the patrol car. When I entered my automobile, I could-
> n't drive off immediately, though there was a great im-
> pulse to flee. I was in no condition to drive, for my heart
> was racing, and I was sweating profusely. It took me
> about five minutes to calm down.

Sherlock pointed out that this incident outside his friend's
house was not an isolated case. He has lost count of how many
times he has had similar experiences in his life. And the fact that he
anticipates more worries him, because he never knows when it will
happen. Having to live with that fear, he says, is a form of torture.

So genocide in America does not resemble the Holocaust. It is preventing people of color from realizing their potential as human beings and creating the impression that they are, by nature, lesser creatures than Caucasians. In other words, the aim of America's genocidal efforts is to eliminate enough of the human spirit in people of color that they will recognize, if not consciously, certainly unconsciously, that they are indeed inferior to those who set the political and economic agenda in America. Imagine, if you are white, having to live with doubts about one's humanness!

Malcolm X was aware of how effective the genocidal campaign was in the black community. He tried to undo what had been done to most blacks. I witnessed some of his attempts to do it. At times it seemed as if he was trying to replace that part of humanness that was stripped from blacks by whites.

Wherever he spoke he drew crowds. It fascinated me to observe the people listening to him. He was able to do what no other black leader in his time could. He said publicly what the average black in the street wanted, but was afraid, to say. Malcolm X was able to cut through the black's white-influenced view of himself and elevate him to his true human station which was denied him by the empowered. At Malcolm X's rallies black men and women stood tall.

As he spoke, I could sense their fears, doubts and anger leaving them, and a surge of pride and hope pouring into them, at least for the moment. Usually, pride and hope play no part in their everyday lives for they have to perform certain roles in the white man's world. But standing before Malcolm X, or watching him on TV, blacks could believe that they didn't have to play those roles.

"Yes, you are fully fledged human beings," he would assure them. The more they heard him speak, the more courage they gained to try to exorcise from their souls the doubts of being fully human.

"All of our people have the same goals and the same objective," he said, in one of his speeches.

> That objective is freedom, justice, equality. All of us want recognition and respect as human beings. We don't want to be integrationists. Nor do we want to be separationists. We want to be human beings...

> We have to keep in mind at all times that we are not fighting for integration, nor are we fighting for separation. We are fighting for recognition as human beings. We are fighting for the right to live as free humans in

this society. In fact, we are actually fighting for rights that are even greater than civil rights and that is human rights.(3)

Genocide in America becomes physical when people of color, especially blacks, try to leave their prescribed place. In the past, before the era of political correctness, such a deviation was met with force, often brutal in nature. This was most evident in the way the American Indians were treated from Pilgrim times through the day they were awarded U.S. citizenship in 1924, about 150 years after the birth of the USA. By that time most had been herded into reservations, or big city slums, ensconced in their proper place, and haunted by the horrific tales of their ancestors experiencing massacre, murder, mayhem and perpetual hounding by federal troops, as well as the government's treaty violations. To appreciate the effect of the genocidal efforts, it is important to note the decline in the American Indian population since the arrival of Christopher Columbus. While most ethnic groups in America have grown in size, the number of American Indians has decreased, from an estimated 9-12,000,000 in the early 1500s to about 350,000 in 1960.(4) As for the blacks—there were more than 200 years of a bestial form of slavery, another 100 years of Jim Crowism fraught with lynchings, house bombings, beatings, race riots, humiliation, rejection and hopelessness.

And now that physical force is illegal in perpetuating racism, whites employ more sophisticated ways of maintaining the degradation of beings designated inferior by the Founding Fathers. Avoidance is one way. If you can't employ physical force to preserve the racial status quo, whites move away. That's what has been done, for the most part, in America's larger cities. Whites have fled to the suburbs, leaving the core of the cities inhabited by people of color who are usually poor and undereducated; when middle class blacks move into a suburb, whites tend to flee to a different community. This pattern is part of the 1990s version of genocide. Though outwardly different, its message is the same as when genocide was practiced in a cruder fashion. The message is that the inherently inferior belong in their "proper place," not only geographically but socially and economically as well. Thus by moving away, the "proper place" is preserved, and the whites' racial obsession remains intact, as does the blacks' white-induced notion of being a lesser human. The White Flight is interpreted rightly by blacks as whites not wanting to have anything to do with them. With some blacks, the rejection reinforces their suspicion of being inherently inferior to whites; for they reason, "There must be something wrong with me if they don't want to be with me." This suspicion, I'm afraid, stirs even in the hearts of those who pretend they are not phased by the white slight.

Many people of color, especially blacks, sense in varying degrees the effects of the 400-year-old practice of genocide in America. Because many don't like the feeling of always being a victim, they try to construct a lifestyle free of reminders of being trapped within the jaws of a genocide that the ruling whites are oblivious of. Most blacks have given up crying for help, because whites aren't listening. To maintain some semblance of sanity, many black adults steel themselves to make the best of a situation they are powerless to alter. When they enter a restaurant in a white neighborhood, they expect to be stared at, or when shopping they expect to be watched by the store's security officers. Most refuse to make an issue of these slights, because they know it won't really change the condition. Based on experience, any protest on their part ends up hurting them more than those committing the racist acts. Their anger and frustration levels rise, exacerbating whatever physical ailments that plague them. Since survival is their watchword, they try to overlook the indignities they experience every day by being black in a racist society. They slip into a form of denial, devising means that would keep them from dwelling on the reality of their social pressure-cooker situation. Burying themselves in their work is one way to escape. So is immersing themselves in church activities, as well as sports and music. Taking advantage of every opportunity to improve their material lot by buying clothes, cars, radios, TVs, CD players, items that give the impression of "making it"—is another form of escape. Many who are underemployed or unemployed find escape through alcohol, drugs, and sexual promiscuity which leads, in turn, to a high rate of infants born out of wedlock.

I have learned from many conversations with blacks across the country that while involved in various escapist modes, they can't escape from the resentment and rage stirring within them; the kind of resentment and rage that stirs in the heart of a prisoner who has been unjustly convicted. Deep down there is a burning urge to get back at their oppressors. But there are very few opportunities to do that. Certainly not at work, at school or in a restaurant or cinema in a white neighborhood. The need to survive keeps most blacks from erupting and releasing their true feelings. So they continue to expend most of their energy trying to restrain themselves, and weave and live in a world of pretense they try to convince themselves is real. But continually trying to find ways to make the best of an oppressive way of life takes its toll on those who are forced to resort to such measures. I remember at an *Institute for Healing Racism* dialogue session, a participant, who had just finished pouring his heart out, pausing for a moment and finally saying, "I'm so sick and tired of being sick and tired."

From time to time certain events occur that catapults many blacks out of their fragile, carefully crafted comfort zone which they have struggled to create and maintain. It is a time they can express their real feelings and not give a damn of what whites think or feel about them. It is a time of great exaltation, a moment of freedom, a rare victory in a lifetime marred by defeat after defeat, humiliation after humiliation. The "not guilty" verdict in the O.J. Simpson criminal trial is a case in point. One of their "own" had beaten the system.

Most blacks hailed the "not guilty" verdict as a victory against their oppressor. The core of black reaction was expressed at Howard University's Law School. When the assembled students heard the verdict, these highly educated, bright, black young men and women literally jumped for joy, embracing each other, kissing each other, shouting praises to the Lord. It was an underdog's last minute Super Bowl touchdown that won the game. It didn't matter that two whites had been murdered, because thousands, hundreds of thousands of blacks in the past had been murdered, and their killers never prosecuted. This was sweet revenge. To them the American criminal justice system had been on trial, not O.J.; the system had been rightly exposed as a legal force to keep blacks in their proper place, resorting to illegal, and if need be, brutal measures to fulfill their real but unofficial purpose.

Certainly, the verdict couldn't undo the pain resulting from centuries of white injustices directed at blacks. But it was satisfying to know that whites, perhaps for the first time, had become aware of what blacks have had to endure at the hands of the criminal justice system; that their protests through the years were not empty complaints of congenital complainers. They weren't crazy. There was merit to their charges, and the whole world was privy to the indisputable evidence.

In a life where victories are rare, the O.J. verdict in his criminal trial was a black victory of watershed proportions, comparable in some ways to the 1954 U.S. Supreme Court decision declaring the "separate but equal" legal position as unconstitutional.

But the jubilation soon faded. It was back to the familiar, to the drudgery and uncertainty of trying to make the best of a bad situation. And there was the price to pay for a victory at the expense of whites' feelings—most whites had been outraged at O.J.'s criminal trial verdict and incensed at the blacks' reaction. Since the payback had always happened, it was expected in the black community, but not through murder and rioting as was the case prior to the 1960s. During the era of political correctness there are more sophisticated ways to punish a recalcitrant minority and keep "them" in their "proper place."

One way is to intensify the process of eliminating or cutting back benefits granted during the heyday of the Civil Rights period. Political scientist Roger Boesche of Occidental College has identified some of the aims of the process: Nothing violent, mind you. Just things like the elimination of affirmative action, denying minorities services like education and health care, eliminating 50,000 staff members from Head Start, cutting money allocated for summer jobs for inner city youth, cutting funds for low income housing, and building more prisons and putting black men in them. Nothing violent, just acts of deprivation that will make life for blacks even more insecure and difficult to endure, and in the end intensify the degree of violence in the black community.(5) Which, in turn, will justify officialdom's decision to employ harsher measures in cracking down on black violent crime, which is viewed by those who commit the crimes as acts of rebellion performed by freedom fighters. In the meantime, white onlookers, through the medium of television, silently applaud the action of the police. This feeling and other feelings generated by observing the black social chaos portrayed on TV fuels the whites' repressed obsession in regards to blacks. This cycle has been in operation for a long time.

There is an element of blacks, mostly young men and women, who instinctively know they are potential genocidal victims, and they will do everything in their power, including resorting to violence, to keep from being crushed by the genocidal steamroller. They see what has happened to previous generations of blacks, like their parents and grandparents, and they refuse to submit to that kind of dehumanization process/They would rather die resisting such humiliation than accept it. As a consequence, they are fueled by such rage and hatred of whites that they can't distinguish between friendly and hostile whites. They are prone to strike out blindly and violently at their oppressor, their enemy, the violator of their human rights. Having absolutely no faith in their government, they don't vote, refuse to go to school or work in mainstream businesses. I have watched them create their own economies, usually illegal, like those based on selling drugs, and gain some satisfaction from being suppliers of the whites' dope

habit. It is their way of helping to destroy the enemy, of dismantling a system that has caused them and every other black so much
pain. Seeing whites cower before them is also a source of satisfaction.

While governmental agencies are aware of this element of violence prone, disenfranchised blacks and are bent on crushing it,
they fail to ponder what has led this element to resort to such desperate, mean action. They are confronted by a rebellion and don't
know it. More prisons won't eliminate black rage and restore their
faith in their government. Doing time in jail only reinforces black
rage.

America's leaders are hopelessly ignorant of black pain and
aren't inclined to find out what it is like. They are not interested, because the plight of black people is a low priority issue in the grand
scheme of things. And it is low priority because their repressed obsession toward blacks' "inherent inferiority" influences their behavior and commitment toward action. Deep down they believe that
governmental assistance is a waste of money, because blacks will
never change. Therefore, there is little motivation to explore the
root causes of the blacks' pitiful condition in America. Though
they won't admit it, deep down most white leaders who have read
The Bell Curve: Intelligence and Class Structure in American Life by
Richard J. Hernstein and Charles Murray subscribe to the book's
thesis that blacks are inherently less intelligent than whites.(6)

The nation's leadership shows concern about blacks only in
times of crisis and impending peril to the community at large.
Washington responded when South Central Los Angeles went up
in flames in 1992, promising to repair what was destroyed and
build better educational and medical facilities, bring jobs to the
high number of unemployed and restore hope to a community
drowning in hopelessness. Few of the promises have been kept,
and little has changed.

Because the white leadership and most of the black leadership
have failed to alter the degenerative pattern of racial conditioning
in America meaningfully, many blacks are openly or secretly
drawn to a figure like Minister Louis Farrakhan. He, like Malcolm
X, says what they wish they can say, but are afraid to. It is more
than his forthrightness that makes him appealing to so many
blacks of all walks of life. He, more than any other black leader, can
articulate with great accuracy and poignancy what it feels like to be
black in America. Farrakhan helps blacks to be honest with themselves and to generate the courage to break out of the shell of denial, to find the incentive to deal with their true condition. In that

process they gain some self respect and self worth, which no other contemporary black leader has been able to do for them. What has also impressed many blacks is Farrakhan's influence in transforming drug and alcohol addicted hopeless men and women into human beings free of addictions, focused on family, job and community service, and enjoying a sense of self-respect never before experienced. In the eyes of the downtrodden and disenfranchised, the ability to change someone like that provides hope, something no one else has been able to provide. The fact that he scares whites is a highly prized bonus, because within most blacks there is a hidden desire to get back at their oppressors. To see whites squirm is the source of some pleasure. And when Farrakhan blasts the white establishment, many blacks outside of the black community are secretly cheering on the charismatic head of the Nation of Islam. The proof of Louis Farrakhan's appeal in the black community is that he was able to put together the Million Man March, something no other living black leader did, or could do. He is today, in the eyes of many blacks (not the majority of other black leaders who may be jealous and envious of him) one of the few persons they deep down embrace as the legitimate spokesmen of America's blacks. It is important to keep in mind that he didn't inherit this position; he wasn't appointed by some influential board, or elected to this high office. Let's face it, he's earned the right to speak for a large segment of the great masses of black Americans.

It is absolutely shameful the way governmental officials and the news media react to Louis Farrakhan. It is as if he were the devil incarnate. Many journalists dismiss him as a "nut." Even the normally level-headed panel composed of black and white newspaper editors and columnists on the distinguished *McNeil-Lehrer Report* branded him a full fledged member of the "lunatic fringe." Not one of them saw any redeeming feature in the man, nor his message, despite his ability to accomplish what no other black leader has been able to do in the past 32 years.(7)

Frankly, the news media's haste to paint Farrakhan a thorough "bad guy" was not only irresponsible; it was one grand capitulation to the campaign of highly influential vested interest groups desiring to discredit the head of the Nation of Islam as a demonic figure bent on destroying America.

Not that Farrakhan is a saint. His propensity to overstate and lash out at his critics troubles me. And there are aspects of his philosophy that I cannot accept. I was irked by his ill advised tour of the Middle East, where he met with and praised a number of ruling despots. Nevertheless, he's a human being, complex (like all of us) with foibles, faults, virtues, talents and endearing qualities; a walking, talking collection of contradictions.

Instead of quickly stigmatizing the man, journalists should have tried to answer the questions that arose naturally from the historic march on Washington. For example: What qualities does Farrakhan possess that make him so appealing to so many blacks? What in his message is able to evoke such a positive and passionate acceptance of him?

I think if the journalists had probed fairly, without bias, they would have found a brilliant man, finding difficulty to contain deep-seated anger that sets off shock waves of fear in most whites. His anger is no different than most blacks' anger, except he enjoys a freedom to express it and not be fired or suspended from school. So many blacks holding respectable positions in white-run institutions silently cheer Farrakhan for vicariously telling off their "white oppressors."

What is the source of Farrakhan's anger? I believe it is the way whites view and treat him and other blacks. His anger is so deeply rooted, so intense, that the desire to hurt his oppressor—especially when he's challenged by whites—overcomes him from time to time, resulting in outrageous remarks that explode onto the front pages of newspapers. Those outrageous remarks, by the way, could be a genuine cry for justice.

But not everything Farrakhan has to say is outrageous. In fact, most of what he says is painfully true. The trouble is his reputation triggers journalists' adversarial instincts every time he speaks; they zero-in on the potentially inflammatory remarks they sense he is uttering—and report it to the public in the guise of objectivity. Consequently, they miss much of his commentary that isn't outrageous; that is, in fact, incisive, like the explanation of the nature of white supremacy in America, shared at the *Million Man March*. Had journalists heard it with an open mind, they would have gained an understanding of why he and many other blacks are so angry. It was no harangue, as the public was led to believe. Basing his talk on solid historical fact and incisive sociological and psychological understanding of the past and present, he explored the origin and nature of white supremacy in America and purposely avoided the word racism, a term he knew would upset many whites. Listening to the commentary, I gained insights into why many blacks behave and feel the way they do; I found myself wanting to reach out in genuine friendship, wanting to say how sorry I was for their past and present condition. It wasn't an exercise in assuaging guilt; nor was I being patronizing. An urge to be with blacks swept over me.

Not that I had the power to change their condition. I wanted to make a statement in action. I wanted them to know that being with them was being with my family.

My wife felt the same way. So I have made a practice since hearing him to share openly my feelings on Farrakhan in all my speeches and continue to do so.

Not only journalists, but politicians and educators missed an opportunity to gain insights into the gravity of the American racism problem. Without such insights, it is impossible to diagnose accurately the social illness. As a result politicians and educators of good will were left groping for solutions to a problem they don't understand, a problem which frightens them.

The attempt by some narrowly focused men and women to compare Farrakhan with Adolph Hitler is unfair. It is, in fact, a blatant case of attempted character assassination. First of all, Farrakhan has not carried out a genocidal campaign. In fact, in his *Million Man March* speech, he proposed a meeting with the American Jewish leadership and himself, to resolve whatever differences exist between them. But instead of following the example of Israel's late prime minister, Itzak Rabin, the American Jewish leadership rejected Farrakhan's offer.

I know that Farrakhan has made some anti-Jewish remarks, which have angered many Jews, as well as non-Jews. But Yasser Arafat has done worse things.

I don't profess to be Farrakhan's apologist. I am, however, concerned with fairness, and the need for communities to live in peace. People in the best of families make outrageous statements under stress. Feuds develop, some lasting a lifetime. But it takes wisdom and spiritual enlightenment to recognize the futility of feuding, and make a genuine effort to end it—and live in friendship. It wasn't an Arab or a member of the Nation of Islam who killed Rabin; it was a devout Jew.

Chapter Nine

The Roots Of Black And Jewish Friction

The friction between African Americans and Jews doesn't make much sense, for both have suffered at the hands of the same oppressors.

When you review what African-Americans and Jews have had to endure through the centuries, you wonder why there is so much tension between both groups in the United States. They have had good reason to be allies. But for a few cases in the past of joint assaults on the forces of bigotry, and a few individual supreme sacrifices like the 1960s KKK murder of three civil rights workers—two Jews and one black, the gulf between Jews and African-Americans continues to widen. Minister Louis Farrakhan's harsh remarks about Jews in recent times haven't helped. Nor have the Jewish Defense League's late leader Rabbi Meir Kahane's strident pronouncements against blacks.(1) He often referred to them as "Neanderthals." There is much ignorance on both sides about the other's culture. African-Americans and Jews have formed opinions of each other based on erroneous information, which they believe is factual. It is a classical example of one people's deep-rooted prejudice pitted against another people's deep-rooted prejudice, producing a climate of distrust and resentment between both groups.

Where does the anti-Semitism among many blacks stem from? Much of it has to do with religion. Not the basic teachings of the prophet-founders of religion, but in the interpretations of so-called prominent theologians that devout religious adherents have embraced as divine truth. The theologians' public proclamations and writings about Jews, as well as actions directed against Jews throughout the centuries, created a widely established tradition of anti-Semitism within Christendom. For example, The Roman Catholic Church's Inquisition was used as a weapon to punish, and in many cases exterminate Jews, who were denounced as "Christ Killers."(2) Martin Luther, who led the Protestant Reformation in

Germany, openly reviled Jews as the enemy of God, describing them as lecherous creatures, undeserving of acceptance within the fold of the human family. At one point he called for all Jews to be condemned to hell.(3) To be faithful, most Christian congregants embraced the views of their church leaders. Obviously, in our politically correct era, churchgoers have repressed what they learned about Jews while growing up. But it doesn't take much for the venom of anti-Semitism to surface. I believe Luther's views as well as the Roman Catholic Church's views of the Jewish people helped prepare the soil for Nazi anti Semitic seeds to sprout in Germany, which eventually produced the poisonous fruit of the holocaust.

A foundation of anti-Semitism was laid within the black community with its acceptance of Christ as their Lord. In embracing Christianity, slaves, ex-slaves and free blacks and their descendants not only embraced the basic teachings of the white man's religion but the church sanctioned twisted views of Jews as well. I sense that there is an underlying belief among many blacks, and white Christians as well, that in God's eyes Jews are inferior to them because of their refusal to accept Jesus as His son. With each celebration of Good Friday and Easter, black churchgoers have been reminded of who had killed their Lord. So when Louis Farrakhan denounces some Jewish landlords in Harlem as "bloodsuckers," he is arousing within blacks the latent anti-Semitism within their religious belief system.

Unfortunately, the bridges of understanding built between both sides are so fragile that few possess the courage to go to the other side in the spirit of wholehearted friendship. In reality, these bridges stand today as monuments to human misunderstanding.

Whatever has been done in the past to create peace among the two sides has not been done with a sincere desire to embrace each other as family members. The efforts have been superficial, designed to establish as long a truce as possible, the greatest concern being the prevention of physical clashes. Nothing meaningful has been done to overcome the ignorance of each others' cultures and the suspicion that rules hearts—in other words, an experience that can produce a change of heart among African-Americans and Jews about each other.

Having been brought up in a Jewish home and in a Jewish community, I have experienced race prejudice among Jews. It is deep-rooted and widespread. Certainly not as flagrant as expressed by the Ku Klux Klan. It is what I call the "schwartza" mentality. The word "schwartza" is a Yiddish word meaning "black one" or "black person." However, when used, it has a negative ring to it, usually springing from the gut where "schwartza" receives an emotional boost, and its true meaning emerges: a black animalistic inferior being.

As a child I heard this word used often among my parents, relatives and their friends, even in the synagogue. While there were many incidents, one in particular stands out. It stands out because it demonstrates how innocent children are poisoned with prejudice by people of good will who aren't aware that they are poisoning children, including their own.

I must have been eight or nine when most of my relatives came to our home to celebrate a high holy day. It was a joyous occasion, a time to play with all of my cousins. When my father picked up a spoon and tapped the glass before him, we all stopped what we were doing and all eyes were focused on him. My father, who could do no wrong in my eyes, stood at the dinner table laden with all sorts of Jewish delicacies, and announced a big moneymaking scheme that he was seriously considering." I am thinking of opening a liquor store in the schwartzas' section."

"Why there?" an uncle asked.

My father smiled and said, "Because schwartzas love liquor."

Everyone, including my favorite aunt—Sonia—cheered and agreed that my father had a great idea. One uncle cried out: "Louie, you'll become a rich man." Everyone shook his hand and toasted his success.

Most Jewish men and women of my generation, I believe, have had similar experiences, which contributed to the development of their "schwartza" mentality. And they passed on their attitude toward blacks to their children, not consciously, of course. Usually through a slip of the tongue statement about an issue like interracial marriage; or an angry expression on a parent's face while watching police arresting a black man on TV. Most Jews today would deny possessing the "schwartza" mentality, because they are decent people. But when you take the time to describe the condition, many honest and open-minded Jewish men and women admit having it, and want to know how to rid themselves of it. Here is a case in point: After giving a lecture on racism at Wesleyan University, three Jewish students approached me with a concern. They wanted to know why they were unable to establish genuine friendships with blacks on campus. Every time we approach a black, they complained, his guard comes up and shows no interest in interacting with us. When I said that perhaps the black student saw something in you that he resented, one of the students asked, "Like what?"

"A superior attitude toward him."

"No way!" one of the students shot back.

"You are probably not even aware of possessing such an attitude."

"So you think it's unconscious on our part," the female student said.

Sensing some bewilderment among them, I asked if they had ever heard of the "schwartza" mentality. When they said they hadn't, I explained what it is. As I spoke, I sensed an awareness overcome them that researchers experience when they discover something new. They had become aware of feelings toward blacks they never knew they had. It didn't take long before they admitted having heard the word "schwartza" used, and always in a negative way. They realized that deep down they did possess a superior attitude toward blacks and that they were afflicted with the "schwartza" mentality, something they did not choose to have. When they asked how to get rid of it, I suggested they seek out an *Institute for the Healing of Racism* and get involved in it. An explanation of the Institute will be made in a later chapter.

Now, I don't know whether the schwartza mentality stems from the Book of Genesis' image of the sinner Ham, who was black and cursed and destined to be "a hewer of wood." That may or may not be a factor. But I do feel that the Old Testament's reference to the Jews being God's Chosen People is evidence enough for certain elements within Judaism to sport a superior attitude toward everyone else, especially people of color whose culture is very different than theirs. When Israeli commandos airlifted thousands of Ethiopian Jews to Israel, leading rabbis refused to accept the African refugees as legitimate Jews, calling for them to undergo a religious conversion process. A few years later, probing journalists revealed that Israel's Public Health Department had ordered all the blood given by Ethiopian Jews at blood banks to be thrown away. When pressed as to why they resorted to such action, health officials responded that it was their way of screening AIDS contaminated blood from Israel's transfusion pool. But that turned out to be a lame excuse, because the Health Department's action was not based on any scientific testing. The Ethiopian Jewish leadership cried out for an end to racial discrimination in Israel. Protests followed, some of them violent. Finally, Prime Minister Shimon Perez publicly apologized to the 60,000 Ethiopian Jews living in Israel.

This inherent sense of superiority harbored mostly by the ultra conservative segments of the Jewish population was publicly displayed at the funeral of Bauruch Goldstein, the right-wing

American born Israeli physician who massacred 29 Arabs while they were praying in a Mosque during the Muslim Sabbath. During his eulogy of Goldstein, Rabbi Yaacob Perrin proclaimed before a thousand mourners: "One million Arabs are not worth a Jewish fingernail."(4)

That public display of racial superiority was reminiscent of the 1930s, when Nazi theoreticians proclaimed the glorious destiny of the superior Aryan race before throngs of "sieg-heiling" supporters. After reading the account of Goldstein's funeral in the New York Times, I became convinced that you don't have to be German to be a Nazi.

Though most American Jews would never reveal their true feelings about blacks in public, there are a few who have the courage to do so. It is not something they are proud of, and they wish they weren't burdened by such bigotry. But they know they are. And being honest and honorable, they can't withhold their true feelings. Take for example Norman Podhoretz, a Jewish intellectual and former editor of the *Commentary Magazine*. He admits growing up in Brooklyn fearing and hating blacks:

> The hatred I still feel for Negroes is the hardest of all the old feelings to face or admit, and it is the most hidden and the most overloaded... It no longer has... any cause or justification... I know it from the insane rage that can stir me at the thought of Negro anti-Semitism, I know it from the disgusting prurience that can stir in me at the sight of a mixed couple. (5)

As a child growing up in a predominately Jewish neighborhood in the Bronx, I witnessed, and was affected by, a form of race prejudice within the Jewish community. The Ashkanazis who hailed from northern and eastern Europe, and were generally fair complected and spoke Yiddish, viewed the Sephardics as inferiors for they hailed from North Africa, the Middle East and southern Europe, and were generally olive complected and didn't speak Yiddish, but rather Ladino. My parents who were Ashkanazis forbid me to set foot in a Sephardic synagogue, which I grew to believe was foreign as a Christian church. I remember my mother warning me never to eat food prepared by Sephardics, for "they fry with olive oil and not schmaltz (chicken fat)." As a child and youth I obeyed my parents and never set foot in a Sephardic synagogue or tasted Sephardic food.

This form of race prejudice even exists in Israel. While working as a journalist in Minneapolis in 1958, I remember interviewing Israel's Interior Minister, who startled me when he said that the animosity between the Ashkanazis and Sephardics was so intense in his homeland that if it wasn't for being preoccupied with its hostile neighbors, Israel would be engulfed in a civil war. In 1971, I gained a sense of what he was talking about. While in Israel I learned of street clashes between both groups, and of Sephardic social activists forming a Black Panther Party.(6)

In analyzing the ancient feud between Ashkanazi and Sephardic Jews, one can deduce that it is the lighter skinned Ashkanazi Jews that American blacks are feuding with, because Sephardics don't speak Yiddish and the word "schwartza" is a Yiddish word. Though in the main that is true, there is evidence that American Sephardics may harbor negative, though not overt, racial feelings toward blacks as well.

Most of the first Jews to come to North America were Sephardics, many of them settling in the South and taking on southern cultural characteristics including the whites' attitude toward blacks. In fact, some of the Sephardics were slave holders and fervent supporters of the Confederacy during the Civil War. The Secretary of State of the Confederacy, Judah Philip Benjamin, was a Sephardic. As was David Camden De Leon, the Confederate Army's surgeon general.(7)

While some may argue that the background material I have just shared stirs up existing prejudices between African-Americans and Jews, my counter argument is that in principle it is always good to know the truth. I know that exposure to the truth can be painful, especially if it has been hidden a long time, and you have become emotionally attached to a belief you suddenly learn is false. When this happens, a person usually feels betrayed and is often consumed by suspicion. I know while in that state of mind it is more difficult to embrace the truth when exposed to it. Nevertheless, we must embrace it—pain and all—if we are to make an accurate diagnosis of why tension exists between Jews and African-Americans. As I have mentioned earlier, without such a diagnosis, it is impossible to address the heart of the problem.

Yet many people of good will on both sides still shy away from lifting the veil of denial to learn how they truly feel about the other side. They prefer expending their energy and funneling their money into projects that will ensure a degree of tranquillity between both sides. Those who engage in such exercises aren't stupid. They are just fearful of discovering something about themselves they don't have the courage to face; or are fearful of creating a situation that could lead to violence. To make it easier for themselves, they try to persuade others who show an inclination to lift the veil of denial to abandon that impulse, and pursue, instead, the safer course they have carved out for themselves.

Blacks and Jews, including close friends, have urged me to stop talking about the tension existing between both groups, claiming that it only exacerbates the situation. Shortly after appearing on the *McNeil-Lehrer Report*, I received a heartfelt letter from an old friend of Jewish background, expressing deep concern over my sharing the "liquor store" story with a national television audience. Doing that, she said, fuels the flames of anti-Semitism and discourages Jewish participation in the *Institutes for the Healing of Racism*, a movement I'm committed to.

I didn't take her letter lightly, because she was obviously sincere and the points she raised were not frivolous or self serving. What she feared could happen. And that troubled me. The fact that I have never forgotten my Jewish roots, has made revealing the race prejudice within the Jewish community a painful exercise. My initial impulse was to keep secret what I knew, for I did not want to hurt a people who have suffered so much through the centuries. Besides, I was always proud of Jewish accomplishment, and still am. So being in the position of opening the lid to family secrets isn't something I relish. Especially since it means being criticized, and at times vilified, by people I love.

But after much reflection, I realized I had a greater loyalty than to my heritage—and that was to the human race, my global family. At this point in my life, I no longer harbor any suspicion toward Sephardics; all Jews, regardless of where they live, are my relatives. As are all blacks in the world, and everyone else.

Being members of the human race, African-Americans and Jews should be caring for one another and not suspicious of each other. To overcome the suspicion and the warped view they harbor for each other, it is necessary for men and women on both sides to be forthcoming about their true racial feelings. Breaking out of denial would be healthier for all involved, for they would no longer have to live a lie. Willingness to find out the origin of their prejudice will allow them to begin to heal the virus of racism festering in their hearts. In time, it will become possible to start a fresh dialogue on how to forge a lasting bond.

Significant progress will be made in race relations only when all sides are honest with each other and are willing to express their true feelings in a full and frank ongoing dialogue. That is the first step necessary for the reconciliation of the races. Anything done without taking this first step would end up being a charade, another failed attempt at fostering racial unity.

Chapter Ten

The Role Of Education In Perpetuating Racism

American formal education has played a mighty role in the creation and maintenance of racism in America.

An outrageous charge, most well-intentioned people might think. Well, I can appreciate that reaction, because in the recent past I would have been among the most ardent protesters. I have spent more than twenty years working as a teacher, and have worked with many dedicated educators. And I know many other educators who are forward thinking and instinctively progressive in regards to social issues. But after reading anthropologist Jack Weatherford's books, *The Indian Givers* and *Native Roots*, after learning about the enlightened civilizations the ancestors of today's African-Americans came from and gaining a more comprehensive understanding of US history, I have a clearer grasp of reality. I have come to the conclusion that the European settlers, who quickly assumed the role of rulers in North America, operated schools in America in which boys and girls were indoctrinated with falsehoods that were hailed as the truth by their teachers. And this is still going on. These falsehoods that were promulgated as reality have been expressed with such conviction and authority over the past 300 years—they have become sacrosanct. Those few individuals who dare to question the authenticity of these sacred beliefs are usually branded as saboteurs of America's heritage.

Brainwashing in our schools

In effect, we have been brainwashed into believing that when the Europeans came to the Americas, they found a total wilderness, inhabited by humanoid type creatures devoid of respectable intelligence and culture, devoid of a belief in God, given to inhumane social practices, and incapable of functioning in a civilized society. Plainly put, they were depicted as pagans and savages, summarily dismissed by the European settlers as being outside the human family.

Therefore European historians could rightly proclaim Christopher Columbus the discoverer of America. By making that pronouncement, they were also stating non-verbally that Columbus was the first human being to set foot in America, relegating those who greeted the European explorer as subhuman beings. Teachers through the decades have trumpeted that falsehood as the truth. Columbus' alleged feat has been so highly acclaimed that the federal government has declared his birthday a national holiday, and hundreds of cities and towns across the land have celebrated that day with magnificent pageantry and parades. Not to mention that many towns and cities have been named in his honor.

The truth of the matter is, when Columbus reached "the New World," he had no idea of where he was. He thought he was on an island off the coast of India. And the Arawak people, who greeted him and his crew with much warmth and hospitality were viewed by the Europeans as simple-minded, two-legged animal-like creatures who could easily be enslaved because of their innocent and pure-hearted nature. Columbus exploited the native people's kindness and generosity by making many of them his slaves. Through his rapacious lust for gold, silver and diamonds, he was instrumental in the extermination of most of the Arawak people in the Caribbean Islands he plundered.

What we have overlooked in education is that there were many civilizations in the Americas, made up of human beings who had families, cultures and religions long before Columbus' arrival. There were even great urban centers. In 1250 AD the city of Cahokia, which was larger than London, England, at the time, rose out of the plain of what is now southern Illinois, on the Mississippi River.(1) Though the Indians there used the mighty waterway as a trading artery for centuries, we learned in school that a Spanish explorer, Hernando DeSoto, discovered the Mississippi River. In sharing that "historical fact" with students, teachers have been inferring that the American Indians living on the edge of the Mississippi River and using it regularly didn't count, for they were less than human. And the students usually absorbed the unstated message. What is sad—and quietly destructive—is that the teachers were unaware of the message they were conveying to those they were charged with educating. They weren't aware that they were perpetuating racism by conveying false information in the guise of truth. Imagine believing that Henry Hudson discovered the river that runs between Albany and New York City, when American Indians lived on both sides of the river and used it for trading purposes centuries before Hudson sailed up the waterway.

The message students should have been getting all of these years is that Indians engaged in commerce, operated farms, maintained legitimate healing and ecological practices, devised sophisticated organizational and governance systems, and were capable of discovering not only places but medicines and such materials as rubber and asphalt. The Indians developed foods such as potatoes, chocolate and chilies which revolutionized the cuisine of Asia and Europe—in fact, some 60 percent of the foods eaten in the world today were first harvested by the Indians of the Americas.(2) And that, by and large, the American Indians were highly ethical and principled people, with a deep reverence and love for the Great Spirit (God). None of the Indian languages contained any profanity. Lying was unheard of. After spending some time among the Nez Perce and Flathead tribes, the writer Washington Irving wrote in 1834:

> Simply to call these people religious would convey but a faint idea of the deep hue of piety and devotion which prevades their whole conduct. Their honesty is immaculate, and their purity of purpose and their observance of the rites of their religion are most uniform and remarkable. They are certainly more like a nation of saints than a horde of savages.(3)

Though we have been led to believe that all of our political system's roots are in Europe, some important ones are in North America. Crucial contributions to our federal system and democratic institutions were made by the Indians. In fact, if it wasn't for the advice given to Benjamin Franklin by Iroquois Chief Canassatego, the political structure of our country would most likely be different than it is today. Instead of being a nation of united states, it would be a land made up of separate and sovereign states, each with its own army, currency and tariffs. Canassatego, who found it difficult to deal with so many different colonial administrations, suggested to Franklin that the colonies speak with one voice. He proposed that the colonies should form a union, using the League of the Iroquois as a model. The League of the Iroquois was made up of six different Indian tribes that had lived in peace and harmony for centuries.(4)

Impressed with the model, Franklin lobbied the other Founding Fathers to adopt a federal system. Finally, after about thirty years of lobbying, the Constitution was written, establishing the United States of America. Incidentally, in drafting the US Constitution, its drafters borrowed several sections from the League of the

Iroquois' Constitution, called the Great Law of Peace. Interestingly, the section which the Founding Fathers did not plagiarize had to do with upholding the principle of the equality of the sexes. For example, the Founding Fathers refused to follow the way of the Iroquois in granting women the right to vote or any other major role in the political structure. In the Iroquois society, women were granted the sole power to select and dismiss the sachem, a council member.(5)

What I have just shared, and a lot more, was not taught in America's schools in the past, and is mostly not being taught today. Because they failed to tell the whole truth, our schools through the decades have perpetuated racism in America. By disregarding the contributions made by the ancient Indian and African and Asian civilizations, and focusing primarily on the achievements of the European civilizations, the schools created the impression that people of color did little or nothing in the process of civilizing humanity; that only whites made meaningful contributions. When children are exposed to what life was like for the average Pilgrim family, and nothing significant is mentioned about the way Indian families functioned, an important unspoken message is being conveyed by the teacher or the textbook. In a sense, by superficially treating or omitting positive references to people of color, the teacher or textbook is not only stating that whites are more important than others, they are, in the eyes of the students, eliminating Asians, African-Americans, Indians and Latinos as members of the human race. The people of color, through the years, have been portrayed by our schools as props, to be used to enhance the whites' ambitions, and satisfy their needs. Most adults living today have been exposed to this kind of instruction, including our teachers and principals and professors who are training prospective teachers. In reality, our schools have functioned as brainwashing machines for more than 300 years, guaranteeing whites privileges that people of color desire but know they will never enjoy in their lifetime. These privileges, which are a product of racism, are very difficult for whites to recognize since they are a part of their natural everyday experience. In a way, it is like a fish trying to get an idea of water by removing itself far enough to see it.

The trauma inflicted on children of color

Through the years, the unstated message on race our schools have conveyed has had a devastating effect on students of color. It leaves them thinking: "If we have contributed little or nothing to the development of humankind," they have reasoned, "then I am ashamed of being who I am, and I want to be associated with the group that is being acclaimed the chief developer of humankind." This kind of reaction among children of color often goes unstated. Out of self-defense they bury it in their unconscious where it continues to churn away, often causing disruptive behavior in the classroom. In essence, what most children of color learn in school is to hate themselves. Being what sociologists call victims of internalized racism, many often daydream about being white, while others seethe, waiting for the opportunity to strike back at "Whitey."

What American children were exposed to in the classroom regarding race through the years was reinforced by the most respectable academic resources outside of school; resources which teachers encouraged their students to use. The *Encyclopedia Britannica*, for example, in its eleventh edition, published in 1911, described the Negro this way: "In certain characteristics... the Negro would appear to stand on a lower evolutionary plane than the white man... The mental constitution of the Negro is very similar to that of a child, normally good-natured and cheerful, but subject to sudden fits of emotion and passion during which he is capable of performing acts of singular atrocity, impressionable, vain, but of ten exhibiting in the capacity of servant a dog-like fidelity which has stood the supreme test."(6)

You can just imagine what impact the highly honored encyclopedia's description of the "Negro" had on the impressionable minds of white children. And what about the black children who read the same description? This, and other warped bits of information regarding blacks were proclaimed with certainty as the truth by the most reputable persons and institutions, year after year, generation after generation. And no one of authority questioned the distribution of such information. It was absorbed as knowledge, knowledge which contributed to the development of the white adult's mind-set toward people of color. And it was the kind of knowledge that influenced, in the main, the black adult's opinion of himself or herself.

Most teachers today, even the well intentioned ones, aren't aware of what a black child endures while in school. If the teacher assumes that the black child is equal to a white child in terms of classroom performance, she's making a mistake. This has nothing to do with native intelligence, or with genetic make-up. It has to do with preschool preparation. Generally, white children entering kindergarten have had more exposure to planned educational activities. A major reason for this condition is economics. White families earn more than black families; they have the money to buy their

children books, take them to museums, obtain various mind development games, including computers, and expose them to a variety
of educational videos on a regular basis.

Therefore most white children enter school with a greater
knowledge base than black children, and are not as traumatized by
the classroom experience as black children. According to Stanford
University social psychologist Claude Steele, a black child starts
school handicapped by two fears: The fear of being devalued, and
the fear of lacking the ability to succeed.(7) These fears are not
imaginary. They are learned through their brief life experiences. By
watching TV, going shopping with their parents in predominately
white neighborhoods, seeing how blacks and whites interact, listening to their relatives talk about whites, driving through white
sections of town and seeing how whites live compared to blacks,
they gain a sense of who really has the power in their country.
Though they will never say so, the majority of black children attend school feeling disadvantaged.

They aren't dumb. And they want to believe they aren't
dumb; but by attending school they eventually learn that they just
aren't as smart as their white classmates, who generally get higher
grades. Of course, the black child isn't aware that his white counter-
part has had a considerable head start. He weighs the evidence before him; feels ashamed and inferior. And when he is consumed by
those feelings, and still has some pride, a part of him rebels. Deep
within his core, he senses he is being wrongly judged, that he's the
victim of an injustice that he can't articulate or control. This angers
him, and the only way he can find some relief is by sassing the
teacher or turning into a bully, who enjoys beating up white guys.
It is his way of gaining respect from people he has learned are supposed to be superior to him. This type of student becomes a ripe
candidate for a street gang.

Unfortunately, the average teacher isn't aware of the trauma I
have just described, or what most black children experience in a
predominately white school. There is something else they are not
aware of: And that is the psychological and physiological impact a
black child experiences in an alien classroom (which isn't meant to
be alien) directed by a teacher, who means well, but has lower expectations of a black child. She's usually experienced and has the
standardized test scores to justify her decisions when classifying
her students. What she doesn't know is that those test scores are a
reflection of an educational system that refuses to seriously take
into account the disadvantages a black child carries with him the
day he starts school and that usually stays with him throughout his

academic career. Educational psychologist Harry Morgan discovered through a series of studies that most black children give up wanting to learn in school by the third grade.(8)

A few years ago, I gained some understanding of what a black child goes through in a predominantly white classroom. It began while interviewing a group of African-American and Latino students who had complained of being the target of racial slurs in their predominately white high school. The first student, Ken, an African American, revealed an experience, which inspired me to do some serious research. He had come from Cleveland, where he was an A student in a predominately black school. His favorite subjects were mathematics and science; he dreamed of becoming an electrical engineer, an inventor. While in Cleveland, he had won a number of awards for several electrical gadgets he had invented.

Ken said he entered the new high school with great expectations. But he soon learned that he wasn't as welcome as his white peers. No one told him that he wasn't wanted, or that he should leave. There were the usual superficial greetings from his white classmates, but no one took the time to engage in deeper conversations. There wasn't a white student he could honestly call a real friend. Though his teachers were pleasant, they rarely called on him in class. That mystified him. Being a veteran teacher, I felt I knew why Ken's teachers didn't call on him. It wasn't a matter of not liking the young black man. The teachers had lower expectations of Ken because of his skin color, and because he had matriculated from a predominately black school whose academic standards, they felt, weren't as high as their school's. They probably felt Ken didn't belong in the advanced track. To avoid embarrassing him, they rarely called on him.

After a few weeks he felt that he didn't belong in the high school. It got so bad that he didn't look forward to attending class. What kept him going was his promise to his mother that he would try as hard as he could to excel scholastically. But it was hard to concentrate. As soon as he would enter the classroom, he would continually glance at the wall clock to see how much longer he would have to endure the pain of being in an alien place. When the period-ending bell would ring, Ken would bolt out of the classroom, and find a quiet place where he could gird himself for the next onslaught. Being in class was pure torture, for he felt like an oddity, always on edge, never feeling that he belonged there; it seemed like he was sliding back instead of moving forward intellectually. Intuitively, he knew it was the not the place to be—but there was his promise to his mother.

The mounting stress triggered a sensation in Ken that he had never experienced before. It was scary. He grew so self-absorbed in class, he could not think or reason. His intellectual capacity seemed to shrink. It got so bad that he began failing his exams. In a few weeks his teachers came to his rescue; to relieve him of the academic rigor they felt he was incapable of handling, they placed him in the lower track, designed for students who weren't interested in attending college, or weren't capable of doing college work.

As Ken was revealing why he was demoted, he began to cry. As I looked at him, I sensed that he was crying because his dream of becoming an electrical engineer had been dashed. Not only that—he had been humiliated, told that he wasn't as good as his white counterparts. The demotion had set off doubts about his intellectual capabilities, something he had never experienced before. There was no one he could go to to erase those doubts. The fact that experienced educational authorities executed the demotion made those doubts stick. As I continued to look at this young black man, who at one time was full of hope, I realized that Ken had been psychologically wounded, that his teachers weren't aware of what they had done to him. I also realized that that very day thousands of other young black students were probably experiencing what Ken had experienced. And I thought of the past—the countless African-American, American Indian, and Latino students who had been psychologically wounded in a place that is supposed to stimulate intellectual and social growth in youngsters.

When the next thought came to mind, I had to close my eyes, because it seemed so extreme. But it wouldn't go away. When my heart intervened, I felt compelled to embrace the thought as the truth. Our schools have been guilty of a crime against humanity; and because our educators aren't willing to accept the responsibility, the psychological wounding of children of color goes on.

When I think of what happened to Ken and the countless other students of color who have experienced similar treatment in our classrooms, I remember author James Baldwin's observation of the fate many black children face in America:

> A child believes everything; he has no choice. That is how he sorts out reality. When a child retreats and can no longer be reached, it is not that he has ceased to believe; it is that we, who are all he has, have failed him and now he has no choice but to die. It may take many forms, and years; but the child has chosen and runs to death.(9)

Witnessing what had happened to Ken drove me to unearth what exactly happens psychologically to a child when he becomes a victim of racism in the classroom. It only took a few months before I gained some insights. In Hawaii, I came across the work of human developmentalist Kenneth Yamamoto, who was trying to determine why so many native Hawaiians drop out of high school. He concluded that when a student is made to feel inferior, lacks confidence and doesn't like himself, he eventually has two painful experiences in the classroom, the latter being the most painful and damaging to the ego.

The first is a conditioned reflex. As soon as the insecure student enters the classroom, it turns into a factory for failure. An urge to flee sweeps over him, for he doesn't want to be in a place where he only experiences defeat. That's how Ken felt when he would continually glance at the classroom's wall clock, waiting anxiously for the period-bell to ring. The other experience is more traumatic, for it has to do with the shutting down of the student's cerebral cortex, which is the seat of thought in the human brain. Remember when Ken complained that he could no longer think or reason in class? He was experiencing the shut down of his cerebral cortex. Neither he nor his teacher were aware that this stress-induced phenomenon was taking place within Ken. When it first happened, Ken panicked. This is natural, because when the cortex isn't active, the medulla oblongata, which is on the base of the brain and controls our emotions, sets off two survival emotions—fight or flee.

Anger usually boils up within the student who chooses to fight. His inner voice cries out for help, for justice and, in the end, for revenge. Unable to hear the inner voice of the student, the teacher responds to the outward expression of the desperate young soul, who is behaving aggressively; and out of self-defense brands the youngster a "behavioral problem," placing him in a special track for dummies and the emotionally unstable. Unless he drops out of school, the student remains in the same track and graduates from high school unequipped to function effectively in a democratic but alien society. He finds himself at a crossroads, where he must choose one of two paths. Most choose the path where the student bows to the educators' evaluation of him, and he says to himself, "Yes, I am a dummy," and spends the rest of his life looking for ways to dull the pain.

Our cities are packed with millions of men and women of color who have chosen that path. They are products of insensitive, ignorant school systems, made up of teachers of good will. What are the teachers ignorant of? The pressure, pain, frustration and anger most students of color must endure in the classroom; and how those feelings effect their ability to succeed academically. When a book like *The Bell Curve* is published, many teachers feel vindicated, for the authors' findings support their suspicions as to why black students don't do as well as white students in school. I doubt if the authors of *The Bell Curve* would have written the book had they been aware of the cerebral cortex trauma that most students of color experience in school.

Those who choose the other path, outwardly reject the educators evaluation of themselves. Ruled by anger, they resist the establishment's attempts to control them. This is not an easy task when you consider their struggle in warding off the effects of the seeds of self doubt planted in them by their teachers. Their resistance often explodes into violence, and many of them end up in trouble with the law. It doesn't surprise me that one-third of black males between the ages of 20 and 29 are either in jail or on parole.(10)

The mental shutdown of black students in the classroom has had an adverse effect on the black community. It has spawned an anti-education attitude among large numbers of young black men and women, who equate failure with school. To cover up their shame, they have concocted an excuse for their failure, which they try to force upon other black students who show signs of succeeding scholastically.

The excuse is that "education is a white man's thing." Sadly, to keep from being ostracized from their classmates or friends, many black students embrace the excuse. As a consequence there is a reluctance to go to college; and the intellectual level of the community declines. This has economic ramifications. Communities composed of poorly educated residents will not attract high-paying hi-tech industries. And the students who have embraced the excuse aren't equipped to land employment elsewhere.

There are also social ramifications. The students that harbor an anti-school bias end up losing hope, being embittered, frustrated and angry. A large number of such men and women, when concentrated in a community, usually turns it into a hotbed of violence and crime.

The tragedy in all of this is that those black youth who have embraced the excuse aren't aware of why they fail in school. If they did, they would never go to such lengths to cover up their shame. They and their parents would demand that schools create learning environments and teaching approaches that would not bring about mental shutdown in students. The students would be liberated from the repressed belief that they are stupid and inherently inferior to whites. As a result, they'll gain greater self-respect and hope of realizing the career aspirations they harbored before falling prey to the "excuse."

The "excuse" is a relatively new phenomenon. There was a time when an education was highly prized among adolescent blacks, usually a reflection of their parents' appreciation for schooling. It was felt that an education was a gateway to real freedom. This was especially true in the years shortly after emancipation. The late sociologist and founder of the National Association for the Advancement of Colored People, W.E.B Du Bois, was impressed with the young black men and women's eagerness to attend school during his lifetime:

> They were consumed with desire for schools. The uprising of the black man, and the pouring of himself into organized effort for education... was one of the marvelous occurrences of the modern world, almost without parallel in the history of civilization.

These newly free men and women displayed what Du Bois called "a frenzy for schools."(11)

The school systems in America are responsible for dashing the young blacks' enthusiasm for schooling; and the emergence of the "excuse" as a face-saving device.

Inadequate efforts to redress the damage done

Realistically, much of the government's effort to improve the learning conditions for students of color have met with little success. In too many cases the efforts have backfired. Take school integration, for example. It has failed as a means of wiping out racism in America. One reason is because very few of our schools have been truly integrated. According to a Harvard Graduate school of Education study, 66 percent of black students have never attended an integrated school; and for Hispanic students the percentage is higher.(12) This, despite the 1954 US Supreme Court ruling that school segregation is unconstitutional. The trouble is that the Court doesn't have the power to change human hearts. Those who are emotionally opposed to a law will find ways to circumvent it. Urban white parents who didn't want their children to attend school with blacks fled to the suburbs. Several fears set off their exodus: They felt the appearance of black students automatically lowers the academic standards of a school; and there is always the concealed fear of what could result from black and white student interaction. They weren't ready for interracial marriage, or being grandparents of interracial babies produced out of wedlock.

Unfortunately, many white teachers followed the white families to the suburbs, usually to make more money and work in more pleasing surroundings. Of course, this left the city schools inhabited by mostly black, Hispanic and Asian students, being taught by, for the most part, less experienced and qualified teachers. So the majority of students of color found themselves not only in segregated school situations, but receiving an inferior education.

Whites have found other ways to avoid school integration. In many towns and rural areas, private schools have sprung up, often organized and financed by local Protestant churches. These schools have become known as Christian Academies. Because tuition is required, most black families, who generally are poorer than their white counterparts, send their children to the public schools. As a consequence the great majority of students in the public school system are boys and girls of color. To give the impression they are not fostering school segregation, academies will offer a few scholarships to "deserving" black children who would fit neatly into the school's special environment.

We find that more and more whites who remain in the city are sending their children to either independent or parochial schools. In Baltimore, for example, only 10 percent of the public school population is white, and most of those students are too poor to pay the private school tuition, which runs between $8,000 and $10,000 annually. The bottom line is that the students of color and the few whites who remain in most of our public schools are at a disadvantage when it comes to entering and succeeding in college. The reasons are that those who are fortunate to attend private schools find themselves in smaller classes, being taught by teachers who have more freedom to be creative in their teaching approach. Because the teachers have a say in formulating their curricula, they tend to be more enthusiastic in the classroom and more committed to reaching and motivating their students. Though the students find the academic work more rigorous in private school, they find their learning experience more rewarding not only academically, but socially as well. As a result they tend to be better prepared for college work, and usually score higher on tests than their black and Hispanic counterparts in public schools. The sad fact is that the majority of public school students either don't matriculate to college or start and soon drop out; while the great majority of private school graduates enter college and graduate.

What I have just described is a formula for the perpetuation of racism. Generally, students of color, especially blacks, who can't afford to attend private school, end up not receiving an education as good as their white counterparts. As a consequence, students of color usually end up getting the less skilled jobs, if they get jobs at all; and the whites get the higher paying positions, which puts them within the privileged circle of power, occupying positions that shape institutional policy and programs. In the end, this formula assures people of color remaining in their "proper place." And all of this is achieved by whites without breaking the law.

It is no accident that there are more black males in prison than in college. The racism within our school systems is a factor in the existence of this statistic.

Deep down, most poor blacks whose children are stuck in decrepit ghetto classrooms are aware of the formula, but their complaints are rarely heeded by those who create and maintain the rules of conduct in society. This, of course, is the source of resentment and anger and frustration among people of color, whose patience is wearing thin. Of course, those affluent African-Americans concerned about their children's future are placing their sons and daughters into high-priced private academies, thus contributing to the deteriorating quality of education most poor black, Hispanic and American Indian students are receiving at their underfunded public schools. And sadly, most of the privileged blacks show little or no interest in doing something that would improve the quality of black children's schooling. In fact, they shun any involvement with the ghetto.

There are school systems that claim they are fully integrated, but upon close scrutiny are functionally segregated because they operate a tracking system. Some of the more sophisticated systems no longer use the term tracking, preferring the term "grouping." Nevertheless, behind the titles are the same social and academic results. Black, Hispanic and American Indian students are channeled into the less academically challenging classes, usually taught by teachers who would prefer teaching the advanced classes made up primarily of white boys and girls. And the tracked students of color usually know this; they also know they have no control over what is going to happen to them. Worst of all, they have no control over a momentum that will influence the shaping of their destiny.

Over a period of time they find themselves becoming accustomed to being in the lower track, and in the end learning to believe they are inferior to those in the advanced classes. Besides the football field and basketball court, there is little interaction between black and white students in the "fully" integrated schools.

Even attempts to bus black students to white schools have not achieved well-intentioned goals. For the most part, the bused black students have found themselves in a foreign setting, viewed by the regular student body and faculty as outcasts, interlopers or wards of the state. Though rarely physically harmed, the black students have been forced to hang out together, for they have not been welcomed into the school's existing social circles. And the few who have managed to be accepted in one of these circles, because of their prowess on the athletic field, have usually paid a price for the privilege of having white friends. They have been the object of patronizing behavior and considerable backbiting on the part of the whites, and rejected by blacks as traitors.

Academically, there have been few rewards. Most of the time the bused black students have entered the white school lacking the academic background of their white classmates. This has been true of even those who have done well in the predominately black schools they have come from. Not only has this kept them from being channeled into advanced classes, they have found themselves trying to survive in an academic ghetto, stigmatized as mentally inferior by the whites they see everyday. This isn't something whites proclaim openly; it is, rather, a belief beating in their hearts. And most black students sense it. To avoid it, they usually cluster together in places like the school cafeteria, which becomes an oasis of moral support, a place where they can heal their psychological bruises, and reclaim some self-esteem.

School busing hasn't really worked, because the students and teachers in the white schools aren't ready to accept black youngsters as fully equal to them, despite their support of Black History Month. And it doesn't matter if the whites are conservative or liberal. It is just a matter of one being open about his or her racial feelings, and the other trying to hide them. In the final analysis, the inability of white students and teachers to accept black students as equals stems from their race prejudice, which most refuse to acknowledge. When the bussed black students complain about the treatment they are experiencing at the hands of students and teachers, it is usually greeted by various forms of defensiveness and denial that reinforces the black students' sense of anger and hopelessness. In time, they give up complaining, and their instinct to withdraw from everything white is reinforced.

Many educators in the American Indian community are aware of the failings of the school integration movement. To avoid further damage to their students, they are trying to come up with educational alternatives. One initiative has been recognized as a work of genius by the MacArthur Foundation.* Patricia Locke, half Lakota Sioux and half Chippewa, has been named a MacArthur Fellow for the work she has done in helping seventeen tribes develop colleges on their reservations.

Though an avid advocate of the principle of the oneness of humankind, Ms. Locke feels American Indian youth will gain more by attending an all Indian school that is culturally geared to reach its students. For what the Indian student usually learns in the white run school isn't going to help him function effectively in his community. In fact, for most it is a counterproductive experience. He usually learns that he and his culture are inferior to white people and their ways. Hating the feeling that evokes in him, the student resists going to school, and eventually drops out, unequipped to survive while tormented by self doubt and confusion in a society that has little respect for him. For most American Indian elders this is an all too familiar pattern their children follow. People like Ms. Locke are determined to break that pattern, a pattern which has led to abominable social conditions for most Indian families in America.

Ms. Locke points out that if those running the public schools were all seriously involved in internalizing the principle of the oneness of humankind there would be no need for all-Indian schools. But that is not the case. Therefore, she reasons, to send an Indian child to a white run school is like placing him on a moving conveyer belt heading toward a classroom buzz saw, that ends up slaughtering him psychologically.

The same can be said for most Latino children. Hector Lopez, who managed to escape the buzz saw, remembers being on the conveyer belt. It was a bleak period of his life. Going to school was a dehumanizing experience. When he looks back, he realizes that because of his ethnic background, he was being programmed to end up doing what his father did:

---

*   The MacArthur Foundation continually searches the country for individuals who are making significantly positive changes in the life of the community. When they find such individuals, whom they call geniuses, they award them between 250,000 and 300,000 dollars, to be spent in whichever way the recipient chooses.

My upbringing had a big impact on my life, basically because of the school system in which I was raised. The
Napa Valley is a high-class society of grape field owners
and wine owners, and then there's the working class
which is usually Mexican-based. It's socially segregated
in many ways. The school system is very segregated. I
was a victim of what they call the tracking system. I was
placed in a lower track and never quite excelled. My first
language in this country was Spanish. My father had
been here legally for 40 years but he never quite grasped
the English language. Since I spoke Spanish and dressed
in boots, farm worker style, I got placed into lower class
English as a second language (ESL) courses. This eventually brought me problems. I never quite learned algebra
and my reading courses were almost coloring-book
style. I got out of high school with probably about a fifth
grade reading level, and at the same time, I was going to
school with children of the Coppolas—Francis Ford Cop-
pola's children. They were all taking very college-
oriented courses, but those were never introduced to me
by counselors. So I came out ready to return to the fields
right after high school. This form of thinking was introduced to me early—being an American, yet having no
mobility because of who I was... (13)

The state of the problem in American higher education

Things are not much better in the domain of higher education. Appalled at the high rate of drop out among Indian youth at
predominately white colleges, Ms. Locke has helped to establish
seventeen tribal colleges where the attrition rate is practically nonexistent. While the teaching approach is sensitive to the students'
cultural needs, academic rigor is not compromised. Every effort is
made to help those students who want to pursue law, medicine or
engineering get into graduate school and succeed there.

In contrast, most American universities and colleges, instead
of being the breeding ground for solutions to problems like racism,
have become racial battlegrounds. I am not only referring to the
number of physical clashes that have taken place in recent years on
some campuses. It is the countless nonphysical clashes that occur
daily in the classroom, in the dinning hall, in the editorial room of
the college newspaper, on the athletic field, in the student senate
and faculty congress, and any other place where professors and students gather. Wherever I have lectured in the past few years—and

that has been at scores of colleges in every section of the nation—I have sensed tension between the races. While on some campuses it is more apparent than others—it has always been there. It is more subdued in those places where the administration has expended considerable energy and funds to create an extended campus-wide truce, which, in reality, is a cover-up of a simmering situation that is potentially explosive. This is particularly true among the elitist colleges. Many of their administrators are aware of the fragile nature of the truce they have been able to fashion through skillful negotiating and capitulating to some minority student demands. It is a precarious situation, because if they give in to every demand made by a racial or an ethnic group, white students and faculty will often protest, claiming unfair treatment, and they'll make their own demands, which usually intensifies the existing friction between the races. Maintaining a workable balance has turned into a collegiate art form.

There are no officially integrated campuses that are racially serene. It is important to keep in mind that the college is not an academic oasis; they usually reflect the social conditions on the outside. Students and faculty that come to a university to study and work don't leave their prejudices at the campus gate. Also, if there is racism in the city where the college is located, there is going to be racism on campus, as well. It may not be dealt with the way it is dealt with in the city—but it is there, rooted and virulent.

The trouble is that in academe those with the greatest power don't want to believe the race situation on their campus is bad. They don't want to think about the unthinkable. As a consequence, they will resort to all sorts of measures to convince themselves and those around them that they are right. What fosters the self-deception maneuver as the only rational alternative they can take is an underlying belief that there is no solution to the racism problem. So they channel their intellectual and creative powers into devising schemes that will prevent physical clashes and construct mechanisms that will minimize nonphysical conflicts. To do this they find ways to keep potential disputing parties separated as much as possible. What they have resurrected is the "separate but equal" technique as a way of maintaining social order. To keep from being accused of doing what white supremacists resorted to in the past, they have concocted a convenient spin to their actions: "What we have done for the minorities," they claim, "is provide them with opportunities to become acquainted with their rich cultural heritage—and provide places where they can be socially comfortable."

To assure continuance of an inter-ethnic truce, university administrations have organized and assiduously promoted campaigns calling for campus civility. Which is not designed to uproot the cause of racism, because—again—deep down they don't believe that this objective can be achieved. Why promote civility? Because it is safe, thoroughly politically correct—a condition which they believe all civilized men and women would support. And who in their right mind would not consider themselves civilized?

Through a well thought-out and financed scheme, the top campus decision-makers create an atmosphere where all "isms" have the room to express themselves fully without interfering with each other's aims, and are guaranteed equal treatment by the administration. It doesn't really matter to the guardians of this scheme that each "ism" is only concerned with carrying out its own agenda, and has little or no interest in networking with other "isms", unless they can gain something from such a venture. To the administration, what matters most is the creation and preservation of campus social order. And whatever means is necessary to achieve the desired end—will be employed. The rationalization used to support the Machiavellian approach is that no decent person would countenance an outbreak of violence on campus, therefore any measures used to prevent that from happening should be taken. In the meantime, no thought is given as to how to eliminate racism.

To maintain control, all of the "isms" are lumped together into a single organization and given a name that has a human rights ring to it. The fact that each group is given funding is an incentive for them to be well behaved. Of course, this gesture is meant to be viewed as democratic and just. And the university's public affairs department makes sure that the organization is perceived that way, not only by the student body but the Board of Trustees and the public and private agencies that fund academic research projects. And the college's applicant pool is also a target of their upbeat message of campus civility. After all prospective students will shy away from attending a college afflicted by chronic racial problems.

The sociological safety net created by the administration, which includes all of the "isms" represented on campus, is designed to neutralize those groups the administration fears the most—like black activists groups. For example, should a black organization complain that a Lesbian-Gay group is receiving preferential treatment, it will gain a reputation of being an irritant within an organization that is widely accepted as democratic and

just—and the complainant is usually shamed into being compli-
ant. Of course there is always the unspoken threat of being cut off
from university funding.

To keep all of the "isms" happy, the administration will try to
accommodate many of their desires in a splashy fashion by holding news conferences and special assemblies. This, again to reinforce the democratic and just image it has developed in the way the
university is treating all of the "isms" on campus.

To launch a civility campaign, a university will stage a three
or four day special conference for its students at the beginning of
the fall semester. That time is chosen because it is the start of the
academic year, the best time to set the right tone for the implementation of its campus wide civility scheme, which, in reality, is a
propaganda venture. This is just what the University of Massachusetts at Amherst did in 1993.

Among the top priority goals was to make certain that every
"ism" on campus would have the opportunity to share its philosophy through workshops, debates, panel discussions, and speeches.
A special place was set aside by the university where each group
could set up a booth, manned by some of its followers, who were
free to pass out pamphlets and field questions of student and faculty inquirers.

To assure universal participation on the part of the student
body, and that included "ism" followers and independents, the
conference shapers decided to have Bill Cosby, a distinguished
alumnus, who earned a doctorate degree from the university's
school of education, give a public talk at the campus coliseum,
which seats nearly 10,000 people. Since the talk was free and Bill
Cosby was speaking, almost every seat was filled the night of his
performance. Obviously, the administration was thrilled at the
turnout. And more than satisfied with the number of students who
participated in the plethora of workshops, speeches and forums
that solicited questions from the audience. To stimulate student
participation, the university squeezed a variety of food fests and
concerts in between the barrage of philosophizing, emoting, propa-
gandizing and proselytizing. For nearly a week the campus was
highly energized—and entertained. But in less than three weeks
the conference-generated energy and emotional high had dissi-
pated, everything was back to normal: The racism that existed on
campus before the conference was still in tact—just as rooted and
virulent as ever.

Since the conference planners were convinced that racism
couldn't be eradicated, they didn't try to find out what progress

was made to eliminate the social disease. What impressed them was that the proper social tone had been set for the students and faculty; that they had succeeded in weaving an aura of toleration and a degree of contentment across the campus. All of the "isms" had gained some respectability, as well as some converts. The fact that the campus was more divided and polarized than ever before didn't bother the administration. What mattered most was that the different "isms" weren't warring against each other or against the university's leadership. What has resulted from the campus-wide civility campaign is a tolerable system of apartheid masquerading as a harmonious community celebrating diversity.

At some universities the need to create and maintain some degree of campus-wide social tranquillity carries over to the academic side. An unofficial policy of evaluation is applied to students of color, especially African-Americans and Hispanics. Why those two groups? Because they are considered the most potentially volatile. Remember, preserving the existing truce is an important priority of the administration. By avoiding racial conflict on campus, they rationalize, the majority of students (who are white) will be able to pursue their studies without being harassed by external forces or events.

The idea is to pass African-American and Hispanic students even though they are failing. Graduating with a "C" average and unprepared to function effectively in a job reserved for college graduates, they realize their degree is worthless, and end up working in jobs that don't require a college education, or collecting welfare checks.

Deep down those who apply such an evaluation policy do not believe they are compromising academic integrity by carrying it out. They probably believe that it is a benevolent way to deal with those students who aren't endowed to do college work, until they realize they aren't qualified to further their education.

This grade evaluation policy, which is designed to make minority students feel good while they're on campus so they won't be disruptive, reinforces the existing racism in the job market. When a large percentage of minority college graduates fail to perform adequately in the workplace, the employers' suspicion that African-Americans and Hispanics are inherently inferior—is reinforced. Consequently, they'll hire and promote minorities only for cosmetic purposes.

The compulsion to keep peace on campus at all costs is reflected in the way minority faculty and staff members are treated. Often times courageous and creative black professors, who go out of their way to make their courses culturally attractive for minorities, end up skirting university academic policies. The professors resort to such tactics because they know the university's policies are stifling minority students' ability to learn.

The department chair won't fire the professor, but instead begin a process of making life uncomfortable for the "nonconformist" instructor—like dropping the professor's favorite course, or having him or her teach an unpopular course, or apply extra pressure to write articles for publication. The process continues until the minority professor seeks employment elsewhere. The administration hopes the decision to leave is made before it has to judge whether the instructor is worthy of tenure. Otherwise, deciding to deny tenure could set off a racial conflict at the college.

As for the minority staff member—someone who is viewed unorthodox in his or her professional practices is usually relieved of his or her duties and promoted to a higher-paying position that has high visibility but requires little responsibility. This strategy accomplishes two things: On the one hand, it reveals to the world that the college has a minority in a high ranking position. On the other hand, it limits the minority person to a position which has little or no power in altering existing academic or social policies and practices.

Schools of Education as potential centers for the dismantling of racism

Within every university operating a school of education, there is an opportunity to reverse the spread of racism. Since these schools are training prospective teachers and educational administrators, and provide in-service training for practicing educators, they are in a position to replace curricula and teaching approaches that are perpetuating racism with curricula and approaches that will help eliminate racism—and create truly harmonious communities.

The first thing that must be done is to acknowledge that the existing approaches to overcoming racism in education haven't been effective. Obviously, that will take some doing on the part of school administrations, for it is difficult to admit that what you have been doing doesn't work—that, in fact, it has had the opposite effect on what you have been striving to achieve. Some professors have invested a great deal of time and energy into devising multicultural educational approaches; in fact, their professional reputation hinges on what is being asked of them to scrap. They would be faced with having to choose between saving face and rejecting the proposed changes, or taking a courageous step and expressing a willingness to become wholeheartedly involved in implementing a program that is aware of the nature of the problem, of how it came into being, and of how to solve it.

A Solution for Educators

As far as I'm concerned there is no choice. For to continue what is being done in our schools—despite the efforts being made to make minorities feel good—is a crime against humanity. I know that is a harsh indictment of an entire professional class. But the facts are plain. Our schools—elementary to university—have not only failed to eliminate racism in their institutions, but have contributed to its spread, as was described earlier in this chapter. What is being done now must be scrapped, because students are being psychologically wounded in the classroom, and the virus of racism in others is being nourished by teachers who are ignorant of their own racial conditioning and the racial conditioning of their community. What we are faced with is a social catastrophe few educators realize exists.

A revolutionary change is required in the way schools deal with racism. What must be debunked is the belief that the school is no place to solve social issues like racism, that it is meant to be only a learning center. Learning is not a neutral process. As we saw, millions of black, Hispanic, and American Indian children have learned to dislike themselves and feel inferior because of their experiences in school. White kids have learned in school that whites are superior to people of color through textbooks and instruction based on myth, not fact. Teachers unconsciously perpetrate the racism that children of color face daily in the classroom. Since formal education is responsible for perpetuating racism, it has a responsibility to eliminate it.

The School of Education is the logical institution to spearhead the revolutionary changes. By training educators who understand the deep-seated nature of racism, it can lead the way for the rest of university campuses and society. The School of Education should offer a required course that describes in detail how formal education helped to institutionalize racism in America; showing how teachers as way back as the 1600s inculcated within all students a belief in the superiority of the first European settlers and the white immigrants who followed over the indigenous people and those other people of color who came from other parts of the world, most of them against their will.

Not only should the blatant examples of racism be exposed, but the subtle forms of racism should receive thorough exposure, because currently that's what most teachers manifest, and that's what does the most harm to students of color. That includes teachers who observe Black History month willingly, teach tolerance, show kindness to children of color, but who haven't dealt with their own racism which is festering in their unconscious. It is these teachers who unconsciously hurt students of color the most. How? Through the teacher's kindness, the black child's guard will come down, and is crushed when the teacher puts down the student in a patronizing or condescending manner, or overlooks involving her in a class activity because deep down she feels the child is inferior to white kids. The black student is crushed because she doesn't expect to be treated as an inferior human being by someone she has learned to trust. Examples of such classroom behavior should help promote an understanding of how the crushed student usually reacts to a subtle classroom put-down. Often times a university student of color taking the required course will volunteer to explain how it felt being put down in elementary or high school. Such revelations have a way of quickening the latent compassion in a white person's soul.

By taking this course, prospective teachers will most likely be motivated to deal conscientiously with their own repressed racism. They will also gain insights as to how to avoid mistakes made by educators in the past. And it will inspire and encourage them to want to participate in implementing the revolutionary changes necessary to eliminating racism within our schools, and turning them into healing and unifying centers within their community.

Training prospective teachers to discover, release and develop human potential in a student is a must. For when some of a child's potentialities are discovered and released and he recognizes them, he is usually impressed and develops self-respect and self-worth, a condition that is often missing in students of color. He begins to understand who he really is. With this knowledge, a child starts to feel good about himself—which generates internal strength and security. Instead of directing his energy and attention toward his ineptness and insecurities, he's enthusiastically focused on the world outside of himself, exploring it and experiencing a sense of fulfillment through his discoveries. He is motivated to want to learn more and often develops a passion for learning. By engaging in such a process, a "minority" student usually overcomes his low self- esteem and truly believes he's a member of the human race, and he acts accordingly. I have witnessed this transformation take place while teaching at Springfield Technical Community College. (A detailed explanation can be found in my book, *Education on Trial*, One World Press, Oxford, Britain)

A separate course should be offered which unearths and describes the realities underlying the principle of the oneness of the human family. Genetic, anthropological and biological proof should be provided, since the evidence is irrefutable. When the students finish this course, they will understand that, in reality, there is only one race—the human race, and there is only one human color, comprised of different shades. To help students gain some understanding of how most people have embraced the multi-race theory, a concerted effort should be made to explain how this distorted view of reality came into being. The mistakes of earlier scientists need to be understood in the context of contemporary scientific discoveries. While the major emphasis should be on having students understand and internalize the principle of the oneness of humankind, they should also gain a healthy understanding of why the human family is so diverse. In other words, they should be exposed to the principle of unity in diversity and how it is manifested in all levels of nature.

In this way, prospective teachers will become aware that we all belong to the same family and will see the need of becoming a unifying force in the community. They will also be inclined to seek help in overcoming whatever racial prejudice is festering within them. As a result, they will be more willing to engage in a racial healing process offered by the school system or the community. They will look upon all children in their classes as members of their family. With that understanding, they will be more committed to serving all of their students equally. In fact, they will most likely put forth extra effort to helping the child of color, because they will look upon that child as a family member in pain. Therefore they will no longer approach a student of color with lower expectations. But most of all, they will be able to overcome their subconscious belief that European-American students are superior to students of color. As a consequence, they will find themselves able to reach students they once viewed as beyond reaching.

After internalizing the principle of the oneness of humankind, the prospective teacher would be ready for a course on how to integrate that principle into the school curriculum from kindergarten to the twelfth grade. Why the saturation approach? Because changing attitudes and behavior isn't easy. For nearly 400 years, Americans have been saturated with a lie, which most of us have accepted as the truth; and that is, that whites are inherently superior to people of color. In this course, the prospective educator will learn how to weave the principle of the oneness of humankind into mathematics, science, history and every other subject a school child is likely to take, including physical education. Armed with this training, teachers will be inoculating their students against the disease of racism.

Harvard Psychiatrist, Dr. John Woodall agrees:

> If the principle of the oneness of humanity were taught to children from the earliest age, a foundation would be laid for the social cohesion we desire. By teaching this principle as the first essential lesson, we would be able to demonstrate the context within which an ethical life based on the need for justice for all makes sense. The principle of the oneness of humanity gives a context for ethical decision making. It provides a context for examining communication styles that foster cooperation. It serves as the only sure basis upon which diversity can be truly appreciated for its necessity to the whole of society, and not simply tolerated. The principle of the oneness of humanity denotes a cohesion and transcendence of the human spirit that is not captured in the idea of tolerance.

> Because it eliminates the perception of others as fundamentally different in nature, the principle of the oneness of humanity abrogates the law of the struggle of survival. When this principle is internalized in one's emotional and intellectual life, one's highest values become the preservation of the best interests of all people. It becomes a natural desire to abandon the use of force as the preferred means of social interaction. Instead, the natural social graces become possible and valued. It becomes possible to see the loss of others as a loss to oneself. Similarly, the gain of others becomes one's own gain.

> This principle grounds one's ethical life in the widest possible embrace. In its sphere, the value of each part of society becomes evident. Since other ethnic groups are not seen as intrinsically inferior or superior they are not perceived as threats. By putting the value of the entirety of humanity first, the sense of fear and need is diminished. Free from these emotional pulls, one's thinking is free to explore the world without resort to defensiveness. Psy-

chologically, the mind is free to abandon the primitive defenses of projection and denial and move into the mature character skills of reciprocity and empathy.

By giving priority to study of the nuances of the oneness of humankind, a safe context is provided which makes an exploration of human diversity meaningful. It provides an antidote to our diseased racist thinking by providing the context in which primitive psychological defense mechanisms can give way to mature personality development. Taught in ways that show its applications on the personal, interpersonal and institutional levels of human activity, the principle of the oneness of humanity provides the vaccine to prevent future generations from acquiring the infection of racism.(14)

If applied to every student in every school, I believe, the principle of the oneness of humanity would wipe out the epidemic of racism in America in two generations.

Because every educator should be aware of how racism has affected them, all future educators should take a course on the pathology of the disease of racism. Since most women and men engaged in formal education aren't aware of racism being a psychological disorder, they lack an understanding of the nature of a social menace they are opposed to. Without a proper understanding of what racism is, it is impossible to be an effective healer of the disorder. In this course, students will be exposed to the scientific literature, describing how the disorder comes into being and manifests itself. The prospective teacher will realize that while the disease can spark evil behavior, it in and of itself is not evil, but rather an illness. Cure the illness and there will be no more evil behavior. Also, by taking this course, the prospective teacher will recognize in him or herself some of the symptoms of the disease and will be motivated to want to participate in a racial healing workshop set up by the school of education. In this course, the student will learn how racism impacts on children of color, how it thwarts their development, and inhibits them from trying to discover and develop their intellectual potential. They will be exposed in greater detail to the physiological and psychological trauma most students of color undergo while in the classroom. I only touched on it earlier in this chapter.

After taking this course, the prospective teacher will be more willing to participate in creating curricula and teaching approaches that will make school life more comfortable and stimulating for students of color. For they will have gained an understanding of the trauma most students of color have had to endure through the years. Because the teachers will be aware of how the white kids were infected by the virus of racism, they will be in a position to help them heal.

Earlier in this chapter we saw how most students of color function in the classroom, why so many of them don't do as well as their white counterparts. I pointed out that they suffer from a deep, festering wound, which is a lack of confidence, a lack of self-esteem, that they suffer from conscious or unconscious feelings of inferiority, and in many incidences, self-hatred. Those who are planning to be teachers must understand what the "wound " is and what they can do to heal it. Therefore, every student at a school of education should take a course that will explain how the wound comes into being, how it affects a student of color psychologically and physiologically. Equal emphasis should be placed on guiding prospective teachers to become healers of the "wound." They should be exposed to the kind of teaching approaches and curricula that will help them become classroom healers. With this kind of training, school teachers will no longer deepen the wound that afflicts most students of color. They, instead, will be playing a significant role in ending the psychological racial genocide that has been going on in America for nearly 400 years.

Another mandatory course will operate as a laboratory. Students will become well grounded in how the *Institute for the Healing of Racism* functions. The course will be set up in such a way that the participants will have an opportunity to heal their own infection or wound of racism. They will bond with people they would have never bonded with had they not taken this course. In other words, they will be exposed to a way on how a community made up of many different ethnic groups can be truly unified.

The students who take this course will not only find a reliable means of healing their own infection or wound of racism; they will want to organize an *Institute for the Healing of Racism* in the school where they end up teaching. And they'll know how to set one up.

After taking this course, the prospective teacher will be more sensitive to the needs of all of her students regardless of color or ethnic background. As for the philosophy, psychology, goals and objectives and structure of the *Institutes*—that will be described in a later chapter.

Ideally, every school of education faculty member and administrator should take this course. If they participate with an open mind, they will come in contact with their own infection or wound of racism, will be motivated to become involved in the healing process, and will realize that what they had been doing in the past to overcome racism wasn't achieving what it was supposed to achieve. They will become committed to instituting the revolutionary changes needed to free our school systems of racism.

Because parents are a child's first teachers, special courses should be offered to help prospective teachers work effectively with parents in educating their children. Ideally, parents should identify their child's potentialities and talents and share their findings with a school teacher. With that information, the teacher's effort to discover, release and develop her students' potentialities will be enhanced. The teacher would share his/her insights with the parents, establishing an ongoing interchange of information and suggestions designed to aid in the intellectual and social development of the student. If done properly, this teacher-parent alliance can only help the teacher carry out her responsibilities in a more thorough manner.

Of course, realistically, most of today's parents aren't equipped intellectually or psychologically to participate in such an alliance. This condition presents another challenge to the school of education, which is to establish a special program that will produce certified teachers who will train parents on how to become educational partners with their children's school teachers.

There should be a course on becoming a loving teacher. I know those educators who view education as a science would reject the idea of offering such a course. Too emotional to be academic, they would claim. But teaching is more of an art than a science. In order for a teacher to succeed, he must be able to reach his students, stimulate them, motivate them, win their confidence, open them up for learning. To do that requires a caring nature. And caring is a byproduct of love. We need to understand more deeply the origin and nature of love.

Even if a school of education student masters all of his courses and yet lacks love in the classroom, he'll fall short of becoming a successful teacher; for love is an irreplaceable bonding agent. The most effective teachers are those who are able to bond with their students. "Minority" students in particular respond positively to the genuine expression of love. If a teacher fails to bond with her students, there is usually distrust between the two, and the students' cerebral cortex is affected. When unqualified love is expressed in the classroom, both teacher and students are caught up in a wavelength that transcends material differences and barriers.

In that kind of atmosphere, students are more than attentive, they like the feeling—and can't wait until class meets again.

In all these ways discussed above, and probably many others, the school of education could become a force for community reconciliation. It could also offer to the community at large an elective two semester credit course for both undergraduate and graduate students. This course would take place on campus the first semester, and in the field the second semester. During the first semester, students will become well grounded as *Institute for the Healing of Racism* participants and facilitators; in the second semester, they will establish an institute in different community institutions, like churches, synagogues, businesses, police departments, hospitals, as well as schools, head start programs or youth centers.

I know it is much easier to propose change than to execute it, especially in a school of education where many different educational philosophies are espoused, and many philosophical fiefdoms have been established. Traversing through this intellectual minefield with the message I propose wouldn't be easy. The chances of setting off an explosion are great. But the trek through the minefield must be made, because the psychological wounding of students of color in our schools must stop. The role our schools play in perpetuating racism must come to en end. Whatever the schools of education have produced in terms of anti-racism programs has been ineffectual, because the drafters of those programs are unaware of the psychological wounding taking place in the classroom; they have not taken seriously the fact that formal education—which they are a part of—has played a mighty role in the creation and maintenance of racism in America.

Chapter Eleven

Disunity: The Fracturing Of The Black Community

It is rare for people of color, especially blacks, to feel free in America and to have a sense of belonging. As a consequence, an alarmingly high number of blacks are resigned to never attaining what their government proclaims all of its citizens have a right to enjoy. Though they try not to dwell on this hurtful deprivation—this injustice—blacks are reminded of it every day when they interact with whites at work, at governmental agencies, even while shopping or eating at restaurants in white neighborhoods. To lessen the chronic pain of not belonging, there is a tendency for blacks to avoid, as much as possible, any social interaction with whites. For to be with Euro-Americans is a reminder of what African-Americans are permanently denied: a situation that fuels black rage.

Well-meaning whites are baffled by some blacks' rush toward separatism and their resistance to assimilating into mainstream America. This reaction has come after decades of earnest efforts by blacks to integrate into every avenue of white society—and being rebuffed. Today, many blacks refuse to budge in the direction of integration, fearing rejection again. Others view any association with whites as a sign of weakness.

Many young black men and women today reject assimilation as a way to win their freedom, because of the high price they would have to pay to achieve what their parents and grandparents have always longed for and never achieved despite valiant attempts to be like white folks. Assimilation, they feel, means adapting to a system that was originally intended to exclude people like themselves. And that—through the decades—influenced the shaping of the social attitudes and behavior of those meant to be included in what is hailed as the finest democracy known to man.

Today, many college educated young blacks welcome the change of mind on the part of many whites on race matters, but they sense white *hearts* haven't changed. And because of that, they believe, whites are still unable to understand the plight of black people in America. African-Americans bristle when they hear well-meaning whites wonder aloud why blacks can't do what the Polish, Irish, Italian and Jewish immigrants did to improve their lot. With a change of heart, they say, whites would understand that such a comparison reflects not only a narrow view of American history, but more importantly, a profound ignorance of the gravity of America's racism problem. The European immigrants did not come in chains, and were not cut off from their rich cultural heritage, deprived of schooling, enslaved, and treated as animals; the Europeans came as free men and women and as soon as they arrived were able to find some kind of job and send their children to school.

Whatever hardships the Europeans endured—living in cold-water flats and working in sweatshops—paled in comparison to what the ancestors of today's blacks had to endure. For generations black slaves were subject to not only harsh physical treatment, but were the target of endless dehumanizing techniques, designed to convince them of their "divinely ordained" subservient role in whatever relationships they had with whites. Regardless of the screening maneuvers slaves employed, the brainwashing had an adverse effect on them, which, to a degree, was passed on to their descendants in the form of low self-esteem, a lack of confidence, feelings of inferiority and self-hatred, a condition many blacks pretend doesn't exist. But it does exist! Unless these deep, open and festering wounds inflicted on blacks are healed, their anger and sense of hopelessness will intensify. Just as whites need to recognize their infection of racism, blacks need to recognize their wounds.

To young blacks, inclusion in the white man's world would mean giving up aspects of a culture that they were raised in, that they are familiar with, that they trust, and that has been the source of comfort during countless moments of uncertainty and impending danger. To give that up would be an act of cultural treason. Besides, they have witnessed what usually happens to those who try to live as whites with black skin. Acceptance is never complete, and there's always the lingering sense of having sold your soul for something you can never have.

It isn't that young blacks would reject assimilation under different circumstances. If there were, for example, a legitimate attempt to overhaul the present system (which many whites also sense is failing), and blacks were involved on an equal basis in shaping a more just one, they would become a part of it. But young blacks know the chances of that happening in their lifetime—if ever—are exceedingly slim.

It isn't only young blacks that are gravitating toward separatism; more and more older blacks are moving in that direction as well. In recent years, I have met a good number of older African-Americans who have had a change-of-heart regarding racial integration. Not that they oppose the principle. But based on experience, they have learned that in some respects integration has been more harmful to the black community than the type of segregation experienced during the "separate but equal" era. With the advent of integration in the 1960s, they have witnessed the unraveling of the black community.

Prior to the 1960s there was more community cohesion in the black neighborhood. There was less familial breakup, single parenthood, crime and violence, and reliance on drugs and alcohol. The churches were a stronger moral influence on the people. Black fraternal organizations promoted community cooperation and solidarity. There was less unemployment, because there were more black-owned businesses and banks in the community. Though segregated, the schools taught black pride. And that was reinforced at the neighborhood youth centers. In the segregated community, there were outstanding role models for the children. The black professionals hadn't fled to the racially mixed middle class suburbs that eventually turned all black.

The older blacks know why integration hasn't really worked; it's because white racism won't allow it to work. This, despite all of the money and effort put forth by public and private agencies to try to make it work.

So old and young are confronted with making the best of a situation that seems to be worsening for most of them. True, there's a small percentage of black millionaires making more money than any other black of the past. And there are some black politicians who have risen to high office. But for blacks in general the prospects aren't very promising. Although there has been growth in the black middle class, its relative percentage in relation to the rapidly growing black poor and underclass is shrinking. To make matters worse, the social fabric of the black community is deteriorating at an alarming rate. It is beset by mounting problems like teenage pregnancies, single parenthood, street violence, accelerating school drop out rates, suicide, wife battering, high chronic male unemployment that leads to despondency, homelessness, or involvement in illegal economies like drugs, car-jacking and store-bashing. And for many youth there is a dependence on street gangs for fellowship and a sense of self-worth.

There doesn't seem to be any meaningful help forthcoming from the government, which seems helpless in solving some of the same problems plaguing whites. Nor is there a reliable force within the black community to alter the degenerative course many blacks find themselves involuntarily following. The black church, which is fragmented, is unable to change the course in a more positive direction. In a way, it is part of the problem. With the exception of a few churches, most are doing little or nothing to improve the social and economic lot of those living in their neighborhoods. Nor are they fortifying the spiritual core of most of their congregants. Too often, the pastors use the pulpit as a means of securing personal financial stability and building a political power base. The greatest service they provide is a weekly opportunity for a parishioner to release his frustrations and fears, his anger and resentment through communal prayer, singing and a rousing sermon that helps him to forget his deeply ingrained sorrows and woes for a few hours. Because the sorrows and woes don't really go away, the parishioners return to the church for an escape and a moment of ecstasy the next Sunday.

The role of black Christian churches in maintaining the status quo

Although there are many preachers who are truly wonderful and are accomplishing a great deal in their churches through their honest and straightforward manner, some black preachers resort to demagoguery as a way to assure operating a prosperous church. How do they do this? By exploiting their parishioners' fears, anger and the burning need to strike back at "Whitey." In New London, Connecticut, for example, some black ministers are discouraging their parishioners from involvement in an interracial city-wide effort to foster greater racial unity. In fact, they are preaching hatred of whites from the pulpit. Most blacks are so polarized in that city, that when a few whites tried to join the Martin Luther King Jr. Day parade, they were greeted by black hostility and told that "This is our (black) day and our parade, and whites aren't welcome." Of course, this sort of thing isn't happening everywhere in America, but it is happening in more and more places. It has become a popular trend, a trend that Dr. King would deplore, for it runs counter to everything he stood for. In some respects, the black church is becoming a formidable obstacle to implementing Dr. King's dream of a racially united America. Not that the great majority of white churches are doing a better job. In referring to Christian churches in general, Dr. King said, "As a minister of the gospel, I am ashamed to have to affirm that eleven o'clock on Sunday morning, when we stand to sing 'In Christ there is no East or West,' is the most segregated hour of America, and the Sunday School is the most segregated school of the week."(1)

The black church in America wasn't established to promote segregated worship. It was born out of a desire to worship as free men and women. In 1787, Richard Allen, a free black man, led a group of other free blacks to withdraw from Philadelphia's St. George Methodist Church. They quit because they refused to pray any longer in a segregated gallery. In time, Allen helped to organize a separate branch of Methodism—The African Methodist Episcopal Church.(2) Other denominations followed, like the African Methodist Episcopal Zion Church, and the Christian Methodist Episcopal Church. Three major Black Baptist Churches sprung up, as well as hundreds of independent Pentecostal-type sects.

For its parishioners, the black Christian church quickly evolved into an oasis of psychological security surrounded by a desert of white hostility. It was more than a spiritual power station they could plug into. It was their social center as well; a place where they could be themselves, where the white man wasn't around to impress—and judge them, or humiliate them.

There were times the black church rose to heroic heights, even in recent times. From 1955 to 1956, Dr. Martin Luther King Jr.'s church, along with several other black churches in Montgomery, Alabama, organized a year long boycott of the city's bus system that forced the white establishment to end its segregated seating on public buses.(3)

A few years later Reverend Louis Sullivan of Philadelphia got 400 black clergymen to persuade their parishioners and non-church affiliated blacks to boycott those businesses that catered to blacks but refused to hire them. Not only did the boycott work, it demonstrated to blacks everywhere that, when united, they had the power to change what seemed unchangeable.(4)

Unfortunately that message didn't prevail. There was more disunity than unity among the African-American churches. Today, they seem incapable of preventing many of the youth within their neighborhoods from joining street gangs, committing crimes, engaging in promiscuous sex and dropping out of school. They are no longer the moral force they once were.

In the black community, the religion doing the most good in strengthening the moral fiber of its congregants—is Islam, a fact the news media hesitates to report in full. This was true in the days of Malcolm X, as it is today. Those who followed him were able to transform their lives, giving up alcohol, drugs, and becoming reliable family members and workers; and their children studied hard, and were well-mannered and full of hope. What today's black converts to Islam demonstrate is that a person living a hopeless existence, steeped in depravity, can find hope, clean himself up, and live a highly disciplined and moral life.

It is sad to think how the American slaves and their descendants were forced to embrace Christianity, which was their oppressor's religion. The first Africans brought to North America weren't pagans. They had their own religion. They were either Muslims or adherents to a native African religion which sensed the spirit of God reflected in all aspects of life. Those that bought and sold them were Christians, as were those who owned them, brainwashed them, whipped them, and killed them.

Many white Christian clergy—from heads of denominations to rural pastors—endorsed slavery, owned slaves and engaged in slave trading. It was a group of white Protestant clergymen who concocted the slave catechism, which was to inculcate in the black man, woman and child the belief that they were inherently inferior to whites, that their purpose on this planet was to do the bidding of their master—the white man. Every time they assembled for church services they would have to recite the catechism. In this religious dialogue, which lasted about 15 minutes, the slaves were forced to participate in exchanges like this:

Pastor: Who keeps the snakes and all bad things from hurting you?
Slaves: God does.
Pastor: Who gave you a master and a mistress?
Slaves: God gave them to me.
Pastor: Who says that you must obey them?
Slaves: God says that I must.
Pastor: What book tells you these things?
Slaves: The Bible.(5)

And there were twelve other calls from the pulpit and slave responses. Imagine what it must have been like for the slaves to recite the catechism every time they attended church services. Stripped of their rich cultural heritage, prohibited from learning how to read and write, and having never experienced freedom, they could do little to ward off the effects of the religious brainwashing technique administered by the spokesman of God. The slave catechism had to be a factor in causing the festering wound that still plagues many African-Americans today.

Frederick Douglass, the courageous black abolitionist, who revealed to the world the existence of the slave catechism, possessed a penetrating sight. This forthright champion of social justice saw through the church's facade of brotherhood, proclaiming that American Christianity functioned as a willing agent for slavery and racism: "The existence of slavery in this country brands... your Christianity as a lie. It destroys your moral power abroad; it corrupts your politicians at home. It saps the foundation of religion; it makes your name a hissing and a bye-word to a mocking earth..."(6)

Yet, the offspring of the first slaves to come to America didn't have much of a choice. Often separated from their parents and subjugated to constant brainwashing, their primary concern was to survive. And in order to survive, they did what made their white masters happy. So they became Christians, hoping that they would be treated better by their masters. Through the years black Christianity in America has taken on its own peculiar characteristics, so much so that most white Christians feel out of place at a black church service.

While there is more and more evidence that the black church is losing its grip on those it is supposed to serve, many blacks await the appearance of another Dr. Martin Luther King Jr. to continue the march to the "Promised Land." But no one, including Jesse Jackson, has been able to replace the late civil rights martyr. Disunity in the black community, which existed in King's time, is one of the major reasons.

In the 1960s black nationalists like Stokeley Carmichael and H. Rap Brown were openly critical of Dr. King's efforts, calling his Ghandian protest methods too tepid, too slow. "Black Power" was their battlecry, a cry that sent a chill through the white community.(7) The Nation of Islam refused to support the Southern Christian Leadership Conference's struggle to end Jim Crowism, advocating an "eye-for-an-eye" attitude in dealing with the white world. In fact, the SCLC clashed with the NAACP. According to historian Stephen B. Oates, certain SCLC people made no secret of their scorn for the NAACP, calling it a 'black bourgeoisie club' that had outlived its usefulness. NAACP men replied in kind. Inordinately jealous of King's popularity, they accused him of laboring under a messiah complex.(8) The NAACP and the Urban League not only had philosophical differences—they also competed for dues-paying members. The tactics of the militant Black Panther Party clashed with Dr. King's nonviolent approach. Many black churches sided with different movements; many others were too timid to take any stand, trying not to alienate the white power structure. This fear kept many churches from wholeheartedly supporting King's efforts. Take, for example, Atlanta's old guard Black leaders, who viewed King as an aggrandizing upstart and a sanctimonious one at that—and vehemently opposed his move to their city.(9) Even the hierarchy of the 6 million-member National Baptist Convention, USA, Incorporated, which King's church belonged to, openly opposed King's philosophy and civil rights activities. President J. H. Jackson led the charge.(10) Even black intellectuals like Dr. Kenneth Clark had differences with King. The eminent psychologist, whose study of the white society's influence on black children's thinking helped to convince the US Supreme Court to declare segregated schooling unconstitutional, called King's philosophy of loving his oppressor "unrealistic and psychologically burdensome."(11)

Dr. King's greatest triumph was his martyrdom. It made many whites pause and reflect about the plight of blacks in their country, something they had never done before. As for black reaction—his murder stoked the fire of rage in many African-American hearts, which led to rioting and pillaging in cities across the land. Shaken, Congress had to do something to quell black passions. As a result, they passed civil rights legislation. And for the first time, the federal government declared the birthday of a black man a legal holiday, quite a few years after his death.

Interestingly, many of those in the black community who were critical of Dr. King, who actively tried to block his efforts, were hailing him a modern-day Moses. And perhaps the greatest praise came from those black preachers who openly called him a troublemaker. Since the troublemaker couldn't make any more trouble, they could use the fallen human rights hero as a rallying point to increase and strengthen church membership. Today, many of those ministers are the most vociferous and passionate observers of Dr. King's birthday, even though at the time they could not embrace his vision of an integrated, racially united America.

The deficiencies of the black Christian church didn't escape Dr. King, especially when it came to improving the social and economic lot of their parishioners:

Two types of Negro churches have failed to provide bread (for the people). One burns with emotionalism, and the other freezes with classism. The former, reducing worship to entertainment, places more emphasis on volume than on content and confuses spirituality with muscularity. The danger in such a church is that the members may have more religion in their hands and feet than in their hearts and souls... This type of church has neither the vitality nor the relevant gospel to feed hungry souls.

The other type of Negro church that feeds no midnight traveler has developed a class system and boasts of its dignity, its membership of professional people, and its exclusiveness. In such a church the worship service is cold and meaningless, the music dull and uninspiring, and the sermon little more than a homily on current events. If the pastor says too much about Jesus Christ, the members feel that he is robbing the pulpit of dignity. If the choir sings a Negro spiritual, the members claim an affront to their class status. This type of church tragically fails to recognize that worship at its best is a social experience in which people from all levels of life come together to affirm their openness and unity under God.(12)

Internalized racism

The black church is not the only reason for the disunity within the black community. Internalized racism is a powerful factor. It is important to understand how internalized racism came into being. Though the slave catechism played a major role in the brainwashing of the slave, so did the stratification of the slave community. Those who worked closer to the white master and his white overseers occupied a higher order than those who didn't. For example, those slaves who worked as cooks, butlers, waiters and nannies within the master's house were viewed by whites and blacks as occupying the highest station within the slave community. The field slaves, on the other hand, were looked upon as the lower caste. But even among them, there was some stratification. Those who functioned as an overseer's deputy had privileges that the others didn't have. One of them was the power to boss the other slaves around, and even whiplash them if they disobeyed his orders. Being exposed to this social order for decades instilled within the slave a belief that being closer to and more like white folks provided you with more power and respect from both blacks and whites. So the idea was to emulate the white man's ways, even his immoral ways.(13)

The abolition of slavery did not do away with the effects of this brainwashing which went on for generations. The slave stratification mentality has filtered in varying degrees into the black community today.

For a long time many blacks weren't aware of the effect racism had on them, because it was too painful to think about it. They had to direct most of their energy at trying to become more like the "superior" white folks. An unofficial status structure was established, with the lighter skinned men and women being envied by the darker skinned. A friend once told me that her grandmother continually warned her to never drink coffee, because it would make her darker. And in most black families, the lighter skinned children were usually favored over the darker sons and daughters. Most of the professional positions in the segregated black community were usually held by light skinned men and women, with the darker skinned working in the fields or in factories as unskilled laborers. Certain black college fraternities and sororities discriminated against darker skinned students. For example, one sorority had a rule that applicants for membership must not be darker than a tan shopping bag; another one wouldn't allow a woman to join if the veins in her hands didn't have the bluish cast that white hands have. The desire to become more like white folks was so great that some people who operated companies that produced skin lightening and hair-straightening lotions became wealthy.

The outward manifestation of internalized racism is not a static phenomenon. It continually changes. With each passing year, it is more difficult to detect. But it is still around in the 1990s, as psychologically destructive as it always has been. It is more difficult to detect, because people of color are becoming more adept at concealing their internalized racism. The most common form of concealment is the adoption of an assertive and vociferous attitude in the promotion and defense of one's culture or ethnic group. Unlike previous post civil war generations, many blacks today, especially the youth, emphasize their racial background through a distinctive speech pattern, through the clothes they wear, and through their hairstyles. It isn't uncommon to see women with cornrow braids and men with dreadlocks. As for the conked hairdo (a very painful hair-straightening process) for black men—that is practically nonexistent. The efforts to reclaim African heritage have led to a tendency among some black intellectuals to prove that blacks are superior to whites, and to embellish historical black

African accomplishments. The desire to rid themselves of the deeply ingrained feeling of degradation is expressed in a fearless determination to promote black power.

In spite of all this, many blacks have been unable to purge themselves of internalized racism. In a way, their pro-black activities anesthetize the pain that internalized racism produces. It isn't that an African-American can never heal this wound; it's just that it's difficult to do. You can't wish it away. While you can block it out of your conscious mind, it remains festering in the unconscious, setting off unconscious behavior that a perceptive social observer can detect as a symptom of internalized racism. A painful example is the tendency of some well-known African-American figures, many of them millionaires, to conceal their full lips. This is especially apparent during television interviews. I'm sure they are not aware of such behavior, and would be horrified if they knew they were doing that. Yet, it is a classic example of being ashamed of what you are, of not liking yourself, of wanting to look like a white person—"the real American."

I have met some African-Americans who are willing to admit that they are afflicted by the wound of internalized racism. Here is how one woman, Thelma Khelghati, a director of graduate studies at a New England college, discovered her internalized racism. She mingled freely, and with self-assurance, among whites, wherever she lived and worked. Her marriage to a prominent white man seemed to make her acceptable in most quarters. She was so busy pursuing a successful career and running a secure and healthy home, that she didn't have time to think about her wounds.

But Khelghati was wounded, all right. And that realization took place in the most unlikely place—in a duplicating center in Cambridge, Massachusetts. Wanting a perfect photocopy of an important report she and her husband had written, she took her manuscript to what she heard was one of the best duplicating centers in the Boston area.

When she stepped into the center, she thought she was in the wrong place. All of the personnel, as well as the owner, were black. Her immediate impulse was to leave, because her gut feeling was, "These people are incapable of the kind of job I want done." It didn't matter that she was black, that as a college youth she was a member of a black power radical organization that preached black separatism.

Because the shop was in Cambridge—the site of Harvard University—she had assumed that white people would be operating it, people she would feel had the expertise to do what she wanted done. The woman didn't leave. She stood near the entranceway in sort of a trance for a few moments, stunned that she—a college educated black woman—could feel that way toward blacks, including herself. And there was nothing she could do to overcome that feeling. In some ways, that sense of helplessness to rid oneself of something one knows is wrong is worse than the wound itself. Refusing to conceal the wound anymore, the college administrator directed her attention to healing her wound by establishing an *Institute for the Healing of Racism* at her college and becoming involved in it.

But her display of courage is rare. Understandably so. In order to do what she decided to do, one must be willing to undergo the pain of healing. In the end, she will be free of self-doubt and will walk with dignity, a truly liberated human being. However, I have also met black people who prefer to take a different route. An African-American lawyer whom I met at a conference told me he wasn't going to take the negative route to overcoming racism. He said the solution to the problem was for all sides to learn to love each other. Who could disagree with that? The problem is that in order to love others, you need to learn to love yourself first. Besides, learning to love everyone you encounter isn't easy. You just can't will it. It isn't like turning on tap water. We are all complicated creatures with fears, anxieties, resentments, jealousies and insecurities, as well as repressed anger—all of which stand in the way of expressing unqualified love. For us to become true lovers of our fellow human beings, we must strive to rid ourselves of those inner impediments. The more progress we make along those lines, the easier it will be to love. Liberating oneself requires self-knowledge. And that means breaking out of denial and being willing to face your true inner condition.

It was apparent to me that this lawyer was in denial, that deep down he was hurting badly. I was aware of his ghetto upbringing and angry youthhood, when he was deeply suspicious of whites and wanted to dismember the establishment. Today he is a respected member of what he once wanted to dismantle. And I doubt if he is free of what disturbed him as a youth. Perhaps for that reason, he refused to listen to a lecture by Dr. Paul Herron, a neuroscientist who is exploring what oppression does to the human brain. Herron, who is a faculty member at the University of Tennessee Medical School, reveals how internalized racism affects black children's ability to learn in the classroom. The fact that Herron was an African-American didn't matter. The lawyer was steadfast in his refusal to listen to anything pertaining to internalized racism.

But I have come across some black intellectuals who will speak openly about internalized racism, even as to how it has affected them. Dr. Franklyn Jennifer came to the college where I taught to bid farewell to the faculty and administration. He was retiring as Chancellor of the Massachusetts Board of Regents of Higher Education to become president of his alma mater, Howard University, a predominantly black institution.

Dr. Jennifer spoke from the heart. He appealed to the professors to make a concerted effort to help students of color overcome their lack of self-esteem, their sense of inferiority. Using himself as an example, he demonstrated how the wounds affect a person.

He shared with us an incident that had occurred shortly before he came to our campus. A distinguished academic organization had asked him to address a conference it was holding in Philadelphia. When he and his party arrived at the airport, they were told that the major airlines weren't flying to Philadelphia because of inclement weather. Only a commuter airline, located in a different terminal, was flying. After about a fifteen-minute wait, the pilot showed up. Dr. Jennifer's immediate reaction was not to board the small propeller-driven plane, because the pilot was black. He wanted a white person in the driver's seat, especially since the weather was bad. He knew it was wrong to feel that way, but that feeling was real, and there was nothing he could do to overcome it. And it didn't matter that he was a Ph.D., a noted microbiologist and the head of the state colleges and universities in Massachusetts—he was unable to repress that feeling that had been a part of him ever since he was a child. With great trepidation he boarded the plane. Of course he made it.

Intraracial violence as an expression of internalized racism

Internalized racism goes so deep that it is increasingly expressed in growing black-on-black violence. The black church and black political leaders have been unable to curtail the killing going on in African-American neighborhoods. What makes putting a stop to this intraracial violence even harder is the fact that it involves young and disillusioned black people. In a 1992 editorial of the black-owned *New Pittsburgh Courier,* questions were raised that many African-Americans want answers to today:

> When racist violence caused injuries to or deaths of various blacks during the 1980s, the African-American community would often rise up in anger and demand the culprits be found, prosecuted and properly punished.

Statistics show that African-Americans kill more of their own race than are killed by members of other ethnic groups. Where are the ongoing demonstrations against such abhorrent violence? Why aren't the airwaves filled to an appreciable percent with an outcry to stop activity that seems headed in the direction of racial suicide? Could the black media, churches, community groups, lodges, fraternities and sororities be doing a lot more to protest, oppose and, hopefully, diminish the degree of black-on-black violence?

Are we afraid or ashamed to hold our race accountable for the harm many of us inflict on each other? Are we too hopeful that the problems of drug trafficking, gangs and illegal handguns will just go away someday, leaving us to live happily ever after? Are some of us just too lazy, too apathetic or too trapped up in our own personal problems to unite and oppose black-on-black crime?... With prisons bursting at the seams with black inmates, hospitals treating more black trauma victims and cemeteries seeking new space to bury the dead, we, as a people, must be willing to do more to stop black-on-black crime. It is a very touchy issue, but it must be faced for our own long-term good.(14)

Much of what has led to black-on-black violence and other manifestations of black disunity can be traced to white manipulation, conscious and indirect. Not that there are special governmental bureaus today working day and night at fomenting dissension among African-Americans. That's not needed, because there are other ways to achieve the same end without being conspicuous. It goes on despite living in a politically correct time. Because white manipulation is not that obvious these days, it is more difficult to detect, and therefore it is more difficult to eliminate the real causes of black disunity. But it is in operation all right.

While the causes are hard to find, the results are easy to identify. We know about the bickering between conservative and liberal blacks, the friction between black Christians and black Muslims, the tension between those who defend use of the black dialect and those who champion the use of standard English. There's also the distrust and antipathy between inner city blacks and the suburban middle class blacks. The college educated and the school dropouts don't see eye-to-eye on most social issues. And, of course, there are the warring gangs that terrorize the inner city neighborhoods and those African-Americans trying to eliminate the gang system. Black educators are in conflict over whether to expose black children to an Afro-centrist curriculum or the standard American centrist curriculum. There are those who clash over whether to draw inspiration from Africa or not.

Why are whites, for the most part, to blame for what I've just described, and more? Because they created a social and political system that did not intend to include blacks as equals to whites; even after the signing of the Emancipation Proclamation, blacks were discouraged to pursue the "American Dream;" they were, instead, placed in the position of constantly struggling to survive in an essentially hostile society.

Since the image of the so-called real American hasn't really changed in the minds of most Americans, it doesn't matter whether blacks have gone to college, mastered standard English, bought a house with a white picket fence, or joined a white church, they still remain outside of the privileged circle reserved for those who best reflect the highly revered Anglo-Saxon attributes. Blacks, including those who seem to have "made it" like Arthur Ashe, are still made to feel like "foreigners" in the land of their birth. This form of deprivation, which has become a powerful unwritten element of the American culture, has caused considerable divisiveness among blacks. There are the gradualists, who point to the advances made in eliminating racial segregation in public places; they feel it is just a matter of time before they are welcomed into the privileged circle. On the other hand, there are those who out of a pride laced with anger and bitterness wouldn't step into the circle even if they were invited to enter. While many blacks refuse to be a part of either camp, they try secretly to break into the circle by trying to be more and more white-like. Oprah Winfrey revealed in one of her shows in early 1997, how, as a youngster, she dreamed of being like Shirley Temple, the white child movie star. To try to narrow her nose and give it the "real American" turn-up-look, she would spend hours with a clothespin clasped to her nostrils. (Oprah, April 7, 1997, WFSB, Hartford, CT)

It is the racist American social system that has entrapped blacks, causing anger, frustration and resentment. With many, a repressed rage churns away. In many black communities there are no safe outlets. Yet outlets are needed. Since striking out against the white power structure would be suicidal, blacks strike out against each other. The self-hatred is so deeply entrenched among many blacks that the term "nigger" is used more in the black community than among whites.

In America blacks can go just so far. If they get out of line, they can get into serious trouble. Take what happened to Dr. Martin Luther King Jr. Some powerful whites like the late head of the FBI, J. Edgar Hoover, felt that King's activities were a threat to America's established social pattern. His agents hounded the civil rights leader. And there are many blacks who believe Hoover ordered King's assassination; they also believe that the CIA has played a leading role in the white controlled drug trade in the black community, which has not only stifled social and economic development there, but has contributed to much of the black-on-black violence and other forms of intracultural conflict.

There is the less subtle example of what powerful white individuals and organizations can do if black groups try to even consider altering the prevailing white dominated social pattern. Influential foundations and organizations will threaten to withhold their funding of black social programs if they are suspected of exceeding the invisible racial boundaries set by white rulers generations ago. Several high ranking officials of the NAACP were planning to participate in the *Million Man March* which was organized by Louis Farrakhan, the leader of the Nation of Islam. To my knowledge, these persons did not attend, and subsequently, were soundly criticized by some African-Americans. Controversy over this, as well as constant criticism and condemnation of Minister Louis Farrakhan by influential Jewish organizations, the American news media, some U.S. Governmental officials and numerous others has, to a certain degree, caused some friction within the overall African-American community. As an example, basketball legend Kareem Abdul-Jabaar, author of *Black Profiles in Courage*, was interviewed by a reporter from *USA Weekend*. When asked what he thought about Louis Farrakhan, Abdul-Jabaar said, "Ignore Louis Farrakhan. He's part of the problem. He's not part of the solution." Many blacks have criticized Kareem for saying this, while others have commended him.

The white controlled liquor and tobacco industries have not only contributed to retarding black social and economic community development, they have been the cause of some dissension among African-Americans. These industries have exploited the need-to-escape syndrome in the black community. Their flashy ads in black magazines and neighborhood billboards continue to encourage and entice blacks to consume their products, which are not only physically harmful, but stimulate antisocial behavior as well. To assure that their products will remain popular in black neighborhoods, these industries contribute heavily to various black charities and educational foundations. Despite the donations made by these white firms, more and more blacks, especially parents, are voicing displeasure with the tobacco industries' influence in their neighborhoods. There have been clashes between them and those blacks who are benefiting from the status quo.

Another cause of disunity is the tendency by many whites to favor and hire lighter-complexioned African-Americans. This can create a division much like what existed during slavery times where the slave owners purposely set up a slave caste system based on skin color, where the lighter-skinned slaves were usually given easier jobs and more privileges than the darker ones. By causing division and disunity within the slave population, the white masters were able to maintain greater control of their slaves.

Much of white America tends to hold negative feelings and perceptions about Negroid features, dark skin color, and various aspects of the African-American culture. When whites appear to be more accepting of those blacks who seem to be more like them in physiognomy, education, culture and speech, this actually—inadvertently or otherwise—sets the scene for dissension and division among African-Americans. Jealousy and envy comes to the fore; self-hatred is reinforced, causing more intracommunity conflict.

Relative to speech, white denunciation of the way some African-Americans speak has often caused tensions between those who choose to speak the black dialect and those who do not. Teasing of those who talk standard English has often caused dissension among blacks. Many African-Americans who speak English correctly are frustrated that so many other African-Americans believe that speaking articulately is a white characteristic.

The fact of life is that in America a black's chances for success in the arts, sciences, business, or the technologies are tremendously enhanced when he or she masters English. The notion by some blacks that clear and grammatically correct speech is a "white" trait is a dangerous form of self-abnegation, and to reject success as a "white thing" not only is frightening but self-defeating. Yet, this is a fact of life in the black community and has been, and still is, very effective in creating dissension among educated and non-educated blacks.

Black disunity is continually fueled by the support of black conservatives, by powerful and influential whites in corporations, government, and in the news media. This has caused a barrier between black conservatives and liberals. And the two black factions continue to bicker and argue over how the plight of the African-Americans in general can be handled and ameliorated.

There is also a tendency for certain whites in power and of influence to "pick"or designate who they consider to be black leaders. The people they choose are those African-Americans who represent the least threat to upsetting the social status quo, and who are easily manipulated. Thus, it is to these people that white aid, assistance, support, opportunities, and favors go. This is another way of fueling dissension and disunity among African-Americans.

Some blacks are finding ways to transcend the disunity and deal candidly with the effect of being black in America. Every summer since 1987, African-American men from different parts of the country, as well as the Caribbean, gather for a week at the Louis G. Gregory Baha'i Institute in South Carolina. Led by an African-American clinical psychologist, they pray together, sing together, share together in a fashion they are incapable of doing elsewhere. In that setting they are free to be themselves, free to share their pain—and free to cry. They are free to do all of that, because everyone there truly understands why they need to release what they have been forced to hold back for most of their lives. The toxins of internalized racism are being shed. At the gathering, the men listen more with the heart than the ear. They embrace each other with caring tenderness. A real brotherhood emerges, producing a living fountain of love and understanding that fortifies them to cope with the racism they encounter every day back home and at work.

They are no longer living a lie. They have broken out of the shell of denial, and are able to accept the fact that they are wounded, and to articulate accurately the general plight of the American black male. Two faithful participants of the annual gathering, James A. Williams and Ted Jefferson, have written about it in a booklet entitled, *The Black Men's Bahá'í Gathering: A Spiritual Transformation.*

> In order to begin to fathom the effect slavery, racism and racial discrimination has had on our race of people a person only needs to look at any adult who was abused as a child. Years of counseling and therapy are necessary to heal the emotional and spiritual wounds such abuse has caused and to eradicate the misconception that the individual, as a child, was somehow responsible. Now look at an entire race of people who were not just in slavery but, ultimately, abused in every way imaginable, not just during their formative years but from birth until death, century after century. How do you heal an entire race?

Although American history treats slavery as a normal outgrowth of empire building, there is no place in history that records any instance of a people entering slavery voluntarily. Traditionally, slavery, as an institution, was sustained through the subsequent subjugation of the conquered people. American slavery was radically different: one race destroyed another race's cultural and religious identity and rationalized their oppressive and inhumane acts with the ideology that all dark-skinned people were "divinely-ordained" as inferior. To be human and not be treated as such then, and for many of us, even now; to be living in the "land of freedom"; to carry our individual yearnings of our race and forebears; these are the burdens we carry. This is the primary cause of our pain, this is our plight. We have so much to unlearn about "who" we are before our collective healing can begin and a new identity created.

Out of necessity most American black males have become artful in disguising the contents of their hearts. Though our bodies were enslaved, it was our hearts that were scarred and shattered. We learned all too well the lessons a racially divided society imposed upon caring, loving hearts encased with dark skin. Now, it is generally accepted that anyone who possesses even a modicum of common sense will not betray the full degree of attraction he feels toward something or someone, lest he be manipulated or perceived as weak or naive. We have learned to guard ourselves and our loved ones by employing a highly developed cynicism and skepticism against what has proven to be inevitable failure or betrayal by well intentioned "change" institutions, including our own. We have also learned to guard ourselves against optimism—too many of our leaders have been slain. We have learned to withhold our trust.

Ironically, we tend not to trust or love other black men, deemed to be on the bottom rung of society's ladder even though shared suffering typically results in the formation of strong bonds of loyalty and emotional ties. Whether due to the maladies of self-hatred, the social necessity for avoiding others who also have the stain of powerlessness, or the extreme competitiveness among black men, our emotional deprivation can be directly traced to the fragmenting social mechanisms imposed by slavery, and later, by our inability to find healing in a society which is, itself, disintegrating.

Although the greatest source of our singular and collective pain stems from the effects of active racism upon our fragile souls, we readily acknowledge that very little in our personal and collective lives can be achieved without the "permission" of "the man." Perhaps the crude saying, "the only thing a Black man can do for me is point towards a White man," represents the prevailing, unspoken creed that many of us practice.

Tremendous amounts of psychological and emotional energy are expended resisting while simultaneously acquiescing to this social arrangement. Black men remain in a state of constant, multifaceted conflict. One source of conflict stems from the choices the upwardly-mobile or established Black male sometimes is forced to make. How often have we decided to do nothing when another "brother" is swept under by the racist tide? We know the ruthless power of that tide and frequently choose, instead, to seek our own safety. White America often rewards Black men and women who look away. And we are very much aware of it.

Essentially, we have become survivors, and at times, as in the above example, survivors at the expense of other Black men. These are the rules we must play by. We do not have time for games or dreams or "feel good" kinds of things. Racism is quite alive and well; we sadly are aware that the unique position we earned through suffering has been diminished by the willful lessening of our sense of outrage and justice. We justify this by the greater need to survive and prosper. We have become masters of "selective accommodation" in order to attain our personal objectives.

Our hopes for social acceptance into the cultural mainstream of White America were once conveyed through the voice of religion. However, the Black church, the most powerful social institution in the Black community, began its decline decades ago. Sensing its demise, we abandoned the church and found ourselves gathering in the arena of politics and business, hoping these would lead us to the "Promised Land," or, at the very least, allow us to utilize our talents and creativity in potentially rewarding endeavors. We have won victories at an incremental pace. We have made some personal and collective inroads, and some of us finally found a sense of attainment, as evidenced by an ever-expanding Black middle-class and the high visibility of Black people in politics, entertainment, sports, the media and so forth.

Perhaps we have been lulled into complacency by the victories we have achieved. Or, perhaps we have just become tired. Regardless of the reason, our attention span for our still-grave plight has suffered. Behind our middle-class homes are dark alleys littered with the fading lives of our drug-infected "brothers." The walls of federal prisons are burgeoning from the wharehousing of our young. Standing upon the slippery slope, we offer pity and words of compassion, but we dare not extend a helping hand for fear that we, too, will be pulled into some bottomless pit.

Because of the psychological and social conflicts we carry constantly within ourselves due to our assigned position with predominately White America, some of us may not be able to accommodate normal, day-to-day problems, and commonly occurring crises in a healthy and systematic manner. Such opportunities for personal growth and self esteem enhancement are filtered by the prevailing sense of helplessness that we, more often than not, feel to some degree. Though our problems may eventually be resolved, their effects remain to serve as a constant reminder that our position in life is tenuous and quite fragile.

One sad reaction to the uncertainties we face in our daily lives is the search for self-reliance. Even if this search is never carried out actively due to a lack of financial resources and opportunity but instead is contemplated continually in our minds, the quality of our interpersonal relations with other Black men still deteriorates. Our need to bond with other Black men is relegated to secondary importance. We may even reject an extended, dark-skinned hand of friendship solely because it was offered by someone whose profile is not consistent with "where we want to go." Or, we may perceive it as being too needy with nothing to offer in return. The search for self-reliance is a primary factor in the erosion of the prerequisites for healthy community life and in the chronic increase in alienation and loneliness that we feel.

Another sad consequence of the racial discrimination acting upon our daily lives is that our family life may suffer. Rigidity often becomes the norm in family affairs instead of consultation and compassion due to our inability to challenge and to conquer the racism outside of the walls of our homes. Anger develops into an easily accessible emotion, and our fears are sometimes disguised in unreasonable forms of behavior and decision-making. We watch the young developing minds of our children attempt to grasp the reasons for unwarranted denials and rejections meted out by White society when they have done nothing wrong. They cannot comprehend the insidiousness of racial oppression, even as it predictably and gradually envelops their daily social interactions. Although we individually strive to present an image of strength, our children cannot help but sense our weakness, resignation, and inability to conquer these forces we cannot even see. They may grow up resenting us. Many of us have lost our teen-age sons and daughters, not to death, but to shame and pity—theirs. Many of us have lost them due to our inability to build walls of love and financial security that are strong enough to protect them from the traps designed solely to catch a wandering child. Should not real men be able to maintain and protect their families? Are we 'men' in the truest sense of the word? And, just as important, do our mates see us as men when their personal development moderates their anger at our plight?

Total self-reliance is largely an illusion. It remains a psychological goal that most of us have in common, in spite of the fact that the "dangling diamond" and even most of its lesser variations will be out of reach forever. Another form of "self-reliance" is the attempt to embed oneself within a socially and financially secure strata of White society to the extent "reliance" upon Black institutions, culture, and friends is no longer necessary. Of the two, the latter has the most serious personal consequences, due to the enormity and complexity of the mental and emotional denials one must sustain relative to one's true cultural identity. Not many of us intentionally seek this form of escape, yet because of movement to "better" neighborhoods, upward mobility, the work and social environs dictated by our professions, or just life's circumstances in general, many of us are discovering that we are losing contact with Black community life, its problems, its pains, its mind-set, old friends, and the cultural identity we once claimed.

This situation creates both a cultural void as well as a dilemma because the traditional degree of conformity required by a predominately White environment denies the validity of and, in most cases, rejects Black cultural values—those limited to and based upon class, exclusivity, and materialism—for conformity's sake. Because of prevailing attitudes regarding skin color, White society can not fully welcome and embrace us as equals; it extends itself superficially while it denies us entrance into its inner sanctum of families, intimate friendships, and social interactions where its own cultural roots are found. Genuine racial harmony in America does not exist except in limited situations.(15)

There is a tendency among many African-Americans who don't feel fully free in their homeland to live elsewhere. There's a natural pull toward Africa. To satisfy that impulse, Joy Leary of Oregon, accepted an invitation to do a two-week lecture tour of South Africa.

It was a very emotional experience. Wherever she lectured, in large cities and rural communities, she would break into tears. She discovered why in a small, filled-to-capacity village hall. Standing before the eager audience, and seeing those beautiful black faces, she began to cry before uttering a word. As she cried, the audience sang love songs. When she stopped crying, the singing subsided, and a middle aged woman in the back of the hall stood up and in an emotion-charged voice said, "Joy, I want you to know that when an African leaves his homeland for five years, he's still an African; when he leaves for forty years, he's still an African; and if he leaves for 300 years, he's still an African." The woman extended her arms toward Joy and cried out, "Welcome home, Joy."

The struggle for self-respect among blacks is not to be criticized by whites, even if the struggle takes on what whites perceive to be strange twists and turns, painful to themselves and others. Breaking completely out of bondage often requires unusual and strained movement. What whites need to exhibit is patience. And compassion. For whites have not had to endure what blacks have had to endure in the past and present. It is a miracle that African-Americans are not extinct considering what they have been subjected to; despite the harshest of restrictions, they have been able to contribute meaningfully to America's development.

The day African-Americans overcome their obsession with being black and view themselves as humans first, they will be free of the shackles of internalized racism. But doing it alone is extremely difficult. Assistance from the white community is required. Not by expressing pity. Not through material handouts. Not through enthusiastic involvement in multicultural activities and mastering the etiquette of political correctness. When whites are able to overcome their obsession with being white, and view themselves as humans first, living on a planet made up of a great variety of people who are all related to them, they will genuinely embrace a black as an equal. And—in time—the black will sense that. And the more he experiences that kind of embrace, the more his self-hatred will dissipate, until it evaporates, and he becomes a free man in a country that glorifies freedom. But not only will the black person gain something significant from this human interchange. The white person will become truly free as well; no longer a bondslave to an obsession thwarting his development as a human being—and the progress of his country.

Though this is a simple process, it isn't easily executed. For this to happen, whites need to acknowledge that they live in a fundamentally racist society and that they have been affected by the prevailing racism. They need to explore their hearts for the infection of racism that is there, and commit themselves to healing it. Only when they become involved in such a healing process will they eventually look upon a black and other people of color as equals. If this isn't done, even the most well-intentioned white men and women will continue to alienate blacks through their patronizing and condescending manner and end up unintentionally furthering the cause of black separatism.

What most whites are not aware of is that they have an obligation to treat people of color as equals because are related to them. That's right, related to African-Americans, American Indians, Latinos and Asians! As we stated earlier in the book, science now recognizes that all five and a half billion humans on Earth are at least fiftieth cousins. Because whites are related to people of color, they have a responsibility to help heal their cousins. And the most effective way to help is by healing themselves of the infection of racism.

One of the remedies is the internalization of the reality of the oneness of humankind. Eric Erikson, the noted psychologist and philosopher, believed that the unification of the human race was the greatest deterrent toward man's steady gravitation to global obliteration.

> The question is: Will mankind realize that it is one species—or is it destined to remain divided into "pseudo-species" forever playing out one (necessarily incomplete) version of mankind against all others.(16)

Chapter Twelve

The Institute For The Healing Of Racism

A lot has been written about racism by scholars and activists, describing what the social scourge has done and is still doing to our society. So much has been expounded from the pulpit about the evils of racism, that the message is perceived by most of us as just another holy platitude. And whenever there is a bloody racial conflict, the news media swarms all over the story, often concentrating on the superficial aspects of the incident, like who did what to each other. This only serves to reinforce the fears and anxieties in the community concerning the 400 year old unsolved social problem. Predictably, the conflict results in television panels composed of race relations experts that produce more confusion than compassion, more entertainment than enlightenment. Radio talk shows, especially those that encourage listener participation, reduce the racism issue into a heated argument bordering on insanity. Politicians usually respond by passionately uttering nothing that will offend any segment of his or her constituency. School principals decide to hold in-service workshops on diversity that the participants know will do nothing to change the racial conditioning in their school. And worried community leaders keep experimenting with, and searching for, ways to maintain some sense of peace between potential warring ethnic groups in town. As for the rest of us? We hold our breath, hoping the politicians find what they are looking for.

All of this activity! All the promises, pledges, protests and hand-wringing! And yet the racism problem not only remains unsolved, it is heating up as more and more people of color grow more impatient with the subtle and overt discrimination they experience daily. Ironically, the civil rights victories in the 60s have made the racial situation in America potentially more explosive. More aware of their rights than ever before, people of color have grown more assertive, which scares most whites—who now advocate employing harsh punitive measures for lawbreakers as a means of preventing a bloody race war from spreading beyond the borders of the black and Latino neighborhoods. And the whites' reaction infuriates people of color. The trenches are being dug on both sides of the color line.

Because none of the vapid political pontificating, the incessant *mea culpas* by a wide assortment of "do-gooders," has led to a solution; because none of the hundreds of sociological studies and strategies has led to a solution; because of the pitiful performance of our government in trying to find a solution; and because of the worsening racial situation, a number of us attempted to seek a meaningful solution. Only after-the-fact did we realize how presumptuous it was on our part to undertake a challenge that the mightiest institutions in the land were failing to meet. After all, none of us were race relations experts. None of us were sociologists. Or psychologists. I, for example, had never taken a psychology course in high school or college. While we had a mission, we were terribly unfocused in the beginning, as to how we would carry it out. By we, I mean those who created the *Institute for the Healing of Racism* concept. We came from different parts of the country—Asian-Americans, Hispanics, American Indians, African-Americans and European-Americans. What drove us to form the Institute for the Healing of Racism was a common concern and recognition that what was desperately needed was something positive, creative, healing and unifying; a new reality-based approach that gets to the core of the problem. Otherwise, we felt, America's racial problem would deteriorate into an irreconcilable hostility, culminating in a ferocious bloody internal war.

What makes the *Institute for the Healing of Racism* different from the general run-of-the-mill diversity training programs are the following principles:

The *Institute*'s view of the nature of racism. It views racism as a disease (psychological disorder).

The *Institute* provides a person with an ongoing timeless healing experience. One- or two-day workshops have little impact in overcoming the infection or wound of racism within us.

The *Institute* provides the participant with a transformational experience, whereby one releases the poison of race prejudice and replaces it with the reality of the oneness of humankind.

An *Institute* participant also gains an awareness of the realities underlying the principle of the oneness of humankind.

The *Institute* stresses more than toleration. Its primary focus is helping participants to become more loving and unified.

When the *Institute for the Healing of Racism* in a particular community or institution becomes well-grounded, it develops an urge to want to help other communities and institutions (public and private) to set up institutes. The idea is to get every institution in a community healing and unified.

In the beginning, the only thing the members of the *Institute for the Healing of Racism* had going for it was this set of shared beliefs. We believed that the existing race relations experts didn't have the answers; nor did the professors in the finest research universities. We also believed that the experts and academics were not aware of the true nature of the problem. Consequently, whatever solutions they proposed were based on an erroneous diagnosis. Concentrating on pushing through social, economic and political reforms as the way to eliminating racism was not enough—in fact, it was off the mark. Hence, most of their proposed efforts to solve the problem have met with, at best, only superficial success in relieving some of the symptoms of the disease, leaving the disease as virulent as ever.

Intuitively, we believed that racism was more than what conventional wisdom felt it was—it was a disease, a psychological disorder. Before we could explore how to heal the disease, we needed to know its pathology. Through the help of psychiatrists, John Woodall of Harvard and Manichur Manshad, who teaches a course on racism at the University of Louisville's Medical School, and Price Cobb, who wrote *Black Rage*, as well as neuroscientist Paul Herron, at the University of Tennessee's Medical School, and other behavioral scientists, we became aware of the origin and nature of the disease of racism, how it spreads, and how it affects the oppressed and the conscious and unaware oppressor.

We believed that if the participant in the *Institute for the Healing of Racism* were to understand the pathology of the disease of racism, she/he would no longer view someone afflicted with the disease, including himself/herself, as evil, but, rather as a sick person who is capable of curing what ails him or her. Such a view of racism would not be used as an excuse not to rid oneself of one's racial conditioning, but as an incentive to find a cure. By accepting this aspect of reality, the participants would be more sympathetic toward one another during their sharing sessions and would be more willing to help each other. Through this approach a lot of the hollering, cursing and name calling that often occurs in many race relations workshops would be avoided. Generally, people who share the same illness don't yell at each other; on the contrary, they try to comfort one another; they try to do everything in their power to help each other recover. We were determined to create and preserve this kind of spirit and atmosphere within the *Institute for the Healing of Racism.*

We also believed that the internalization of the principle of the oneness of humankind is the vaccine that can wipe out the epidemic of racism that has permeated every community in America. When the great majority of people believes that everyone they see is related to them, they would be less likely to hate or hurt anybody. They would be more willing to get together, to work to unite their community. The enthusiasm to carry all of this out would stem from a realization of an aspect of reality they had never known before. The discovery of a truth has a way of turning the discoverer into an enthusiastic sharer of what he or she had discovered.

The idea was to establish an organization that would involve a participant in the process of ridding oneself of the poison of race prejudice and replacing it with a genuine belief in the oneness of humankind. This was the formula, we believed, that could transform the United States from a fundamentally racist society into a country where true community unity is practiced.

We realized that this organization had to be more than an arena for catharsis; it had to be a human transformation center; where, in a friendly atmosphere, the participant is inspired to identify the infection or wound of racism within himself, and is exposed to the means of healing it. Simultaneously, the participant is being exposed to, and internalizes, the realities underlying the principle of the oneness of humankind. In other words, the participant is involved in a process whereby he or she is replacing the poison of prejudice with the healing balm of reality.

In devising an effective format, we had to take into account that to complete the transformation process we envisioned, sufficient time was required. Accomplishing it in a one day workshop, even a week long workshop wouldn't do. The mechanism that we were to establish had to provide the participant with an ongoing healing and unifying experience, within a nurturing atmosphere. After all, what is developed and continually reinforced over one's lifetime, especially a deep rooted obsession, takes some heavy duty effort for most; which in the end is extremely rewarding. For most of the participants the rewards begin to become apparent as early as the third or fourth session, with some even sooner. Experiencing that is a form of encouragement, for the participants keep coming back looking forward to more rewards. When engaged in this cycle, participants find themselves bonding with everyone in the room, regardless of skin color, gender, economic status. As to the nature of the rewards? That comes in the form of a growing awareness of relinquishing once deeply entrenched negative racial thoughts and feelings about others and oneself. Shedding even a segment of an undesirable thought or feeling is a reward. When they experience that, most participants want to rejoice, for it is a liberating experience. Then, fellow participants want to share in rejoicing. As a result, every experienced reward strengthens the unity of the group.

Having begun to participate in an *Institute for the Healing of Racism* program, a person leaves not with a belief that they are healed, but rather, a deep awareness that they are involved in an ongoing healing process that may take a lifetime; in some respects, adopting the attitude of a recovering alcoholic. As a consequence, many participants experience three or four ten-session dialogues before feeling confident enough to join with some others in helping to form an *Institute* in another section of town, or some local institution. In establishing and helping to maintain a new *Institute*, much of what was learned in one's previous experiences is reinforced. Not only that; new insights about one's personal racial condition as well as society's racial condition are usually gained.

The *Institute for the Healing of Racism* has two goals:

1) For the participant to become a healer of racism in his or her community;
2) For the participant to become a force for unity within that community.

Achieving those goals is dependent on accomplishing the following five steps:

1) Understanding and internalizing the principle of the oneness of humankind;
2) Gaining an accurate understanding of how racism came about in our country;
3) Gaining an understanding of the pathology of racism and how it impacts on all of us;
4) Participating on a regular basis in a ten-week sharing session set up by the *Institute*, where, in a nurturing and cooperative atmosphere, everyone is involved in helping each other heal;

5) Social action—in the form of helping to establish *Institutes* elsewhere in the community.

A format has been created, largely by Rita Star of Evanston, Illinois, as to how to achieve the *Institute*'s two goals. Again, it is designed to aid the participant in engaging in the twofold process of identifying and eliminating one's infection or wound of racism and replacing it with a genuine belief in the oneness of humankind. It is important to note that getting involved in one aspect of the twofold healing process and ignoring the other won't result in the desired outcome—and that is, to become a healer of racism and force for unity in one's community. For example, trying to inculcate the principle of the oneness of humankind, without trying to heal one's racial infection or wound will most likely result in a person who intellectually accepts the principle but is unable to internalize it because one's repressed negative racial feelings stand in the way. Our college campuses are teeming with such men and women, both faculty and students. They can speak eloquently about equality and manifest flawless political correctness, but deep down their festering negative racial feelings remain intact. And the traditional targets of racism on campus know this.

Built into the *Institute's* program are several exercises on how to improve one's listening skills. What is stressed is learning to listen more with the heart than the ear—in other words, being able to penetrate the veneer of a smiling face and hear the crying heart, being able to sense the spirit underlying the uttered word, and even sense the reality of the sharer.

Before each session officially begins, a member of the Institute's steering committee takes about five minutes to bring the membership up-to-date on what actions had been taken by the committee at its last meeting. The steering committee* sets Institute policies and coordinates logistics.

There are two parts to each session. In the first part, which is about 30 minutes long, a presentation is made by an *Institute* member or members on some aspect of one of the first three steps. Refer-

---

* The steering committee is composed of volunteers. Decisions are made through consultation. When and how often the committee meets is determined by the committee. The committee earnestly solicits ideas, including dialogue topics from the general membership. Most committees develop an annual plan. It also arranges workshops to train prospective facilitators.

ences are made to the theme, and if appropriate, a printed copy of the presentation is shared with all of the participants. How the presentation is made is left up to the presenter or presenters. It could be a lecture, a facilitated discussion, or a video followed by a brief question and answer period.

The participants shouldn't take the 30-minute presentation lightly, for the *Institute* seeks to educate the mind as well as the heart. The *Institute* hopes to produce balanced healers, who can articulate convincingly the nature and origin of racism, and what is needed to overcome it. The *Institute for the Healing of Racism* is not another "touchy-feely" program.

Before the 80-minute dialogue session begins, the facilitators remind the participants that the *Institute* doesn't promote any political, economic, social or religious ideology; that it is not a debating society; nor is it to be used as a place to build a political power base. This reminder is made in order to prevent outside forces from interfering with the participants achieving their goals. Also, a review of the dialoguing guidelines is made before every session, since old dialoguing habits take time to break. (The guidelines are listed in the Appendix in the back of the book.) We have discovered that the more faithful the participants are to the guidelines, the more rewarding is everyone's experience at the dialogue session.

After the 30-minute presentation, the next one hour and twenty minutes is devoted to dialoguing on a question related to what had been presented. For example, if the presentation was centered on a particular aspect of the pathology of the disease of racism, the participants might wrestle with the question—What emotions are generated within you, and what images come to mind, when you hear or see the word racism?

Before the sharing begins, each participant takes about five minutes to meditate on the question. This helps everyone get in focus. After the meditation, the group is broken up into pairs. In this one-on-one arrangement, each person attempts to answer the question in about five minutes. This is not a discussion or consultation. No questions are asked. It is a sharing, with one person speaking and the other listening. The role of the listener is crucial. For if the sharer is listened to wholeheartedly, he will be more forthcoming and eventually break through psychological barriers: Certain repressed feelings suddenly surface; and the sharer becomes aware of what he has to work on in his healing. To assure that this kind of breakthrough occurs, the listener must listen without judging or evaluating what is being shared, nor take what is being said personally, or become defensive. The listener listens supportively. In time, what was buried in the unconscious—surfaces, which usually results in a combination of relief, and some fear. The listener's support and sympathy often helps the sharer neutralize the fear, and he goes on working on the hurt that had been resurrected. When the sharing is done properly, bonding between the two occurs, regardless of skin color, gender, economic status or one's ethnicity. This, because each one learns something about each other that perhaps no one else, even their spouse, is aware of.

Following the one-on-one sharing, the group reassembles in a circle, and everyone has an opportunity to answer the question. Though there is no time limit, everyone is aware of the importance of not monopolizing the group sharing session. There will be times, however, when someone, who is experiencing a breakthrough, is encouraged to continue sharing. An astute facilitator is able to sense when this is happening.

Usually in sharing with the group, feelings and thoughts will be revealed that weren't revealed during the one-on-one session. This occurs because the participant feels less inhibited. Sensing the pain and anguish of others helps to quicken the flow from the unconscious to the conscious mind. You also get to know a part of a human being that most other people, including family members, never get to know. As a consequence, a bonding occurs between persons who conventional wisdom would never expect to bond, like black and white or Arab and Jew.

The quality of facilitation will determine how rewarding the dialogue session will be for everyone. (The facilitator's guidelines are in the Appendix.)

Ideally, two persons of different ethnic groups and gender should facilitate each session, in order to make all participants feel comfortable. If this can't be done, then those who do facilitate must be sensitive to the concerns and feelings of those representing all of the cultures in the group.

An effective facilitator is someone who cares about people, who likes to be with a wide assortment of people, who is basically altruistic, has strong refereeing instincts, is a good listener, and possesses a highly cultivated intuition. It is the latter that is especially important. Why? Because she can sense when a person wants to share, but hesitates out of shyness, or fear.

I remember one time, at a session I was facilitating, my friend, an African-American, was sitting with his legs crossed and his arms locked across his chest. He seemed extremely tense. While he hadn't uttered a word during the previous hour, I sensed that he wanted to say something but was hesitating, so I called on him.

After a lengthy pause, he declined to share.

"I must have been wrong," I said to myself, and called on someone who had her hand raised.

But it turned out that I was not wrong about my friend. About ten minutes before the end of the session, he spoke up: "Ever since I took my job as Associate Dean of the Engineering School I have felt uneasy on campus; constantly being judged and evaluated by whites, even by freshmen. Though I have been at the university for eight years I still feel like I don't belong. Every day I find myself having to prove my worth to people, even those I have to interact with on a regular basis.

"Even the church I have attended for the past eight years, which is predominately white, is a place where I feel like an alien because of my skin color." There was a lot more that poured out of my friend.

I was surprised. And so was everyone else in the room who knew him. For he seemed so well adjusted; so happy-go-lucky, without a care in the world. Having known the man for five years, I thought I knew him very well. But it was obvious that there was a lot more to the man than I realized. Especially the pain.

When I got home I phoned my friend, told him that what he shared that evening moved me, and that I wanted to deepen our friendship. We decided to have lunch the next day.

It was a wonderful get-together. We didn't talk much about racial issues. We talked, instead, about our children and grandchildren, shared pictures and grew closer as friends.

Incidentally, what happened at the dialogue session between the Engineering school official and myself, and what followed at lunch the next day is not unusual. That kind of bonding occurs often. What usually occurs is a soul-to-soul connection between the participants. Lasting friendships are forged between people most social observers would never expect to become close friends. It's interesting that during the one or two month hiatus between dialogue sessions, the participants usually get together socially; not just once or twice, but regularly, going to a game, having each other over for dinner or lunch, picnicking together. When out socially, they tend to generate stares from passersby on the street, or from other patrons at a restaurant. And they know why—most people are not accustomed to seeing such a racial mix of men and women having fun, and obviously enjoying each other's company. While the IHR participants know that their social mixing is viewed

as abnormal by most, they, however, believe that what they do together is normal, and those who stare at them are the abnormal
ones; that what they represent is meant to be the norm for the community. In a way, they are experiencing what it would be like living
in the future, when racial mixing will be so commonplace that no
one will view it as unusual.

Actually, when genuine racial mixing occurs among the IHR
participants, they are making a nonverbal statement that they are
unaware of making—and that is, that they have achieved the *Institute's* two goals. And no one reminds them of it. Why? Because it
might detract from the naturalness of their growth experience.

Their genuine racial mixing is a demonstration, in micro-
cosm, of the unity of humanity. They had been able to achieve
that, because they had internalized the principle of the oneness of
humankind. It is impossible to do it otherwise. I know there is a lot
of energy expended by well-meaning people to try to unify a community, and they never succeed in doing it. The reason for their failure is that they don't realize that oneness and unity are not the
same. They may have done a lot of work in trying to bring about
unity through dinners, marches and picnics, but have done little or
nothing to gain an understanding of the realities underlying the
principle of the oneness of humankind. Actually, oneness is a principle, a fundamental truth; in other words, no one is going to establish the oneness of the human family, for it already exists. What
hasn't been achieved is the family's unity; which is a process. In a
way, oneness is like a seed, with the mechanics of unity inherent in
it. Under the right conditions, growth, which is a process, takes
place; and the seed is on its way to fulfilling its destiny. In the human condition, when a person understands, internalizes and puts
into practice the principle of the oneness of humankind, the inherent mechanism of unity is activated within him. He develops a joy-
ful will to bring people together wherever he may be—and does it.

Of course, there are always cynics who have never undergone
a full dialoguing experience, who are quick to brand the *Institute for
the Healing of Racism* a "do-gooder" brainwashing program. Well, it
is not brainwashing, because no one is coerced or manipulated
into participating in the program. It is purely voluntary. And during the dialoguing session there is no attempt to drum into a participant a belief that is masked as the truth, but, in reality, is
fundamentally false. On the contrary, the *Institute's* program provides the participant with a **de-brainwashing** experience. All of
the misconceptions learned in school, church, at home and on the
street that helped to make up and nourish a participant's infection

or wound of racism are exposed and drained. Replacing them are the realities underlying the principle of the oneness of humanity. In actuality, the participant undergoes a transformation experience.

Institutes for the Healing of Racism are springing up all over North America. There are about 200 of them, some using different names but employing the *Institute*'s system of healing. No concern is expressed over the use of different titles, because no one desires to develop a monolithic organization that's centrally controlled. In fact, the *Institutes* are loosely connected, because those of us who have been involved in IHR work from the beginning feel that a tightly controlled administration would stifle spontaneity, draw our energy away from healing, and divert us from the grassroots movement path.

Since 1989 we have held two conferences, with representatives coming from more than twenty states, as well as Britain and Canada. No officers were elected; no administrative streamlining strategies were discussed. Our primary aim was to share what works and what doesn't work, and to collect names, addresses and phone numbers so that we could continue our sharing long distance.

We have been criticized by traditional organizational development specialists as being irresponsible for not establishing a board of directors and an executive council that directs operations, publishes a newsletter, and trumpets IHR accomplishments through a professional public relations office. Frankly, the demand for racial healing has been so great, we haven't had the time to even entertain the idea of carrying out what the specialists suggest we do. Personally, I feel that this has been a blessing, for the time spent organizing would have been at the expense of healing.

One of the reasons for IHR's success is its flexibility. Though a basic format has been forged, every *Institute* is free to reshape it to suit the particular characteristics of its community. In other words, the format functions as an operational framework. What isn't altered in any way are the Institute's goals and the five steps to achieving them.

Some skeptics, who have a superficial understanding of what IHR is, accuse us of "preaching to the choir and not reaching the admitted bigots who need the most help." First, who is to say that the choir members don't need help. Anyone living in America is affected by racism. And if the so-called choir members make headway in healing their infection of racism, the anti-racism forces will be strengthened. As for admitted racists attending our dialoguing sessions, more and more are showing up. Granted, not voluntarily. Certain institutions are ordering them to participate in our sessions.

I found that out when I arrived in Vermilion, South Dakota to speak at one of the state universities. During dinner two representatives of the local *Institute for the Healing of Racism* filled me in on what they were doing with the school system and some of the governmental institutions. What impressed me most was how a county judge was using the *Institute* to rehabilitate hate crime offenders. Several months earlier, ten white teenagers were found guilty of desecrating an American Indian holy place. All ten were ordered to attend every session of the IHR's eight-week dialoguing program. At the end of the program, the teenagers were genuine believers in the oneness of humankind and began teaching their friends, relatives and parents.

There's no one way to finance an *Institute*'s operations. In the beginning, all of the participants pitch in to help defray the cost of renting a meeting place, photocopying, purchasing postage and maintaining a phone. As the *Institute* becomes more established, its steering committee will find sources of funding. Receiving favorable news media coverage makes it easier to solicit funding from local or regional public and private agencies that want to be associated with organizations doing some social good. For example, in Ithaca, New York, the Central New York Power Company funds the workshops given to local people who wish to become IHR facilitators. In Kalamazoo, Michigan, the Kellogg Foundation supports the IHR's local pursuits, and in early 1996 funded a week long regional conference on racial unity that featured nationally known speakers and workshop facilitators. Some IHRs, like Houston, Texas, and the San Francisco Bay area, have gained nonprofit status and are receiving grants from different sources. In 1996, the national leadership of the Unitarian Church awarded the Houston group $10,000 for the good work it was doing in the race relations field. The city government of Little Rock, Arkansas, was so impressed with the local IHR's ability to break down racial barriers that it asked to fund the *Institute*'s efforts. The University of Louisville's and University of Kentucky's *Institutes* are funded by the Student Affairs Offices on their campuses. In Evanston, Illinois, the *Institute* sustains itself by charging a fee to those who attend their weekend workshops.

Since its inception in 1989, the *Institute for the Healing of Racism* has undergone considerable refinement. Always trying to improve its healing approach, it has welcomed constructive criticism, and adjustments have been made along the way. One of our most serious mistakes occurred when the *Institute* was first formed. Some of the white members, including myself, were so elated over discovering the infection of racism within us that we proclaimed openly that we were racists. We equated our sharing with the alcoholic's admission of being an alcoholic. We naively thought that by explaining to whites why they were racists, they would immediately step forward to enlist in our healing program. The opposite of what we anticipated—occurred. Many whites were insulted; some were so outraged that they had to be restrained from attacking us. We hadn't realized what the modern connotation of the term racist was. It had become one of the meanest curse words in the English language. To be called a racist was to be viewed as a purveyor of evil. As a result of that mistake, everyone associated with the *Institute for the Healing of Racism* refrains from defining anyone's racial state of being. We use the term racial condition instead of racist.

In the hope of becoming more effective to a larger clientele, the IHR has always been looking to network with like-minded institutions and programs. So was the Conflict Management Group in Cambridge, Massachusetts, the developers of the conflict resolution method, which is used to settle disputes. In 1995, the Conflict Management Group and the *Institute for the Healing of Racism* in New England forged an alliance that is dedicated to assisting individuals and communities heal the wounds and divisions caused by racial conflict. This alliance, called the Unity Collaborative, has received the endorsement of the American Bar Association's Racial Reconciliation Committee. CMG has achieved international renown for its work on dialogue and conflict resolution in places like South Africa, the former Soviet Union, El Salvador, various countries in South America, Cyprus and Canada as well as the United States. CMG is affiliated with the Harvard Negotiation Project of Harvard Law School.

Chapter Thirteen

Exploring The Spiritual Dimension For A Solution

Writing this book has been a painful experience because, to reach this point, I have had to review the human suffering resulting from racism. And what has made it frustrating as well, is knowing that racism need not be, that it is, after all, a deviation from humanity's course. Humans were created to love one another, not hate each other. They were created to respect their fellow beings as equals and find fulfillment in service to others. This attitude, which all humans have the capacity to develop, is not attained through conflict resolution techniques or toleration exercises. Developing this attitude is dependent on an awareness that has—sad to say—eluded the great majority of people in the world. They have, instead, adopted beliefs that have become formidable obstacles to attaining the attitude we were meant to have. Racism is not, as some social thinkers claim, a natural human phenomenon, as unavoidable as the setting sun.

It is avoidable. But that is dependent on a community-wide understanding of certain aspects of reality: For example, an accurate understanding of what a human being is, as well as knowledge of the composition of humanity, and what every human being's responsibilities are in creating and maintaining its unity. Unfortunately, these subjects are not addressed by most of those working in the human rights field. Much of their efforts are directed at extinguishing the fires of racism and not ascertaining their true causes. Discovering the causes is essential, because from that knowledge you gain insights as to how to solve the race problem. *Perhaps the most important insight is that if we really understood what a human being is, and the make-up of the human species, there would be no racism.*

That's right! In the final analysis, racism is the result of a collective unawareness of the true nature of a human being, and the species we are all a part of. Had most people understood what they were endowed with, they would have been motivated to discover and develop the latent goodness within themselves. Armed with this understanding, they would have been protected from falling prey to racist thinking or behavior. They would have, instead, been a force for unity in their community, seeing mostly the good in all people.

Because that didn't happen, it doesn't mean it cannot happen. What's necessary is to believe it's possible. But in order to believe, you need to take two steps, which for most, would be in an unfamiliar direction. The first step has to do with attitude. A sincere, open-minded desire for self-knowledge is required. By self-knowledge is meant understanding the nature of man and who you really are, which requires an honest understanding of your spiritual condition. The second step is finding and beginning the process of discovering and developing the potential goodness within your true self—the soul. When this simple process is multiplied sufficiently, the social soil becomes less conducive for racism to sprout. What begins to grow instead is community unity based on love and justice. It is important to keep in mind, however, that the growth hinges on the will to do good that results from the individual's dedicated involvement in the process of soul development. Through the process a genuine will to see only the good in others develops, as well as a sincere urge to draw people together, all sorts of people. Without this will and urge, which all humans are capable of developing, a lover of the idea of a unified humanity will ultimately fail as an implementer of what he loves, and he will usually conclude deep down that the idea is impossible to implement. The point is—a person who is not engaged in a sustained soul development effort will become so ensnared in the faults of others that they will eventually succumb to feelings of aversion, suspicion and hatred, which keep us from seeing the good in others.

I know what I'm about to offer as the ultimate solution to the racism problem may seem too simplistic, naive, even foolish to many race relations experts. But I insist in offering it for two reasons: One, because the experts have failed to forge a solution. And two, because there is growing evidence that what I'm about to describe is being successfully applied in existing communities scattered across the planet.

Before identifying and describing the make-up of these communities, it is necessary to explore those aspects of reality that must be internalized before the epidemic of racism can be wiped out. The men, women and children in these communities have undertaken this challenge in varying degrees.

The first aspect of reality that needs to be addressed is the question—What is a human being? Unfortunately, this question is rarely addressed today by most women and men. A preoccupation with materialistic pursuits is one reason. Twentieth-century materialism is the offspring of the philosophy of seventeenth century thinkers like René Descartes and Francis Bacon, founders of the Western Enlightenment movement. Through the powerful influence of these thinkers and their disciples the movement took on a religious quality, devoid of spirituality, however. The credo of the Western Enlightenment was based on the belief that, through human reasoning, all problems could be solved and universal happiness could be achieved. Though its founders were believers in God, their disciples strayed from the path charted by Christendom's leading theologians. In fact, in the nineteenth century, when Nietzche declared that "God is dead," some of the most influential intellectuals of the time applauded, including Sigmund Freud and Karl Marx. Through 300 years of philosophical refinement, the Western Enlightenment movement became the leading force in the secularization of the world. It set the standards for academic achievement and the rules for scientific exploration. To this day the great majority of university professors and school teachers adhere to its philosophy. And their students are influenced by their thinking.(1) Worshipping rational thought and action, they dismiss intuition as an imaginary tool of the superstitious. They view words such as spirit, soul, prayer, meditation and religion as the vocabulary of the superstitious and ignorant. As a consequence they don't believe the human being has a soul. They view the human brain the way most devout Catholics view the cross. Western Enlightenment's influence has shaped not only much of the thinking of our educational leaders but our corporate and political leaders as well, even those who attend church regularly.

Western Enlightenment has made some worthwhile contributions to the social, economic and political advancement of humankind. It has led to the development of science and technology, inculcating within scientists and scholars an appreciation for methodical discipline and objectivity. To Western Enlightenment we owe the development of democracy as a form of governance, emphasizing the separation of powers and the protection of citizens from governmental despotism. From its ranks were spawned humanistic psychologists and sociologists who infused in individuals and institutions a sense of social responsibility.(2)

It is understandable why the proponents of the Western Enlightenment, especially those living in the nineteenth and twentieth centuries, rejected traditional organized religion as a legitimate path to truth. In the past 300 years, traditional organized religion has played a significant role in perpetuating superstition, stifling intellectual inquiry and through fear tactics forcing its followers to embrace falsehoods as the truth. For centuries the Roman Catholic Church refused to accept the reality of our planet revolving around the sun and that Earth is not the center of the universe. It took the Church 350 years to apologize to Galileo, whom it jailed for promoting the solar system theory.

The trouble is—the Enlightenment supporters' aversion for religion was so passionate that they have grown as rigid and fanatical about their beliefs as religious zealots are about their beliefs. As a consequence, they rejected everything associated with religion, even those aspects of reality that are fundamentally true—like the existence of the human soul. In other words, they "threw the baby out with bath water." By doing this, influential academics helped to shape many people's distorted view of the true nature of man. On the other hand, Christianity's view compounded the confusion. Deep down most educated people reject intellectually the dictum that humans are born in sin, even though it has influenced the way they think and feel about themselves and others. After all, it is difficult to escape the influence of what has become a powerful part of the prevailing culture. Nevertheless, for many free thinkers and others, the Original Sin concept has reinforced their distaste for traditional organized religion, and there is a reluctance among them to think about the matter. This doesn't eliminate the effect the concept has on them. Burying the effect in the unconscious doesn't eradicate the influence it has in shaping one's attitude, temperament, behavior and outlook on life. The negativity that encompasses the Christian dominated nations is due, in large measure, to the impact of the Original Sin concept on the people of those countries, be they devout believers or agnostics.

To try to ward off the influence of the Original Sin concept, many of us give the question of what is a human being little or no thought and go about our daily chores, taking for granted being human—just as fish view water. But unlike the fish, we have the capability of discovering and developing latent powers and qualities within us that can turn us into a force for good. The trouble is—if we aren't sure or don't know what we really are, we won't discover and develop those qualities and powers and we will end up functioning on an animal level, where the urges to survive and dominate others are paramount. We become ready candidates for racist thinking and behavior, both overt and covert.

But the human being is more than an animal. While the monkey isn't conscious of his consciousness, the human being is. Where does this awareness originate? Not from a bodily organ. It springs from the soul, which distinguishes humans from all other forms of life. Ignoring or rejecting the soul or neglecting its development is to deny what makes us human. It has led to the formation of humanity's warped view on race. It is the major cause of the mess from which humanity is struggling to free itself. In a way, the development of the human soul has been retarded for nearly two centuries. Complex systems for living have been devised which don't take into account the reality of the human soul. They are geared to satisfy only our material needs and impulses.

I know it isn't easy to change one's perceptions of reality. After all, they have been a part of us for so long, becoming an essential part of our comfort zone. But the change is necessary if we are to survive as a species.

Many of us have lived our lives as bodies only, possessing some vague notion of having a soul. Ignorant of its functions, we treat the soul as we might our appendix, and go on living, not utilizing those latent divine powers and qualities of the soul that can elevate us to a truly enlightened state of consciousness, free of race prejudice and the impulse to do harm. That state of consciousness can be realized by first recognizing the reality of being a soul with a body, and not a body with a soul, or simply a body, and, secondly, by becoming engaged in the lifelong process of developing the soul, which is the real you.

The soul is a spiritual emanation from the Divine Essence. In other words, the human being is connected to God, very much like the ray is to the sun. When humans ignore or reject their soul, they ignore or reject their connection with God, which is the constant source of love and knowledge. When they choose not to acknowledge this source, they are forced to rely only on the instincts that propel the animal and are prone to behave in what society condemns as "evil ways."

Being nonphysical, the soul is not subject to the laws of composition and decomposition, nor is it within entropy's path. It is an everlasting spiritual entity whose essence is unknowable.

While the soul is not inside our body, nor attached to it, it is associated with the body much like a light focused on a mirror. The light isn't inside the mirror; nor is it attached to the mirror. Should the mirror fall and break, the light continues to shine. When ignored, the soul functions like a mirror covered with dust. Its' powers and qualities remain hidden to its' bearer and those he comes in contact with. Such a person is extremely susceptible to the virus of racism. On the other hand, the person who is faithfully developing the soul's powers and qualities is on his way to becoming immune to the virus and becoming a force for unity in his or her community.

Inherent in the soul are those qualities most of us admire and wish we could manifest at all times. Truthfulness, compassion, love, integrity, selflessness, humility, fair-mindedness, trustworthiness, and courtesy are some of those qualities. All of them, and more, are latent within the soul, just as the color, the fragrance and the vitality of a flower are latent virtues within a seed. This is what makes us potentially good.

The divine virtues latent within our soul are like seeds. For them to grow and fulfill their potential, they need to be properly and regularly nourished. When they are, they become more prominent in a person's life, eventually becoming permanent fixtures like sturdy branches to a tree; we become virtuous women and men, lovers of all human beings. Imagine a community composed of men, women and children making significant headway in developing the latent divine virtues within them. Due to this process, the community member develops an invisible armor fortified by a love for all humans, who are looked upon as real family members, and the opportunity to serve a person is viewed as an honor and an extreme pleasure. In this setting, the germ of racism is unable to infect the community.

The soul also possesses the powers of thought, comprehension, and imagination. Inner vision is another faculty of the soul. It is the source of a human being's original and intuitive ideas. The difference between the brain and inner vision is that inner vision knows and the brain reasons.

Using their inner sight, many scientists see a meaningful idea unfold, and they know it is right. To prove it to their colleagues, they employ reasoning vehicles like scientific principles and mathematics. Albert Einstein relied on his sharp inner vision to probe the workings of the universe. He declared that his most awe-inspiring experience was to see and contemplate the unknown, which taught him firsthand "that what is impenetrable to us really exists, manifesting itself as the highest wisdom and the most radiant beauty..."(3) Helen Keller, the incomparable blind and deaf early twentieth century poet/philosopher had a keen inner sight; she often saw and felt what most sighted persons will never see and feel in their lifetime: "I sense the rush of ethereal rains... I possess the light which shall give me vision a thousand-fold when death sets me free."(4)

As you can see, the human being doesn't come into existence with a clean slate. The soul is endowed with certain powers and attributes that are to be discovered and developed. Among those powers are the yearnings to know, to love and be loved. To assure good health, these yearnings must be satisfied from birth through old age. When they are neglected, we become emotionally crippled, or worse. Children are known to have died from a lack of love. A poor student wants to know; if the yearning can't be fulfilled in school, she'll seek fulfillment elsewhere, usually on the street. Adults who stop learning and are deprived of a loving relationship suffer from despair.

At the outset, nature assists us in satisfying these yearnings. The infant's need to know and to love and be loved is satisfied when he finds his mother's breast and suckles and is stroked by her. But these yearnings are to be used for an even greater purpose than creating healthy relationships. The soul's impulses to know, to love and be loved are to be used to strengthen our connection with God. Above all, the powers of knowing and loving are to be used to know and love our Creator. Through this relationship we become greater lovers of our fellow human beings and gain a greater understanding of reality.

Even those who reject the idea of a soul, or have a warped understanding of a soul, employ its powers, and not always in a constructive manner. For the soul reflects where it is positioned, and the human being determines the positioning. If it is trained only on the physical world, its powers will be used to carry out only physical desires. If, on the other hand, it is trained "heavenwards," its powers will be used to fulfill spiritual pursuits like developing virtues which turn women and men into the kind of humans they are meant to be—more generous than greedy, more caring than callous, more humble than vainglorious, more thoughtful than selfish—and free of race prejudice. A spiritually developing person attains a penetrative sight, has the capacity to see the reality of others and hear the inner voice of the troubled human being—in other words, she hears more than words; she senses the real meanings behind the words, and is able to learn the real truth.

Though the soul is meant to be developed, humans are endowed with a free will. Those who choose to reject the notion of a soul or ignore its development can do more harm than a beast in the field, because they can use thought, memory, speech, intuition, imagination—all powers of the soul—to do evil things, like engage in racist activities, or harbor concealed racist feelings that lead to unconscious racist behavior. A gorilla can't do what a Hitler or Stalin did, or what the Ku Klux Klan can do.

Though the physical aspect of our nature is the repository and generator of our senses, it has another important function: The physical aspect demonstrates what the spiritual aspect initiates. For example, without our body, a strong desire to help an elderly person cross the street would remain a good intention. So a healthy body is not only necessary to produce a healthy child, it is essential to carrying out spiritual impulses, like becoming a healer of racism in your community, as well as a peacemaker.

In reality, both aspects of our nature are dependent on each other to carry out their ordained purpose, which is to create a loving and caring human being, who in turn becomes a positive influence in his or her community. In order to live a good life, which, I believe, is continually manifesting the attributes of the soul in all of our interactions, both aspects of our nature must be regularly cared for. When this balance is maintained, each aspect becomes clearly defined: The spiritual aspect becomes more assertive, and the physical aspect becomes more submissive—then and only then are they performing their ideal roles. As the soul matures, it not only initiates positive ideas but prompts the physical aspect into action. In other words, the result of such a cooperative union is a highly developed conscience, which acts as a catalyst for doing good deeds.

While it is essential for a person to be developing spiritually in order to be free of race prejudice, it is not enough. An understanding of the composition of humanity is necessary. In other words, we need to know who qualifies as human beings. Though this question may appear absurd in this advanced technological day and age, it needs to be asked, because there are still many well-meaning believers in God who behave as if blacks and whites are different species; some even believe Italians and Irish are different species. And there are many who still use race as a means of classifying people's natural position in society. Blacks, whites, Latinos, Asians and American Indians are usually placed by custom into different qualitative categories, and they find it impossible to free themselves from these social slots. In time, many, unfortunately, act as if they belong in those slots.

This practice was given considerable impetus from men who should have known better. Some highly regarded scientists of the past legitimized the multi-race theory. A particularly horrendous study, done in good faith by a renowned Swedish biologist in the

1700s, was a contributing factor to the development of modern racism. Carlous von Linnaes, who classified thousands of animal and plant species in his lifetime, broke down the human species into four 'distinct' groups based on skin color. For example, he described American Indians as reddish, choleric, obstinate, contented, and regulated by customs; Europeans as, white, fickle, sanguine, blue-eyed, gentle, and governed by laws; Asians as sallow, grave, dignified, avaricious and ruled by opinions; and Africans as black, phlegmatic, cunning, lazy, lustful, careless and governed by caprice. Though von Linnaes had very limited personal experience with three of what he called "the four families of man," his observations of their behavior, personality traits, languages and moral and intellectual characteristics was embraced by the nineteenth century anthropological community, which in turn, influenced the thinking of today's people, including scientists. Though von Linnaes' observations of what was later to be called the races of man were based largely on assumptions and sketchy data related to him by European travelers to Africa, Asia and the Americas, he became known as the father of the science of anthropology.(5)

Today science has exposed the multi-race theory as a flawed view of reality. Scientists have finally discovered what God has always known—that there is only one race, the human race, with one human color, composed of different shades.

As we already pointed out in Chapter Three—from a biological sense all five and a half billion humans are at least fiftieth cousins; and that includes KKK members as well as the blacks, Jews and Catholics they hate. However, from a spiritual sense, everyone living on some land mass in all five continents are more than cousins—they are brothers and sisters. This is based on the fact that all five and a half billion humans are essentially souls; and since the soul is a spiritual emanation from God, that means they are connected to the same Source of Life—God. Which makes God everyone's true mother and father.

As long as women and men disregard the evidence presented in this chapter, racism will continue to fester in human hearts —and well-meaning people will continue to grope in vain for a cure of the social disease. But there are some enlightened souls like South African President Nelson Mandela who are aware of the reality of our connection to the Creator. Because of Mandela's awareness, he was able to overcome every impulse for bitterness and revenge and become a great unifier of his country, viewing even his enemies as his brothers and sisters. This, despite spending 27 years in prison for leading the struggle to establish social justice in a homeland ruled by racists. In Mandela's 1994 Inaugural speech, he revealed to the world his awareness of our connection to God:

We are born to make manifest the glory of God that is within us. It's not in some of us; it's in everyone. And as we let our own light shine, we unconsciously give other people permission to be the same... As we are liberated from our own fears, our presence automatically liberates others.(6)

I know it is difficult for most adults to internalize the evidence presented in this chapter, for it clashes with what has become part of their belief system. Therefore it is unrealistic to expect an overnight purging. On the other hand, this condition shouldn't be used as an excuse not to make some effort to engage in the twofold process of divesting oneself of the infection of racism and replacing it with a genuine belief in the oneness of humankind.

What is plausible is a conscientious commitment to engage in a sustained "chipping away" of the dross of prejudice blanketing the soul. The motivation and energy to "chip away" is derived from the effort made to develop one's soul and internalize the principle of the oneness of humankind. In time, the effort made will make a difference: A new, clearer racial outlook will emerge. An impulse to overcome racism becomes a part of one's nature; so does the desire to unite all peoples, and preserve community unity.

This process has not only made my wife and me more sensitive to the hurt most people of color endure daily; our four children have benefited from our effort to heal ourselves of the infection of racism. We exposed them to the principle of the oneness of humankind through books, songs, videos, our regular association with families representing a variety of ethnic groups, dinner table discussions, international summer camps, and above all our belief that the internalization of this principle is a religious obligation. As a result, our children have grown into active advocates of social justice, without being conscious of playing such a role.

In fact, some of their actions have been learning lessons for me. For example, because of what our oldest son, David, did during his medical residency in California, I will no longer listen to or tell ethnic or racial jokes. According to the nurse anesthetist who witnessed the incident, David was performing surgery when one of the attending physicians, who was evaluating our son's work, cracked a black racial joke. David stopped what he was doing, peered at the physician and said, "That offends me; never say that in my presence again." The anesthesist, who was a good friend of David's, was practically in shock. "How could he do that?" he thought. "That physician has the power to fail him."

Well, the patient survived the operation, and David didn't fail. When the anesthetist inquired as to what possessed him to respond the way he did to the professor's joke, David replied: "I just found the joke offensive, because I believe all humans are members of my family, and that includes African-Americans. It hurt to hear my brothers and sisters demeaned."

David's action was not an act of courage. It was a natural response, inspired by a deep conviction that grew out of consistent exposure to the principle of the oneness of humankind being put into practice. It has had the same effect on our other children, Dale, Tod and Valerie. Their social activism, which is prompted by a deep belief in the oneness of humankind, started at an early age. I'll never forget the time a black family from New York City wanted to buy the house next door to ours; but its owner, an elderly bachelor who was moving to Florida, refused to sell it to them because he didn't want to "spoil the neighborhood." He had longtime friends on our street and was afraid of alienating them. When we learned all of this, our children, my wife and I consulted on what we could do to change the man's mind.

Talking to him proved fruitless. So we consulted again. This time we decided on an action I never expected to take in my lifetime.

Walking the picket line with my wife and children in front of our neighbor's house turned out to be one of the proudest moments in my life. Our children ranged in age from twelve to two. With the exception of the baby, they all understood why they were picketing. They were so enthusiastic about what they were doing that they refused to go inside to eat lunch; they ate their sandwiches on the picket line.

Some of the residents in the neighborhood who agreed with our point of view joined us. News of what we were doing spread, and the local newspaper sent a photographer and reporter to the scene. The police patrol wagon came by several times, but never stopped to ask what we were doing. I suspect our neighbor, who refused to come out, called the police, hoping they would put an end to the demonstration.

It didn't take long for the elderly homeowner to change his mind. In a few months the black family moved into the house next door.

What sustains our children's consistency as advocates of social justice is their unwavering commitment to developing their spiritual capacity, as well as deepening their understanding of what constitutes the human species and playing an active role in unifying it. It is heartwarming for us as grandparents to see our children doing with their children what we did with them—and doing a more thorough job of it.

Chapter Fourteen

Developing The Race Prejudice Free Community

It is encouraging that more and more men and women are trying to build bridges of understanding between peoples who have been hostile toward one another for generations. Of course, while it hasn't reached ground swell proportions—it is a hopeful sign. In Israel, for example, there are some Arabs and Jews who have set up an organization to help the two groups learn to live and work together in peace. In Northern Ireland, some Catholic and Protestant mothers have organized a campaign to put an end to the bloody sectarian conflict in their land, and their organization is growing in number and influence. The Southern Poverty Law Center has been working successfully in getting a few black and white communities in America to respect each other and combine forces to end racial discrimination within their neighborhoods. In South Africa, a good number of blacks and whites are working together to undo the harm done by the apartheid system practiced by the former government. There are non-governmental organizations around the world helping the poverty-stricken learn employable skills, helping farmers overcome the effects of drought, helping with the vaccinating of thousands of children against deadly diseases. And there seems to be an increase in acts of altruism on the part of individuals in a great variety of communities. All of this and more demonstrates a growing desire to do social good.

Yet this isn't enough. More than a growing desire to do good and sporadic acts of goodness is needed. What's necessary is an organized, sustained global effort focused on helping peoples of all walks of life find the means to develop their latent goodness to the fullest and gain an accurate understanding of humanity's composition. When this is set in motion, a collective transformation will evolve, whereby men and women, for the first time, will gain an understanding of what a human being is and who they really are, and what their responsibilities are to develop their potential. With this knowledge, they will gain insights as to why they exist and why humans are meant to love one another. They will realize that the persons they have hated, distrusted or feared because of their skin color are, in reality, related to them. And they will realize, with some sadness, I suspect, all the time spent unaware of their capacity to do good, and they will try to make up for the time lost in developing that capacity. This awareness will, for most people, function as a conscience-prodder to change their attitude toward people they have always hated, distrusted or feared. The monster of racism could never show its twisted face for long in a community composed of such people.

In order for such a community to come into being, its men and women must take to heart the reality of the human soul. Communities are needed, composed of women and men actively engaged in developing its powers and qualities, cognizant of humanity's composition, and involved in internalizing and putting into practice the principle of the oneness of humankind.

While the call for such communities may seem entirely unrealistic, even surreal in some quarters, the fact that some already exist, helping to bind hearts together that heretofore were separated by ancient barriers of hostility, is evidence that they can form and flourish.

Though comparatively few in number, and far from being perfect, they are places where the kind of collective human transformation is occurring that creates an atmosphere of familyhood, not based on skin color, blood line, culture or nationality. Receiving guidance and protection from a divine source, they become centers of spiritual unity in the making, where the blindfold of racial prejudice is being replaced with a vision of humanity united, and an understanding of what role its members have to play in implementing the vision. What those in the community have in common is a desire to fulfill a divine responsibility that they have learned all people were created to fulfill. It is not only that which motivates people within these communities to forge ahead with the implementation of their vision; involvement in the process itself is a great motivating force. Why? Because it frees them from the shackles of prejudice and parochialism, and elevates them into realms of reality never experienced before. With a sense of wonderment, they are able to see clearly why and where humanity has strayed and where it is meant to evolve. That awareness keeps them from repeating the mistakes of the past.

The fact that they have access to inspirational guidelines to carry out the responsibilities needed to unite their communities through the spirit of love is a source of confidence that fortifies their faith and makes living a joy. The future is viewed with optimism, a time pregnant with great promise. Knowing that you have a role in the shaping of a glorious future is the source of deep satisfaction, for it provides you with a sense of meaningful purpose. Much of what seemed important to you before your spiritual awakening is no longer important. Each day is viewed as another positive adventure, an opportunity to do something to unite humankind—and to help spiritualize the planet. Looking through a divine lens, you are astounded at what you see. With great gratitude and humility, you recognize God's plan for humanity, and life is no longer a continuous groping in the dark for meaning, an endless series of scary trial by error exercises. You know what you have to do and what it will eventually lead to. Hope replaces fear; great expectations replace anxieties. You find yourself part of a new paradigm that most people are not aware of because of the energy expended in clinging to the obsolete one, which they are trying frantically to patch up.

Aware of their hopeless struggle, you try to rescue them without offending or scaring them. Not an easy task when the past is littered with the wreckage of numerous utopian schemes, both in the East and West. Buoyed by the transformative power they have experienced in themselves and in others in such communities, these people pursue their rescuing mission with undaunted vigor, not with fanatical zeal, but rather an attitude of a sincerely concerned and humble healer tending to the sick, applying to others the remedy they are applying to themselves.

What is essential is not that all of the members of the community make the same amount of progress during a prescribed period of time, but that all are making a sincere effort to achieve the same goal, which is to heal oneself of the effects of racism and become a force for unity in one's community. That's what matters most. Since everyone has his or her own individuality, and has had different life experiences, it is unrealistic to achieve a uniform rate of progress. What is important to remember is that every spark is a potential flame. Keeping the spark alive is paramount, and that is assured when an entire community is involved in a conscientious effort to grow spiritually and internalize the reality of the oneness of humankind. The energy generated by such a collective effort clears the atmosphere of skepticism and pessimism; you gain a perspective of purpose that makes living meaningful; you find yourself part of a unity you didn't consciously pursue. It isn't forced upon you. Nor is it the result of a carefully concealed manipulative scheme. When you sense it, you know it is where you should be, and you gain an understanding of how you got there. It is the result of an earnest endeavor to apply a set of spiritual principles to one's life, which, in time, transforms your outlook on life, from negative to positive, from fear to hope, and develops within you an inner yearning to bond with others through acts of service. By experiencing this transformational process, you realize that you always possessed the potential of developing your present state of mind, which allows you to see vistas of reality that even the most erudite don't see because they are certain they don't exist. Interestingly, part of what you see is that every human being has the capacity to see what you see, that this potential is part of our natural make-up waiting to be discovered and developed. The unity forged by a community made up of men and women developing this potential is indestructible. For many, becoming aware of being a part of this unity is viewed as a gift from God. And that awareness reinforces the will to stay the spiritual development course, which becomes an act of enlightened faith.

What continually strengthens this unity is a sincere desire that springs from the community members' innermost being. And that is a genuine yearning to be with each other, to be able to serve and help each other. Because you know the origin of the desire, you become even more committed to the twin processes of developing the soul's powers and divine qualities, and internalizing the principle of the oneness of humankind. Through this experience, the community members develop a self-inspired and self-regulated responsibility to do everything they can to preserve unity. And what fuels the need to carry out this responsibility is the awareness that this is the unity our Creator expects of humanity.

What amazes open-minded social observers is that the unity in these communities isn't forged among a special group of people coming from a similar ethnic background and socioeconomic status. These communities are usually composed of a wide cross-section of people, people who normally don't fraternize because they have little in common. They are the highly educated and poorly educated, the introvert and extrovert, poor, middle class and rich, socialist leaning and capitalist leaning, old and young, representatives of a great variety of ethnic groups, men and women born into many different faiths, former atheists and agnostics, and even former clergy. It is important to note that everyone in this broad collection of human diversity enters the community with his or her own assortment of baggage, much of it loaded with the garbage of self-centeredness, greed, biases, pretenses, misconceptions held as truths, and the anti-social practices that usually result from men and women being unaware of what a human being is as well as the make-up of the human species. By applying the two-fold formula for human transformation, the garbage gradually evaporates. What makes the evaporation process possible, is the support of the other community members. Since they are involved in the same endeavor, empathy abounds within the community. There is a genuine willingness to help each other, especially when the struggle becomes difficult. In that kind of atmosphere, people are more likely to break out of denial and come to grips with their prejudices and become inspired to overcome them. They enjoy a sense of freedom never before experienced. The feeling is so exhilarating that every effort is made to keep from regressing.

In essence, the people in these communities are living in a world that outsiders would like to live in but believe is impossible to create. The great challenge then is to find ways to invite the fearful, the timid, and the skeptical to explore with an open mind these communities where over a period of time the diversity becomes less pronounced, because those who enter poorly educated become more educated; the poor gain insights that help them break out of the prison of poverty; the narrow-minded become broad-minded; haters become lovers; the suspicious become trusting; the selfish become selfless. Everyone is expected and encouraged to grow. As a result a human being who always had the capacity to become what God meant for him or her to be emerges fully involved in fulfilling his or her true destiny—and united in purpose and thought with everyone else in the community. To this person, it becomes apparent that he or she belongs to a community that possesses the wherewithal not only to overcome racism, but the other social and economic ills that plague society as well.

What I have described is no fairy tale. It is not the product of some "do-gooder's" wishful thinking. It is not a commune, cut off from the contingent world. The communities I have described—exist! And in the real world. Why they may even be in your city or town. I know it is difficult to believe that they exist, considering the friction that still exists between peoples and the cynicism on university campuses and among society's leaders. Since most have to live and work in a dog-eat-dog atmosphere, the thought of such a community is relegated to the realm of "pipe dream." The skeptics' initial reaction to any information about the community is to brush it aside as a waste of time. After all, they are convinced that as long as humans inhabit our planet there will always be racism.

So they have opted for the pragmatic approach, which means being involved in finding the least painful ways to live and work in a fundamentally racist society. And their suspicion is often heightened when they discover the source from which these communities gain their inspiration and strength. I am referring to the Bahá'í communities all over the world.

The Bahá'í model of community unity can be adapted to anyone's preferred religious setting. In fact, it would be wonderful if churches, synagogues and mosques, as well as secular institutions, organized a program for their membership, where they could become involved in discovering and developing the powers and qualities latent in their souls and gain an accurate understanding of the composition of humanity, from both spiritual and scientific standpoints.

It is not the time to play it safe, not with so many people hurting because of racism, and so many people preferring not to discuss the issue for fear of what would result. There is a sense of fearful desperation gripping the land, an eerie silence covering an ocean of rage and fearful uncertainty. The divide between black and white is widening and growing more formidable. The fear of what happened in South Central Los Angeles in 1992, being only a preview of what is in store for the near future, is plaguing many whites, especially those in leadership roles. Because they have no answers, much of their energy is being devoted to preparing adequately to put down the anticipated rioting, which they sense won't be confined only to the black neighborhoods this time around. Most have given up waiting for a miracle. A sense that there isn't much time left before the explosion takes place permeates the atmosphere—and few are willing to talk about it. That is why I realized that to withhold what I know would not only be a cowardly act—it would be a criminal act.

It is important to keep in mind that the community I am holding up as a model for race unity isn't a Shangri-La where everyone is perfect and there are no problems. People do not experience an instantaneous cure from racism upon entering the community. What sets it apart from most other communities, however, is that everyone is aware that racism is a problem, that something must be done to eradicate it, that they have been affected by it to some degree, and that they are spiritually obligated to heal their racial infection or wound and become a force for unity in their neighborhood. What helps, too, is that they know what they have to do and how to go about doing it.

But the healing process is not always clear cut because people enter the community affected by racism differently, some harboring wounds more obvious than others, while some possess infections tucked away in various depths of the unconscious. And there are times when some members are disappointed because not everyone appears to be living up to the high racial unity standards set by the community. Initially, there's a tendency to judge one another without knowing each others' backgrounds.

For example, a young African-American college student who had been a Bahá'í for about a year was snubbed several times on campus by a fellow white Bahá'í whenever he was with his white friends. The black youth was terribly hurt because he thought he had gotten close with the white youth at community meetings. "Was the white guy two-faced?" he wondered. "How could he call himself a Bahá'í?" When he raised this problem with another community member (never mentioning names), he was urged to take the matter before a special problem-solving council that is charged with preserving and tightening the bonds of unity within the community—and is extremely healing-conscious in its approach. After several sessions, the white youth, who had become a Bahá'í around the same time as the black youth, admitted that he was still infected by the race prejudice virus, and in certain circumstances would avoid association with blacks, even those he was close to, for fear of alienating some of his white friends. During these same sessions, the black youth revealed that he still harbored a deep-seated suspicion of all whites. Both agreed to undergo a program designed to rid themselves of what was preventing them from embracing each other as true brothers. It was an enlightening experience for both. In learning how each was affected by racism, at times digging into their childhood, they grew to understand and appreciate one another and were drawn closer together.

In these communities sticky racial issues are addressed and not purposely avoided to keep the community from being ensnared in controversy. This is possible because the members are aware of the community's standards on race prejudice, and of the negative effect it has on human spiritual development. But that is not the only incentive. The fact that there is a mechanism within the community whereby an individual or a group can receive assistance in winning a spiritual battle is also helpful. What also makes it possible to deal with racial issues directly is that everyone in the community is involved in varying degrees in soul development and internalizing the principle of the oneness of humankind. These processes make people more community welfare conscious than self conscious and able to love those they once distrusted or feared. It doesn't mean, however, that they raise sticky issues without trepidation. While they anticipate pain, they know that in the end the experience will be best for them, and ultimately, the community. In time, people realize that what they have endured were growing pains.

For most Bahá'ís, the quest for a race-prejudice-free heart is an uphill climb. Stripping oneself of feelings and ideas that have been a part of you for so long isn't achieved overnight. It takes time and commitment to a plan you have faith in. What keeps the community members on the quest-path is the plan's vision of what their effort will lead to. Each step along the path results in a boost of confidence that the quest will be won. This occurs because with each advancing step, people discover aspects of a vision never seen before. Anticipation of seeing more stimulates further movement along the path. But the confidence gained doesn't lead to cockiness. It has the opposite effect: It leads to a greater degree of humility. This is the case because those involved in the quest are carrying out the responsibility of developing the soul's latent divine qualities, of which humility is one. In time, those making headway discover that they are experiencing a change of heart and change of outlook. Awareness of the changes is due mainly to the reaction of those outside of the community. They are attracted to the community members' radiant spirit and genuine desire to be helpful to all they interact with. Even the most suspicious are eventually drawn to them.

In other words, not knowing what a human being is will block any attempt to love a person you distrust, hate, fear or feel superior to. Without love you can't bond with another human being. And bonding is an essential element to achieving community unity, a social condition that usually results when the majority of townspeople are making significant headway in overcoming their race prejudice.

Generating uninterrupted and wholehearted love isn't easy. Not only because we live in a helter skelter, dog-eat-dog world, but because most of us harbor hatreds, biases, resentments, pretenses, and fears we refuse to acknowledge. These unconscious negative feelings impede attempts to love.

While it is true to say that love will break down racial barriers, it requires considerable effort before you can be loving to someone you fear, are suspicious of, or abhor. The first step is knowing your true attitudinal condition. And that takes some interior probing—honesty, courage and time. How much? That depends on how courageous and honest you are.

Fortunately, all humans have the capacity to express unqualified love toward everyone they encounter. But that hinges on understanding what a human being is and the composition of the human species. As you gain more understanding of these two questions, those negative feelings that were blocking your ability to express sustainable love toward those you distrust, fear, and hate grow less prominent in your life. They begin to fade away.

While I now know what that feeling of purification is like, I never envisioned myself attaining it. I never felt worthy of possessing that power of becoming a healer of racism and a force for unity in my community. When this happens, all sorts of people are attracted to you, even the most suspicious. For they sense a sincerity and purity of motive that springs from a developing true self.

When this happened to me, I was stunned. At the time, I was in Salvador, Brazil, the capital of the state of Bahia, which is the most African-like state in the country—seventy five percent of the population is black. It was the Salvadorian Bahá'ís who arranged for me to meet with the black leadership of Brazil at the national headquarters of Olodum, the most influential African-Brazilian organization. Leaders of ten black organizations were present. So was an observer from Ile Aiye (House of Negro), which I was told by one of the local Bahá'ís, refuses to interact with whites. During our four-hour meeting, the observer never smiled once, even when I smiled at him. His grim countenance never changed. As a consequence, I tried to avoid his stare.

It was an enlightening session. Not that I had to be told how deep rooted racism was in Brazil. That became apparent as soon as I set foot in that country. What I didn't know was how committed the black leadership was to achieving true equality for its people. Which means not only convincing whites that racism exists in Brazil, but also overcoming what impact racism has had on black Brazilians. It was at this meeting that I learned why Bahia, with its vast majority of blacks, has never had a black governor. The head of Olodum's international department revealed that most blacks in Bahia believe that blacks aren't as smart as whites and therefore aren't equipped to govern effectively. Even that revelation didn't alter the facial expression of the observer from Ile Aiye.

What I also learned was that Brazil's black leadership was waging a national "black power" campaign, which calls for a return to the African religion, which the first slaves brought with them to Brazil. All-black schools and youth centers have been established,

which the government refuses to recognize. Regular all black conferences and festivals have been organized throughout the year.
Various moneymaking schemes have been developed to help fund
the all-black projects. The most effective money producer is Olodum's world-traveling drummers.

After listening to what each black organization was doing to
attain social justice for blacks in Brazil, I shared my views on racism
and what we are doing to try to eliminate it. When we arose to bid
farewell, the observer from Ile Aiye walked over to me and embraced me and kissed my cheek. "Would you come to our headquarters this afternoon?" he asked.

I not only met with the leaders of Ile Aiye, but I was taken on
a tour of one of their schools and youth centers, where black youngsters stared at me, as if I were from a different world. Before leaving
Ile Aiye's compound, which is in an old black section of Salvador,
the observer smiled, and said " I want you to know that we believe
in the principle of the oneness of humankind, which you emphasized in our meeting at the Olodum. The reason we avoid associat-
ing with whites is because they make us feel bad about ourselves."

I am convinced that the observer, Antonio Cortes, was attracted to me because of the effect my religious community has
had on me. He knew I believed that he was my brother.

Chapter Fifteen

Sensing A Solution On The Horizon

In traveling across America and to other countries, doing racial unity work, I have experienced almost every emotion you can think of. The betrayal I experienced, however, was the most difficult to deal with. It was so difficult that at one time I contemplated giving up the struggle. But for some unexplainable reason, I didn't. I kept plodding along, often plagued by doubts about my ability to do any good. Success is difficult to discern when you continuously face resistance and are the object of excessive backbiting, especially from people you thought would be your natural allies. Not only backbiting, but trying to sabotage your work as well. Nevertheless, I'm glad I didn't give up, because I now see some progress being made in healing the disease of racism. Not that the success we have experienced is due to me alone—far from it; it is due to a group of men and women from different parts of the country, representing different ethnic groups, who have the same aim, subscribe to the same philosophy, and draw our power from the same source.

Certainly, we are far away from a total cure. But there are hopeful signs. What is encouraging is that some of us have discovered a way to heal what so many feel is impossible to heal. And that has set off a flame of optimism within me and my coworkers and allies. You can't help but be optimistic when you witness what some would consider miracles. Black and white, Hispanic, Indian and Asian men and women, harboring deep distrust of one another, even hatred, learning to love one another. How could I forget the time when a strident black nationalist and a rabid white racist embraced each other in tears, after undergoing an eight week experience at an *Institute for the Healing of Racism*. To me their tears symbolized the release of the poison of prejudice that had collected and festered in their hearts for a long time. They had experienced an aspect of freedom that had been missing in their lives for more than forty years. If that can happen to those two men, then potentially it could happen to everyone.

Witnessing this kind of transformation, time and time again, in people who according to conventional wisdom are not supposed to associate with one another, let alone love each other, has helped me to gain a deeper appreciation of a particular law of life—and that is, the only thing that doesn't change is change itself.

I have met people along the way who have had similar experiences and have gained the same insight. I doubt if the leaders of their country are aware of what they have been able to achieve in breaking down racial barriers. But if those leaders were sincerely interested in overcoming racism in their land, they could learn a lot from these men and women. Some are no longer with us, but what they did helped to change lives, and some communities, for the better.

****

Poet Robert Hayden died in 1980. He was an African-American who had reached the pinnacle of his profession by being appointed Consultant for Poetry to the Library of Congress, a position equivalent to poet laureate of America. Because he had healed the wound of racism he discovered within him as a child, he refused to view himself a black poet, even though some of his best poems were about the black experience in America. He believed he was not born black. Others whom he had no control over labeled him black. It wasn't that he was ashamed of his heritage. It's just that he saw aspects of reality that others couldn't see. Hayden believed that he and everyone else on the planet were born to live in the universe, first and foremost, as human beings.

His unshakable position on who he identified with culturally in the 1960s made him an easy target of black powerists' mockery. His classes were boycotted at all-black Fisk University where he taught English literature and creative writing. It wasn't uncommon for him to be greeted by a chorus of "Uncle Tom" while striding across campus. He was snubbed by most of his fellow professors.

Though his detractors characterized him a traitor to the black cause, Hayden had a depth of appreciation of one of their heroes that they were incapable of having because of their blinding rage. Attracted by Malcolm X's courage, penetrating logic, integrity, and love of the truth, Hayden captured the essence of the human rights warrior in a poem "El-Haji Malik El-Shabazz:"

He X'd his name, became his people's
  anger,
exhorted them to vengeance for their past;
rebuked, admonished them,

their scourger who
would shame them, drive them from
the lush ice gardens of their servitude.(1)

In the last stanza of the poem, Hayden reveals that in the end he and Malcolm X shared the same view of the reality of man.

He fell upon his face before
Allah the raceless in whose blazing
  Oneness all
were one. He rose renewed renamed,
  became
much more than there was time for him
to be.(2)

In 1968, I had the bounty of witnessing Robert Hayden display a love of the truth and courage that inspired me to try to take a similar course in the struggle to help unite the human family.

On the day of the assassination of Dr. Martin Luther King Junior, I received an urgent phone call from a Teaneck, New Jersey official. He wanted to know if our guest, Robert Hayden, would be willing to participate in a special memorial service for Dr. King the next night. Our town administration knew that the highly-acclaimed poet was in Teaneck because the Bahá'ís had publicized a talk he was to give. Mr. Hayden consented to take part in the service.

The high school auditorium was packed. In fact, people were sitting in the aisles and standing at the back, both in the orchestra section and balcony. Prayers were offered by different clergymen. A church choir sang. And one dignitary after another proclaimed that Dr. King had not died in vain.

Robert Hayden, who was the last speaker, strode to the podium, hunched over it, gripped it tightly with both of his hands, then peered out at the audience through his thick glasses for about a minute without uttering a word. There was no restlessness in the audience, because everyone sensed that they were about to hear something profound. And they were right.

"Dr. Martin Luther King Junior may have died in vain," the poet declared with deep emotion in his voice, "because racism is alive; it roars through the arteries of America."

After a pause to allow what he said to sink in, Robert Hayden recited his poem, *Frederick Douglass*:

> *When it is finally ours, this freedom, this liberty, this beautiful*
> *and terrible thing, needful to man as air,*
> *usable as earth, when it belongs at last to all,*
> *when it is truly instinct, brain matter, diastole, systole,*
> *reflex action; when it is finally won; when it is more*
> *than the gaudy mumbo jumbo of politicians:*
> *this man, this Douglass, this former slave, this Negro*
> *beaten to his knees, exiled, visioning a world*
> *where none is lonely, none hunted, alien,*
> *this man, superb in love and logic, this man*
> *shall be remembered. Oh, not with statues' rhetoric,*
> *but with lives grown out of his life, the lives*
> *fleshing his dream of the beautiful, needful thing.* (3)

The town's leadership was taken aback. They hadn't come to hear that. They had assumed that the distinguished man of letters would eulogize Dr. King, and perhaps even recite a poem that he had specially written for the occasion. Although the service was over, some men and women, black and white, remained in their seats for a while, mulling over what Hayden had presented. Deep down these people knew that the poet had told the truth.

Robert Hayden wasn't naive. He knew that he was being used by those who organized the memorial service as a means of keeping the relatively large black community in town from erupting on the night of Dr. King's assassination. He refused to comply—by telling the truth.

****

Those who are prone to judge people by the way they dress, speak, and what they do for a living would most likely judge Robert Woodrick wrongly when introduced to him. This successful businessman, who was brought up in a conservative Midwestern household, dresses conservatively and lives in conservative Grand Rapids, is one of the most committed human rights advocates I have ever met. He has led a racism healing campaign in the city of

350,000 that has spread to other communities in Western Michigan.

Woodrick, who doesn't have a rabble-rousing instinct in him, cannot pinpoint where his genuine feel for the oneness of humankind stems from. "Frankly," the 63-year-old Chairman of the Board of D&W Corporation says, "I don't have time to find out, nor am I interested in finding out. I would rather channel my energy and time into bringing people together. Why? Because it will make us all, in the end, truly prosperous, and that includes communities, too. And by prosperous, I don't mean material security, only."

After reading my book *Healing Racism in America: A Prescription for the Disease*, he asked me to come to Grand Rapids to help him establish an *Institute for the Healing of Racism* at his company's headquarters. But that wasn't the only thing he had me do. The next day I found myself meeting with some of the political, religious, social and educational leaders of the city, explaining the philosophy and psychology of the Institute and the way it is structured, as well as sharing some of its achievements. I later found out why he had me speak to those community leaders: He was planting seeds of social change. And he was confident that some would eventually sprout.

Three months later I found myself back in Grand Rapids, doing a workshop for all of the managers in D&W's supermarket chain. Woodrick hopes to set up Institutes for the Healing of Racism in every one of the company's stores, inviting their customers to participate in the racism healing process.

I don't know what Woodrick said to his managers prior to my coming out there, because they were the most genuinely enthusiastic workshop participants I have ever worked with. He had opened up their minds and hearts, and had infused into them some of his spirit of the love of humanity. They were eager to carry out Woodrick's dream not because he was their CEO, but because they believed in his dream.

Woodrick's reputation began to spread. The region's news media provided considerable coverage to what he was able to achieve in a field that seasoned human relations agencies had failed to achieve. Grand Valley State University, Aquinas College called for his assistance in setting up Institutes on their campuses. The public school system called for help. Five high schools have institutes. Through the workshops he organized, several Roman Catholic churches decided to establish institutes for their parishioners and clergy; the Western Michigan Episcopalian diocese announced that it was establishing institutes in every one of its churches. The chamber of commerce has established an institute, and more than ten corporations in the Grand Rapids area are doing what D&W is doing to overcome racism within its confines. With Bob's help, the chamber has formed the Employer's Coalition for Healing Racism. There are more than 40 trained IHR facilitators in the city.

Though Woodrick's motive in waging a racism-healing campaign within his company was not sparked by a desire to boost profits, chamber of commerce type audiences are impressed when he tells them his business is booming. Other supermarket chains in different parts of the country have called on Woodrick to help them sort out their race relations problems.

****

It isn't only individuals that are my heroes. There is an institution that has moved me deeply. About 100 miles southeast of Grand Rapids is the headquarters of Starr Commonwealth, an organization started in 1913 to help children at risk become productive and respected citizens. Today it operates seven centers in Michigan and Ohio serving not only children but youth and families at risk as well. Its founder, Floyd Starr, who is deceased, believed there's no such thing as a bad child, that everyone is endowed with an unlimited reservoir of good. He was a staunch believer in the principle of the oneness of humankind. His spirit still drives the life of the organization.

Starr Commonwealth was attracted to the *Institute for the Healing of Racism* when it learned about its philosophy and the results it is producing in breaking down racial barriers. Starr's leadership felt a need to help its more than 500 employees become race prejudice free, and to help all of those it serves become true lovers of all human beings.

Most organizations would never undertake such a goal; they would view it as unrealistic. What they would end up doing it to try to create, at best, a tolerant and civil atmosphere. Though somewhat fearful of failure, Starr Commonwealth refused to take the easier route. What sustained their resolve was the leadership's belief in the innate goodness of humans. With the proper environment and approach, they felt, hearts could be changed.

They tested IHR's ability to overcome people's racial conditioning. First, they asked all of its employees to read *Healing Racism in America: A Prescription for the Disease*; they followed up with a series of two-day workshops. After that experience, whatever doubts some of the management team and staff had completely evaporated.

The changes that took place in only two days was, as one participant put it, "more than remarkable. It was a miracle." I can attest to that, for I was there. In all my life I have never witnessed such transformation take place in such a short period of time. In an atmosphere where titles were left outside of the meeting room, people felt safe to share what they had been hiding most of their lives, and those who listened provided comfort and support to those who were baring their souls. Those who thought they would never cry in public shed tears. Most were astonished when the President and Vice Presidents of Starr Commonwealth broke down. In an instant the leadership became human. Blacks, Latinos and whites who came to the workshop only because of management's insistence, admitted that what they had experienced in the two days was something they believed they would never see happen in their lifetime. What they had experienced was not just another "touchy feely" experience that stays with you for a day or two and then is thrust back into the familiar state of hopelessness.

What kept hope alive in everyone's heart was the fact that an ongoing healing mechanism was established where they work and that Starr Commonwealth was committed to seeing that it continues to function regardless of the financial cost. And the prospect of sharing with the community-at-large what has helped the employees change added another dimension of excitement to their job. The fact that such a diverse group as theirs was able to change provided the participants with the confidence needed to take IHR to the general public.

****

If medals were given to educators for bravery, perseverance and compassionate vision in overcoming racism in our schools, Shirin Selph of Springfield, Massachusetts would be a leading candidate. After producing a master's degree thesis that could be used by schools to break down racial barriers among teachers and students, she set out to get a school to adopt her program, which explains in a convincing manner why it is important to integrate the principle of the oneness of humankind into the existing school curricula—and how to do it. I was so impressed with her work, as were several community leaders, that we urged the Superintendent of Schools to consider Selph for the newly-created post of multicultural Education Specialist. Though impressed with her ideas and methods to implement them, he informed us that the search committee would be making the final decision. Frankly, I didn't think she had much of chance of landing the job, because the search was going to be nationwide, and the fact that she immigrated to America when she was in her late twenties would pose a problem. I felt that some of the committee members might think she would have difficulty communicating with teachers and students. And being from Iran wouldn't help.

Shirin Selph got the job despite the search committee's rejection of her application. The committee's official reasons for its negative decision masked the real reason. The most influential committee member, a leading administrator, was bitterly opposed to Selph's emphasis on teaching the principle of the oneness of humankind in the classroom. She was under the impression that Selph was bent on teaching the principle as a means of promoting her religious beliefs. Aware of the committee's unfounded fear and paranoia, the Superintendent of Schools, Dr. Peter Negroni, overruled the committee's decision.

When Selph met with the Superintendent to be told that she had been hired, he warned that certain members of the search committee would make life difficult for her by trying to obstruct almost every move to implement her racism healing program throughout the school system. Dr. Negroni's warning turned out to be an accurate forecast. In a period of six months, she had four different bosses. For nearly a year, she didn't have her own desk, chair or telephone. She would have to use the desks of staff members who were out sick. The head of the search committee made sure that Selph did not engage in racism healing work during the school day, having her do what a clerk could do—for nearly a year.

While she didn't officially complain about the way she was being treated, there were moments when she felt like resigning. But after a good cry, she would be more determined than ever to stay the course. The fact that she believed deeply in the program she devised was a factor in not bending to the will of her school department enemies. Another factor was Dr. Negroni's moral support. But the most influential factor was her deep faith in God. After a while, the obstacles thrown in her way only intensified her pioneering spirit.

Selph found ways to get her message across to faculty and principals in the system. At first, it was through her outside racism healing activities. In her off duty hours, and not receiving a cent for her efforts, she organized a racially diverse song and dance student workshop that dramatizes racial unity themes. Rehearsals were held several nights a week, and, at times, during weekends. The workshop performed at schools, fraternal organizations and educational conferences throughout the state. It was so effective,

the Springfield School Board honored her for her extraordinary efforts. As one of the founders of the *Institute for the Healing of Racism*
in Springfield, she was often quoted in the newspaper on race matters. And those teachers, whom she persuaded to join the *Institute*,
reported back to their colleagues what Selph was doing in helping
to tear down racial barriers in the community. In time, teachers
and principals clamored for her services. The demand was so great
that much of the opposition organized by the head of the search
committee evaporated. Today, Selph is training teachers within the
system on a regular basis on how to integrate the principle of the
oneness of humankind into the school curricula. And the teachers, for the most part, are enthusiastic about what they are learning
and can't wait to put it into practice. Selph's efforts have been so effective that Springfield's Roman Catholic school system has asked
her to help them implement her racism healing program.

****

Like Shirin Selph, Shirley Pleasant is a racial unity pioneer.
Having lived in Little Rock, Arkansas most of her life, the
55-year-old African-American has seen some social institutional
changes that did away with Jim Crowism. But what hasn't
changed, she felt, were the attitudes of both black and white. In
fact, the attitudes seemed so fixed that Shirley Pleasant noticed the
gulf between black and white in Little Rock widening. She saw
more and more blacks gravitating toward separatism, going in the
opposite direction the civil rights movement in the 60s had been
heading. While she could appreciate the need for blacks to go their
separate way—most of her life had been spent in the segregated
south—she was a firm believer in the principle of the oneness of humankind. Separatism, she felt, might dull the pain for a while, but
in the long run the suspicion and hatred that both sides harbored
would intensify. Shirley felt bridges of understanding had to be
built; some means had to be created to expose black and white to
the fact that, in reality, they were related, that what kept them
apart was based on false assumptions they had embraced as the
truth.

She found what she was looking for in the *Institute for the Healing of Racism*, a program she heard about at a race unity conference
in Memphis, Tennessee in the spring of 1993. Though enthusiastic
about starting an Institute in Little Rock, Shirley received little encouragement, at first. The fact that most of her religious community refused to support her efforts was especially disappointing.
But she persevered.

When she met Katherine Cockrill, a white woman, born and bred in the South, Shirley began to meet some men and women who approved of her ideas, who were willing to seriously consider the idea of establishing an *Institute* in their city. Among those she met were Mayor Jim Daley and members of a special task force he had formed to try to find ways to break down the racial barriers in the city.

Shirley and Katherine were able to convince Mayor Daley to sponsor and fund a race unity conference that would expose the leadership of the city to the concept of the *Institute for the Healing of Racism*. They drew speakers and workshop facilitators from Massachusetts, Illinois and Tennessee, who arrived several days before the conference to acquaint several public schools and the police department with a tried and tested way to heal the infection or wound of racism.

The conference, which drew more than 150 racially mixed men and women, including the mayor, produced an *Institute for the Healing of Racism* that has been officially endorsed by the city government. The mayor's task force was turned into the city's Racial and Cultural Diversity Commission. Both Shirley and Katherine were appointed to it by the mayor. One of the first things the commission did was to announce that it would fund all of the *Institute's* activities and would work with the Institute in establishing *Institutes* in every school in Little Rock, as well as the police department.

Shirley's belief in her dream and her strong faith has helped to institutionalize a dynamic system of racial healing in Little Rock. Hundreds of black and white men and women, representing almost every strata of society, have been exposed to the Institute's transformative power. They now see things and hear things they never saw or heard before. Blacks and whites for the first time are really getting to know each other. Some participants equate the experience to "a spiritual rebirth." Heads of local and state institutions are calling on her to help them set up institutes. The response has been overwhelming, and at times embarrassing, because by nature Shirley Pleasant is a reticent person who does not seek the spotlight. "The fact that Shirley prefers to stay in the background and is so selfless and sincere is what attracted me to her cause," says Katherine Cockerill. "In fact, working with Shirley Pleasant has been a blessing, for I have been able to find a sister I never knew I had."

Shirley Pleasant's work is so deeply appreciated by Mayor Daley that he embraced her before hundreds of black and white onlookers at a special ceremony in city hall, proclaiming to all that she was a pioneer for social good in Little Rock.

While seeing her dream materialize has been the source of joy, it has also been the source of pain she thought she had overcome years ago. By establishing and promoting the *Institute for the Healing of Racism* in Arkansas, her self-created and self-administered anesthesia that dulled the pain of being black in America has worn off. She must now deal with reality; and that means venturing into areas she once avoided, for fear of being rejected or humiliated. Shirley can do that now, because she possesses a strength she didn't have before. It is a strength that springs from a vision that is being successfully put into practice. Shirley is now willing to endure the pain because she now knows what has to be done to really eliminate it: Keep doing what she and her colleagues have been doing in the past two years.

Though basically optimistic, Shirley isn't free of doubts. The one that plagues her the most is whether what she and others are doing across America may be too belated to prevent a bloody black-white conflagration in the near future.

****

LeNise Jackson-Gaertner was always interested in the race issue, because she was a black living in America. But her interest turned into a crusade when her father, Mr. Woodrow Jackson, was accosted by a couple of policemen, while on his way to see his newest grandchild. Accompanied by a daughter, the 67-year-old grandfather was stopped by the Pamona, California police. They were looking for a 25-year-old black man who had robbed a bank earlier in the day. Mr. Jackson was ordered to get out of the car with his hands raised above his head. When he complained that it had to be a case of mistaken identity, he was smacked with a billyclub. The fact that he was a retired Los Angeles Deputy Sheriff didn't matter—the police kept pummeling him. They beat him so badly that the special apparatus implanted in him to contain his failing kidneys broke loose. After Mr. Jackson was thrown into the air and allowed to fall to the ground, semiconscious, the police sped off, leaving him in critical condition. He did eventually recover.

The police department, which never officially apologized, issued a terse statement, describing the incident as "a case of mistaken identity."

LeNise was furious. She wondered, "How could you mistake a 25-year-old with a 67-year-old?" But then she realized, that to many whites all blacks look alike, that the policemen who beat her father were victims of an obsession that had warped their thinking about blacks. That thinking was widespread, she thought, and as long as it prevailed blacks would remain in peril in America.

When she detected it in her children's school, LeNise formed the Mothers For Race Unity and Equality. Its main thrust was to educate the educators about conscious and unconscious racist practices in the classroom. At first it was difficult gaining entry to schools. After all LeNise held no college degree, and her forthright manner scared some teachers.

She worked at toning down her speaking approach, without sanitizing her message. After the first workshop opportunity, word spread throughout her educational district in southern California about her ability to awaken people's consciousness on racism. Not only did public schools seek her help; two universities in the region asked her to teach courses.

While compassionate in her approach, she is uncompromising in her message. "Telling the truth" she points out, "is the key to uprooting the cancer of racism. I know many whites—at first—squirm when they hear what I have to say, but those who don't drop out are usually grateful for what they had learned. They are in a better position to get on with healing their own infection or wound of racism."

In the past few years LeNise has been able to create an approach that evokes in white audiences empathy for the blacks' plight in America. Teachers are especially impressed with her example of how frustration in African-American school children builds over time. Some white teachers become more understanding and empathetic toward their black students and willingly alter their teaching approach to make the classroom experience more comfortable and meaningful for all children of color. The example she uses is an imaginary school where European-American children are treated with the same disregard African-American children experience every day.

> Imagine a school that European-American children have attended for nine years; 95 percent of the teaching staff is African-American from kindergarten through high school. When they enter high school these European-American children are taught by predominately African-American males. This school system's social studies curriculum would concentrate primarily on the contributions, culture, courage, conquest and intellectual achievements of African and African-American male heroes. However, for one week in February, the

school district proclaims European-American history week. European-American history week is celebrated to boost European-American children's self esteem and to pacify their parents. The school would give recognition to European-American people as an ethnic group by pointing out how they excel in sports, comedy and music. John F. Kennedy would be the only European-American male figure discussed in this school and district as an ethnic hero for twenty years. The children would even march in a parade celebrating Kennedy's birthday. There would be no mention of European contributions to the world. European-American children would be told they are a minority group that comes from the Third World, that Europeans and their descendants as an ethnic group started out in America as slaves; that they were backward, barbaric, mentally ill-equipped people who were taken from Europe for their own good. The slave population came from Europe, they would learn, a continent that was made up of savages who were ignorant, and practiced pagan religions. These European-American children would be told that this was why the Africans and African-Americans conquered them—to save Europeans from themselves. And in the end the European-American male children are disproportionately expelled from schools in the district in high numbers when compared with other ethnic groups.

"Considering what I have just described above—how enthusiastically would European-American children approach learning? Would European-American's self esteem be high under these educational conditions?"(4)

****

Eighty-five year old Betty Reid of Northern Ireland is a tireless lover of humanity. Her latest project is evidence of that. After five years of research and writing an educational curriculum on a course on the oneness of humankind, she has been traveling to Estonia training teachers on how to teach the course. The Ministry of Education would like for every school in the country to feature the five year course for 12 to 17 year olds. Her next challenge is to provide something similar for elementary school children.

Whenever I talk to her, I feel energized, full of hope, wanting to do something positive, something that will make the world a better place; in fact, I feel youthful again. I feel confident that when she reaches 90, I'll get a phone call from Betty, declaring that she has completed the oneness curriculum for the elementary school kids.

****

When I was in Texas in early November of 1996, it wasn't the community, academic and political leaders I met that made a lasting impression on me. It was two people I met in Denton, whom I don't think I'll ever forget. They don't hold any prestigious position in that city or elsewhere. Robert Green is an African-American and a college student in his late 20s, and Carol Hinkle is a white divorcee and mother of three grown children. In the past four years, these two humble human beings have had a positive impact on the lives of scores of black and white men and women. In 1992, they established an *Institute for the Healing of Racism* at the Martin Luther King Jr. Recreational Center, which is in the heart of the Black community. Some whites dared to cross the tracks at night to attend the IHR sessions. It didn't take long for the whites to feel at home in the black community and for the blacks' suspicion to evaporate. Genuine interracial friendships were forged. Word of the racial transformational healing that was taking place at the Green and Hinkle orchestrated sessions spread throughout the city. More and more people registered to participate in the IHR sessions. All of this was happening without any foundation, or governmental agency funding. The cookies and tea and coffee provided at the sessions were paid for by Green and Hinkle, who wouldn't classify as secure middle class citizens. They also paid for whatever Xeroxing had to be done. Though the big city news media aren't aware of what the couple has achieved, there are some leaders in Denton who are drawn to them and are seeking their help in breaking down racial barriers.

At the small gathering I attended in Denton, I witnessed a noted university professor and social activist approach Green and Hinkle, asking them to set up an *Institute* on his campus. Then the head of the Wesley Women's Conference, a regional organization with 2,000 members, appealed to the couple for help in building bridges of understanding between black and white women in the Denton area. What drives Robert Green and Carol Hinkle to do what they do? Their love for God. And the best way they can express their love is to help in the struggle to unite the hearts of God's children. Seeing that happen from time to time, they feel, is the greatest reward one can attain.

****

No one has inspired me more than my late friend, Rodney Belcher. It wasn't anything he said that had a profound effect on me. It was the way he lived his life that I will always remember. You could tell by the way he related to people that he had an understanding of the nature of man and had internalized the principle of the oneness of humankind. While in his presence I felt loved; so did everyone who really knew him. You felt a part of his family.

Rod was one of the few people I know who truly believed that the Earth was his country. It wasn't that he had forsaken his native America. (Popcorn was one of his favorite foods.) It was just that his broad vision allowed him to see what most of us can't see, yet—an aspect of reality that future generations will, no doubt, take for granted. What he saw was a planet that had come into being without borders or frontiers, populated by human beings who could adapt, in time, to any climate. As a consequence, Rod could be anywhere on our planet and feel at home.

Because many of his relatives and American friends didn't share Rod's vision, they couldn't understand why he would give up a lucrative orthopedic practice in the Washington D.C. area and spend twenty-six years of his life in Africa. In fact, he is buried on the grounds of the Bahá'í temple, in Kampala, Uganda. After stints in Tanzania and Kenya, Rod spent his last eight years in Kampala, restoring Makerere University's orthopedic center, which he had developed prior to dictator Idi Amin's brutal reign.

Rod was not only a medical school professor; he was in the operating room almost every day, gaining satisfaction from helping crippled people regain the use of their limbs, or find relief from spinal injury pain. He was more than an accomplished orthopedic surgeon in Africa; he was a medical force. Realizing that importing artificial limbs would be too prohibitive for the Ugandan economy to bear, he established a local plant that designed and manufactured artificial limbs. When polio began to sweep through the hinterland, Rod organized a nationwide immunization campaign. To make up for the shortage of orthopedists in Uganda, he persuaded American physicians to volunteer their services in Kampala and outlying districts for a month or two. To avoid high hotel costs, he had a guest house built for the volunteers. And he was successful, for the most part, in persuading his graduates to remain in Uganda to serve their countrymen, instead of seeking more lucrative practices elsewhere. To overcome a shortage of essential operating room materials like light bulbs, he solicited donations from the nation's well-to-do and middle class.

Rod did all of this not as a superior white outsider who pitied a downtrodden population of blacks in a developing country. He never maintained a missionary's mentality. And those he served knew it. They also knew that he loved them, and that they were a part of his family.

For him, living and working in Africa was not a totally giving experience. There was much that he gained from his African friends and colleagues, as well as his students and patients, and those he interacted with in the local markets, schools and garages. It was an exchange, he felt, that made him a richer person. What he admired most was the people's strong spiritual faith, their highly cultivated sense of familyhood, their ability to make the most of the little they had, and their generosity and selflessness.

On March 11, 1996, Rodney Belcher was murdered by two Ugandan anti-American radicals—who did not know him.

Rod's wife Dawn wanted a simple funeral, for she knew that is what her husband would have preferred. But that's not what the rest of his family—the people of Kampala—preferred. The day of the funeral, stores and governmental offices shut down, hundreds of people, many of them on foot, some on crutches, streamed to the Bahá'í Temple, to say farewell to their beloved brother. Originally scheduled to be held indoors, the services had to be held outside because of the throngs of men and women who appeared. Braving the scorching Uganda sun, they stood in respect, many weeping. Some among them were former patients who, before meeting Rod, never thought they would ever stand again. No eulogy was needed, because various religious leaders, governmental officials, Rod's colleagues, and ambassadors representing different nations wanted to share what impact Rodney Belcher had on them. Uganda's Vice President, and Rod's former student, Dr. Speciosa Wandira Kazibwe said that with the internment of Rodney Belcher's body in Ugandan soil, the seed of love had been planted in her country. To nourish the seed, she said, all Ugandans need to follow Rod's example on how to live life.(5)

****

What impresses me more than anything else about my heroes is their ability to do what even their closest friends felt was impossible to do. While obstacle after obstacle was thrown in their way, they surmounted them all; and not without great difficulty.

Though confronted by considerable hardships at times, they never became embittered; they never sought revenge or developed an "us versus them" mentality. Their enthusiasm and dedication to their mission inspired me to keep on going. They inspired everyone around them to draw upon untapped internal powers they never knew they possessed. What these heroes have proven is that something as virulent and deep rooted as racism can be confronted head on—and overcome, notwithstanding the babble of countless cynics who find comfort in human defeat.

There are other beliefs and qualities these heroes, who come from diverse backgrounds, have in common. They have a deep love of humanity, and an awareness of human potential that most others are ignorant of. This awareness stems from an understanding of the true nature of the human being and the composition of the human species. They know that the human being, regardless of skin color or culture, is potentially good, and they have found a way to help others discover and develop their inherent goodness. One of the ways they do that is by exemplifying what they believe through the quality of their relationships and work. Their purity of heart even attracts skeptics to them, and this quality, more than any other, makes them lovable. Only a fool doesn't want to be around people like that and want to be like them.

What also drives them is a burning desire to alleviate the pain that racism afflicts on so many people in the world. A pain that need not be, considering all people are meant to live in harmony. They want to put an end to the needless suffering, mainly because those afflicted by a pain they believe will never end are their brothers and sisters. This is not a belief based on wishful thinking. It is something they believe with all of their hearts and souls. They know the universal kinship principle is not something new; it has been a reality ever since humans appeared on the planet. What hurts them is that the great majority of people are unaware of the principle. The suffering caused by racism, they believe, is a family matter that requires immediate attention. They are troubled by the thought of a black child learning to hate himself while attending school, a white person, in pain, unable to find help in overcoming his negative racial feelings, and Latinos, Asians and Indians being kept out of the inner circle reserved for "real Americans." The hatred manifested by all sides, and what that leads to, disturbs them, because they know it doesn't have to be that way. They know how it should be and have dedicated their lives to that end.

Not naive, they know there is no universal, instantaneous cure. On the other hand, they know there is a cure, that its advance is organic in nature. Because most people have little hope of ever overcoming racism, the heroes' greatest exertions is directed at convincing people it can be cured. Knowing that words alone won't do it, they have demonstrated through deeds, in their own localities, that it can be done. What is encouraging, is people in other localities have heard what these heroes have done, have checked it out, and are trying to do the same thing in their hometowns. So the process of healing continues to grow, despite the pessimism and cynicism that abounds in our society. And the list of heroes expands.

As I see it, there are three aspects to the cure.

1) For people to recognize that racism is a psychological disorder. To engage in a healing process through an *Institute for the Healing of Racism*, or something similar; that this type of ongoing healing mechanism be established in every institution within a community.
2) For people to gain an understanding of what a human being is, and to become engaged in discovering and developing the soul's latent powers and divine qualities. Also, to gain an understanding of the realities underlying the principle of the oneness of humankind and then internalizing what is learned. That communities arise made up of men and women seriously involved in the twofold process of understanding the nature of man and the make-up of humanity.
3) For every school (public, independent and parochial) to integrate the principle of the oneness of humankind into the curriculum of every class a student takes, from kindergarten to the twelfth grade.

I know there will be many dissenters who will expound eloquently why what we propose won't work. And because of the commentators' credentials and reputation, many people who are earnestly looking for solutions to the racism problem will heed the advice and warnings given by these highly esteemed men and women. Unfortunately, when that kind of reaction occurs, the paralysis that already exists in the struggle to end racism becomes more entrenched and hope fades.

Sadly, those heeding the advice of the distinguished social critics don't know that the advice is coming from men and women who have spent little or no time in the racial tug-of-war taking place in our cities and towns and villages. They have never gone through an *Institute for the Healing of Racism* program, or anything similar. Their assessments and appraisals stem from the exalted position of the "ivory tower," where people are honored for disproving curative concepts and theories to social problems conventional wisdom believes can't be solved.

What is needed at this critical hour are not leaders who can think of all the reasons why something can't be done to solve a crucial social problem like racism; what is desperately needed are those who can think of all the reasons why something promising can be done, and proceed with vision, confidence and faith to get it done.

I'm tired of attending race relations meetings that begin with words and end with promises that everyone in attendance knows won't be kept. I'm tired of attending human rights banquets where moving speeches are made and tears are shed, but no one in attendance has the slightest inclination to change their own racial conditioning. I'm tired of engaging in seminars where experts exchange views of how bad the race problem is and haven't the slightest idea of what can be done about it. I'm tired of marching in Dr. Martin Luther King Junior parades with people who no longer share the civil rights martyr's vision and, as a consequence, have no interest in working to fulfill his dream of a racially united America. I'm tired of going to intercultural festivals where people gather to experience aspects of different cultures and have no interest in becoming real friends. I'm tired of participating in race unity conferences organized by well-intentioned individuals or groups who have given no thought to a follow-up program that will take advantage of the energy and enthusiasm produced at the conference. I'm tired of attending race and ethnicity conventions where leading exponents of different schools of thought clash and compete in a seemingly dignified manner for the ear of foundation representatives looking to fund worthwhile programs. I'm tired of attending lectures by renowned race relations experts whose primary intent is to enhance their professional reputation and whose greatest pleasure is dazzling their audiences with poetic phrases and a plethora of quotes penned by great ancient scholars. I'm tired of being around people who express a love for the idea of the unity of humankind, but who refuse to do anything to implement the idea. I'm tired of appearing on television and radio programs that are more show than substance, more heat than light. I'm tired of participating in human rights meetings where representatives of different organizations come with hidden agendas to consult on ways to settle racial disputes through their methods only. I'm tired, tired,

tired of observing all the activity generated by private and public agencies and individuals operating along the outer boundaries of the racism issue, afraid to plunge into its heart with a commitment to stop the bleedings. I'm sickened by the race relations merchants hawking their wares to image-obsessed corporations and universities that are more interested in a diversity facelift than in undergoing the surgery needed to remove the cancer of racism within then.

All of this frenetic anti-racism activity, costing billions of dollars annually—for what? A nationwide condition where the core of the race problem remains destructive as ever. America's traditional targets of racism need no convincing that there have been no meaningful changes. Their sense of hopelessness and rage, in some respects, is greater today then in previous eras. So much effort is put forth in trying to shed those feelings, without much success. Every day they are faced with the struggle of ending the pain they're afraid will never end. The country's ten million ghetto dwellers, for example, are teased daily—through television—of what they are being denied, which continually intensifies their growing appetite for rebellion—or escape. Not that those men and women of color who have attained materially are fully free; deep down they know they are still viewed as foreigners in their homeland by even poor whites.

Looking to the government for solutions to the race problem is a waste of time. Until our leaders begin to face their own racial conditioning, you can't expect any meaningful guidance from them. Most of the members of Congress are locked in denial, as are our state legislators and local political officials. Besides, being successful politicians, their vision is blurred by the need to follow precedent wedded to principles that are the bedrock of obsolete paradigms, and there's always the need to ascertain the population's greatest interests and directing their energy into satisfying them. Overcoming racism is not what the great majority of America's citizenry is most interested in And after reading this book you know why.

Yet something meaningful must be done to put an end to the scourge of racism, for it is eroding the soul of America. The fact that on a conscious level most Americans aren't aware that this is happening only compounds the problem. What will awaken the nation? Sadly, it hasn't been the cry of those who have suffered the most. Nor has the burning of our cities, which has scared our leaders into some reactive action, but hasn't awakened them.

Despite all of this, I remain an optimist. Not all is lost. There is the beginning of a dim glimmer of light on the horizon that has the potential of awakening America. Grassroots movements based on similar understanding of the nature of racism and how it should be dealt with have sprung up in different parts of the country. The transformation taking place among the participants has inspired onlookers, even some critics, to become involved in these movements. In some places, their impact has been so profound that some schools, churches and local governmental agencies are either using their services or joining one of these movements.

What is encouraging is that some of these movements are collaborating with each other, and in some instances joining forces. Should the networking continue, the various movements would evolve into a master movement, attracting the attention of the nation's most powerful institutions that in the past have proven incapable of solving the racism problem. And when the leadership of these institutions, out of desperation, embrace and apply the movement's philosophy and psychology, the pace of racial healing will quicken across the land, for they will encourage their constituencies to participate in the movement.

But more than that is required, because many men and women don't trust their leaders. To them I say: Because the racism problem begins with each one of us, take the time for some honest introspective reflection regarding your personal racial conditioning. If you are sincere and honest in your self-explorations, you will discover your infection or wound of racism. Don't panic! Don't try to repress what you have discovered about yourself. Discovering a part of you which you find disturbing is the first step toward overcoming it. The next step is to find a way to get rid of what you have discovered about yourself. Become involved in a group like the *Institute for the Healing of Racism*, because trying to heal alone is extremely difficult. In a way, it is like trying to recover from alcoholism without any help from others. Support is necessary, especially from those who are in the same situation as you, or are on the road to recovery.

Stay the course, because in time the pain you experience will evolve into feelings of exaltation. You will be able to see and hear things you never saw or heard before. Insights about other people's condition will make you a more effective healer, a role that will bring great pleasure and satisfaction to you and those you serve. You will become a source of inspiration for others to engage in the healing process. And as more and more women and men become involved in the process, the racism that once gripped their community will weaken and eventually fade away.

I know what that's like, because it has happened to me. Not that I am endowed with a gift no one else possesses. I believe that you can do what I and hundreds of others have been able to do, because all of us have been created with the capacity to play a role in unifying all of the children of God.

Appendix

Establishing an Institute for the Healing of Racism

Suggested Topics

In order to galvanize the members into a strong and committed body, it is necessary for several sessions to be scheduled, at which time topics relating to racism can be discussed. No minimum or maximum number of sessions is required. Participants will be ready to suggest a plan of action when they have attained a spirit of love and harmony amongst themselves.

The following topics are suggested:

1. Defining prejudice and racism.
2. How racism is perpetuated—early childhood experiences, misinformation, and segregation
3. The pathology of the disease of racism and the nature of the wound.
4. Unaware racism—how we've all been infected.
5. Internalized racism—when the anger, hurt and frustration turn inward.
6. Stereotypes and how they affect us.
7. Institutionalized racism—examples of its presence in the systems that affect us daily—media, legal, school, health care, economics.
8. Oneness of humanity—achieving unity and preserving diversity.
9. Ally-building as a way to heal racism—an individual commitment.

Guidelines for Sharing

- Sharing is voluntary.
- We want to create a safe, loving, and respectful atmosphere.
- Sharing is about one's own feelings, experiences and perceptions, etc.
- We are not always going to agree, or see everything the same way, and that's okay.
- Each person has a right to and responsibility for his or her own feelings, thoughts and beliefs.
- It is important to avoid criticism or judgment about another person's sharing and point of view or his or her feelings.
- Avoid getting tied up in debate and argument. It rarely changes anything to anyone, and tends to ultimately inhibit the sharing.
- We can only change ourselves. Our change and growth may, however, inspire someone else.
- Refrain from singling out any individual as "representing" his or her group or issue.
- It is important to give full attention to whomever is talking.
- Feelings are important.
- We will surely make mistakes in our efforts, but mistakes are occasions for learning and forgiving.
- We came together to try to learn about the disease of racism and promote a healing process.
- We may laugh and cry together, share pain, joy, fear and anger.
- Hopefully, we will leave these meetings with a deeper understanding and a renewed hope for the future of humanity.

Role of the Facilitator

Facilitators must be able to present both the purpose and format of the healing circle in a clear, concise and attractive manner.

Facilitators must be careful to set an example of the kind of behavior that they are striving to encourage in the participants.

Facilitators should find themselves being excited about the process of healing racism, and plan actions leading their own transformation.

Facilitators should act as instructors by helping participants look for key ideas and find implications for action.

Facilitators should carefully guide the group so that it functions within its intended purpose.

Facilitators must help individuals in the group reflect spiritual attributes, such as personal dignity, courtesy and reliability during sessions.

Facilitators should foster honest communication that is both tactful and constructive, and should themselves be good listeners.

Facilitators must accept in a nonjudgmental manner the values and feelings of the group participants, and be able to feed back to the group in a positive, loving way what they perceive, hear and see without adding their own attitudes, feelings and prejudices.

Guidelines for Facilitators

Become familiar with exercises/outline before entering the meeting.
—What points do you want to bring out in the discussion?
—What issues do you think the group will bring up?

Arrive early to be abreast of any last-minute instructions.
—Create necessary seating arrangement (if applicable).

State purpose of session and begin with introductions.
—Give general outline of events to take place during the workshop.
—Be concise in your statements.
—Do some kind of icebreaker activity to make group fell comfortable, at ease with you. (They will be somewhat familiar with each other.)
—Show enthusiasm.

Use listening skills.
—Listen for content and context of statements as well as affective level.
—As questions to check accuracy of what you're hearing: "Do you mean?"
—Paraphrase the person's comments in nonjudgmental terms: "Are you saying you never thought about white privilege?"

Feedback is descriptive rather than evaluative. By describing one's own reaction, you leave the individual free to use the feedback as he or she sees fit. By avoiding evaluative language, you reduce the likelihood of a defensive reaction.

Be flexible and maintain some control of the group.

—Do not let one person monopolize conversation.

—Do not let one person get ganged up on, or allow a two-way debate between participants.

—Draw the quiet or passive participant into the discussion.

—Be assertive without intimidating.

—Roadblocks may arise in the discussion. Use feedback at times like this. Highlight a group dynamic you see active; be open (yet selective) to sharing from your own experience. You may also want to circle back to a previous comment. People may still need/want to talk, but do not know where to go. In these cases relate their last comment with an inflection that makes it into a question.

—Do not be afraid of silence. Do not put words into participants mouths or succumb to the urge to steer them to what you feel is a right answer. Try and be comfortable with a participant's inability to be articulate about the point, recognizing, however, what the person has tried to say. Be affirming, supportive and directive where possible.

Leave time for closure.

—Try to leave people feeling empowered to change rather than depressed.

-- Stress that this is only a beginning. Encourage them to seek other resources and continue working on these issues.

Some close-out questions.

—What have you learned today?

—What have you thought about in a new way this morning/afternoon?

—What concerns have challenged you? Can we brainstorm about potential things to do?

—How can we stay in touch to discuss future developments involving the diverse issue we explored today?

Notes

Chapter One

    1. Takaki, Ronald, *A Different Mirror: A History of Multicultural America*, p.85

    2. Frady, Marshall, *An American Family*, <u>New Yorker, April 29-May 6 1996</u>, p. 157

    3. Ashe, Arthur and Arnold Ramersad, *Days of Grace*, p. 126

    4. Martin, Waldo E. Jr., *The Mind of Fredrick Douglass*, p. 23

    5. Bouwsma, Angela, *My Turn*, <u>Newsweek</u>, February 24, 1997, p. 15

    6. Takaki, p. 9

    7. *Ibid.*, p. 173

    8. Zinn, Howard, *A People's History of the United States*, p. 153

    9. *Ibid.*, p. 407

Chapter Two

    1. Shepherd, Paul, Associated Press, <u>New Hampshire Sunday News</u>, Manchester, NH, November 17, 1996

    2. Zinn, p. 86

    3. Blais, Madeleine, *In These Girls, Hope is a Muscle*, p. 27

    4. *Ibid.*, pp. 27,28

Chapter Three

    1. Weatherford, Jack, *Indian Givers*, p.135

    2. Ibid, pp. 62, 63

    3. Franklin, John Hope, *Slavery to Freedom: A History of Negro Americans*, p. 27

    4. Hyman, Mark, *Blacks Before Africa*, pp. 55, 56

    5. *Ibid.*, p. 21

    6. Bennett, Lerone Jr., *Before the Mayflower: A History of Black America*, p. 19

    7. Murchie, Guy, *Seven Mysteries of Life*, p. 345

    8. *Ibid.*, pp. 356, 357

    9. Tiger Lionel, *Trump Race Card*, <u>Wall Street Journal</u>, February 23, 1996

    10. Cavalli-Sforza, Luca, *The Great Human Diaspora*, p. 237

11. Robert S. Boyd, *Scientists: Idea of Race is Only Skin Deep*, <u>Miami Herald</u>, October 13, 1996 p. 14A

12. Rensberger, Boyce, *A Look at Race Without the Old Labels*, <u>Springfield Union-News</u> (Washington Post Syndication), February 3, 1995

13. Star, Rita, *Race: How Many Are There*, p.1

Chapter Four

1. Zinn, p. 341

2. *Ibid.*, pp. 339, 340

3. *Ibid.*, p. 230, 231

4. Smith, Charles D, *Palestine and the Arab-Israeli Conflict*, pp. 120, 121, 130, 133

Chapter Five

1. Zinn, p. 15

2. *Ibid.*, p. 33

3. Conrad, Earl, *The Invention of the Negro*, p. 57

4. Fishel, Leslie H Jr. and Benjamin Quarles, T*he Black American: A Documentary History*, p. 54

5. Koch, Adrienne and Eilliam Peden, *The Life and Selected Writings of Thomas Jefferson*, p. 256

6. Conrad, pp. 84, 85

7. *Ibid.*, pp. 102, 103

8. *Ibid.*, p.103

9. *Ibid.*, 105

10. Fishel and Quarles, pp. 204, 205

11. Zinn, pp. 183, 184

12. *Ibid.*, p. 373

13. Popkin, Richard, *The High Road to Pyrrhonism*, San Diego, Austin Hill, 1980, p. 93

Chapter Six

1. Rutstein and Morgan, *Healing Racism: Education's Role*, pp. 4 through 7

2. Burns, Ken, *The West*, a Public Broadcasting Service documentary, shown on WGBY-TV, Springfield, Ma. September 24, 1996.

3. Rutstein and Morgan, pp. 4 through 7

4. Davenport, Frances Gardner, *European Treaties Bearing on the History of the United States and Its Dependencies*, 254, I, p. 23

5. Wilson, James A, *The Cabot Voyages and Bristol Discovery Under Henry VII*, pp. 49 through 53, 204, 205

6. Takaki, pp. 39, 40

7. Conrad, p. 34

8. Goodman, Nathan G., Editor, *A Benjamin Franklin Reader*, pp. 155, 156

9. O'Brein, Coner Cruise, *Thomas Jefferson:Radical and Racist*, Atlantic Monthly, October 1996. pp. 64 through 74

10. Miller Bradford, *Returning to Seneca Falls*, pp. 48, 49

11. Darling, Wendy, OP-ED page, Collegian, University of Massachusetts-Amherst daily newspaper, February 21, 1996

12. Takaki, p.10

13. Rutstein and Morgan, *Healing Racism: Education's Role*, pp. 63 through 65

14. Stossell, John, *20/20*, television program ABC TV, April 19, 1996

15. Rutstein and Morgan, *Healing Racism: Education's Role*, p. 25

16. Brandt, Allen. *Racism and Research: The Case of the Tuskegee Syphlis Study*, The Hastings Center Report, 1978; 8 (No. 6), pp. 21 through 29.

17. Napolean, Harold, *Yauyaraq: The Way of the Human Being*, pp. 12, 13

18, *Ibid.*, p. 14

19. *Ibid.*, pp. 15, 27

20. Morganthau, Austin Wright, McCormick, Manly, *It's Not Just New York*, Newsweek, March 9, 1992, p. 9

21. McCall Nathan, *Makes Me Wanna Holler*, 1995, p.346

22. Cavalli-Sforza, Luca, *The Great Human Diaspora*, p. 244

Chapter Seven

1. DeMott, Benjamin, *Put on a Happy Face*, Harper's, September 1995, p. 33

2. Statistics cited by the Bureau of Indian Affairs, Washington, D.C., 1995

3. Rockwell, Paul, *A White Man's Case for Affirmative Action*, The Dallas Weekly, April 4, 1996, p.8

Chapter Eight

1. Takaki, p. 197; Zinn, p. 259. The TV documentary, *The West*, Public Broadcasting System, segment seven, Ken Burns, ex-

ecutive producer, shown on WGBY-TV, Springfield, Massachusetts, October 1, 1996

    2. Motley, Mary Penick, *The Invisible Soldier: The Experience of the Black Soldier, World War Two*, p. 26

    3. Austin, Lettie J, Lewis H. Federson and Sophie P. Nelson, *The Black Man and the Promise of America*, p. 494

    4. Excerpted from a column by Richard Reeves, O.J. *Aftermath Shows America in Trouble*, Springfield Union-News, October 16, 1995, Springfield, Massachusetts, p. A6

    5. Frazer, Steven, *The Bell Curve Wars*, p.3

    6. *McNeil Lehrer Report*, (A national television newscast) Public Broadcast Service, October 17, 1995

Chapter Nine

    1. Goodman, Gary Scott, *Rhetoric of Meir Kahane of the Jewish Defense League*, a Dissertation presented to the Faculty of the Graduate School of the University of Southern California, Sept., 1978, p. 33.

    2. *The World Book, Volume 1*, Field Enterprises Educational Corporation, Chicago, 1967, p. 215

    3. Marius, Richard, *Luther: A Biography*, pp. 235 through 243

    4. Gates, Louis Henry Jr., *A liberalism of Heart and Spine*, New York Times Op-Ed, March 27, 1994

    5. Lincoln, C. Eric, *Race, Religion and the Continuing American Dilemma*, p. 179

    6. Stroker, Philip, *American Jews: Community in Crisis*, p. 29

    7. Sacker, Howard M, *A History of the Jews in America*, pp. 74, 75, 76

Chapter Ten

    1. Weatherford, Jack, *Native Roots*, p. 6

    2. Weatherford, Jack, *Indian Givers*, pp. 61, 62, 63, 70, 73, 80 through 87

    3. Irving, Washington, *The Adventures of Captain Bonneville*, p. 171

    4. Bigelow, John, *The Complete Works of Benjamin Franklin, Chapter Two*, pp. 210, 365, 366; Weatherford, Indian Givers, pp. 135, 136; Commanger, Documents of American History (6th edition), p. 44

    5. Weatherford, *Indian Givers*, pp. 138, 139

    6. Gladwell, Malcolm, *Black Like Me*, New Yorker, April 29-May 6, p. 77

7. Steele, Claude M, *Race and the Schooling of Black Americans*, Atlantic Monthly, April, 1992

8. Morgan, Harry, *How Schools Fail Black Children*, Social Policy, January-February, 1980, pp. 49 through 54

9. Excerpted from an artcle in Emerge, *James Baldwin Remembered by Wilham Lowe Jr.*, October 1989, p. 55

10. Bureau of Justice statistics, 1995

11. Quoted in a column by William Raspberry, *Statistics Distort Truth About Black Men*, Springfield Union-News, April 5, 1996, p. A15

12. Interview with Hector Lopez by Ala Moshiri, in an article entitiled *Changing Fields*, One Magazine, Vol. 1, Issue 8, p.16

13. Orfield, Gary, *Harvard Graduate School of Education Study—Growth of Segregation in American Schools*, 1993

14 Rutstein, Nathan, and Michael Morgan, *Healing Racism: Education's Role*, p. 35

Chapter Eleven

1. Washington, James M., *The Essential Writings and Speeches of Martin Luther King Jr.*, p.101

2. Fishel and Quarles, *The Black American: A Documentary History*, p.141

3. Lincoln, C. Eric, *Race, Religion and the Continuing American Dilemma*, p. 240

4. *Ibid.*, pp. 100, 101

5. Fishel and Quarles, pp. 114, 115

6. Foner, Philip S, *Selections from the Writings of Fredrick Douglass*, p. 52

7. Lincoln, C. Eric, pp. 107, 108; Oates pp. 197, 400

8. Oates, p. 157

9. *Ibid.*, p. 150

10. Lincoln, C. Eric, p. 99

11. Oates, pp. 252, 253

12. Washington, James, *The Essential Writings And Speeches Of Martin Luther King Jr.*, pp. 501, 502

13. Lincoln, C. Eric, pp. 75 through 76; Fishel and Quarles, pp. 83 through 94

14. Excerpted from an editorial in the New Pittsburgh Courier, February 15, 1992

15. Williams, James A. and Ted Jefferson, *The Black Men's Bahá'í Gathering: A Spiritual Transformation*, pp. 5 through 11

16. Erickson, C. Eric, *Life History and the Historical Movement*, p. 47

Chapter Twelve
(none)

Chapter Thirteen
1. Schafer, Udo, *Beyond the Clash of Religions*, pp. 26 - 28
2. *Ibid.*, p. 30
3. Murchie, Guy, p. 610
4. *Ibid.*, p. 238
5. Haller, John, *Outcasts Of Evolution*, p. 4

Chapter Fourteen
(none)

Chapter Fifteen
1. Poem excerpted from Julius Lester's article titled, *In Memorium: In Gratitude for Robert Hayden*, <u>World Order Magazine</u>, Vol. 16, Number 1, p. 54
2. *Ibid.*, p. 55
3. Rutstein, Nathan, *To Be One: A Battle Against Racism*, pp. 86, 87
4. Rutstein and Morgan, *Healing Racism: Education's Role*, pp. 142, 143
5. Excerpted from a videotape of Rodney Belcher's funeral in Kampala, Uganda, March 12, 1996. The video was produced by the friends of the Belcher family.

Bibliography

Ashe, Arthur and Arnold Rampersad, *Days of Grace*, Alfred A. Knopf, 1993.

Austin, Lettie J., Lewis H. Federson, Sophie P. Nelson, *The Black Man and the Promise of America*, Scott, Foresman and Company, 1970.

Baha'u'llah, *Hidden Words*, U.S. Bahá'í Publishing Trust, 1979, (Reprint).

Bancroft, Fredric, *Slave-Trading in the Old South*, J.H. Furst Company, 1931.

Bennett, Lerone Jr., *Before the Mayflower: A History of Black America*, 5th Edition, 1982.

Bigelow, John, Editor, *The Complete Works of Benjamin Franklin*, G. P. Putnam's Sons, 1887.

Blais, Madeleine, *In These Girls, Hope is a Muscle*, Warner Books, 1996.

Brandt, Allan, *"Racism and Research: The Case of the Tuskegee Syphilis Study,"* The Hastings Center Report, 1978.

Burns, Ken, Executive Producer, *"The West"*, (a TV documentary series), Public Broadcasting System, 1996.

Cavalli-Sforza, Luca, *The Great Human Diaspora*, Addison-Wesley Publishing Co., 1995.

Chopra, Deepak, *Quantum Healing*, an audiotape series, 1990.

Conrad, Eric, *The Invention of the Negro*, Paul S. Erickson, Inc., 1966.

Davenport, Frances Gardner, Editor, *European Treaties Bearing on the History of the United States and It's Dependencies*, Carnegie Institution of Washington Publications.

DeMott, Benjamin, *Put On A Happy Face*, Harpers, September 1995.

Erickson, Eric, *Life History and the Historical Movement*, W.W. Norton, 1975.

Fishel, Leslie H. Jr., and Benjamin Quarels, *The Black American: A Documentary History*, Scott, Forseman and Company, 1967.

Foner, Philip S, Editor, *Selections from the Writings of Fredrick Douglass*, International Publishers, 1968.

Frady, Marshall, *An American Family*, New Yorker, April 29-May 6, 1996.

Franklin, John Hope, *Slavery to Freedom: A History of Negro Americans*, 3rd Edition, Alfred A. Knopf Inc., 1967.

Frazer, Steven, *The Bell Curve Wars*, Basic Books, 1995.

Gates, Louis Henry, Jr., *A Liberalism of Heart and Spine*, <u>New York Times Op-Ed</u> page, March 27, 1994.

Gladwell, Malcolm, *Black Like Me,* <u>New Yorker</u>, April 29-May 6, 1996.

Goodman, Nathan G., Editor, *A Benjamin Franklin Reader,* Thomas Y. Crowell Company, 1945.

Gould, Stephen Jay, *The Mismeasure of Man*, Norton Publishing, 1981.

Hacker, Andrew, *Two Nations: Black and White, Seperate, Hostile, Unequal*, MacMillan, 1992.

Haller, John, *Outcasts of Evolution*, University of Illinois Press, 1971.

Hughes, Thomas, *A History of the Society of Jesus in North America: Colonial and Federal*, Longman and Green, 1910.

Hyman, Mark, *Black Before Africa*, Africa World Press, 1994.

Irving, Washington, *The Rocky Mountains: The Adventures of Captain Bonneville*, USA, 1837.

King, James C., *The Biology of Race*, University of California Press, 1980.

Koch, Adrienne and William Peden, Editors, *The Life and Selected Writings of Thomas Jefferson*, Modern Library, 1944.

Kozol, Jonathan, *Savage Inequalities*, Crown Publishing, 1991.

Leakey, Richard E. and Roger Lewin, *Origins: What New Discoveries Reveal About the Emergence of Our Species and Its Possible Future*, Dutton, 1977.

Lewontin, Richard C, *Human Diversity*, W. N. Freeman and Company, 1984.

Lincoln, C. Eric, *Race, Religion and the Continuing American Dilemma*, Hill and Wang, 1984.

Lipset, Seymour Martin, *American Exceptionalism: A Double-Edged Sword*, W. W. Norton and Company, 1996.

Lowe, Wilham Jr., *James Baldwin Remembered*, <u>Emerge Magazine</u>, October 1989.

Marius, Richard, *Luther: A Biography*, J.B. Lippicott and Company, 1974.

McCall, Nathan, *Makes Me Wanna Holler*, Vintage Books, 1995.

Martin, Waldo E., Jr., *The Mind of Fredrick Douglass*, University of North Carolina Press, 1984.

Miller, Bradford, *Returning to Seneca Falls*, Lindisfarne Press, 1995.

Morganthau, Tom, Peter Austin, Pat Wright, John McCormick, Howard Manly, *It's Not Just New York*, <u>Newsweek</u>, March 9, 1992.

Morgan, Harry, *How Schools Fail Black Children*, Social Policy, January-February, 1980.

Moshiri, Ala, *Changing Fields,* <u>One</u>, Volume 1, Issue 8, 1997.

Motley, Mary Oenick, *The Invisbile Soldier: The Experiences of the Black Soldier, World War Two*, Wayne State University Press, 1987.

Murchie, Guy, *Seven Mysteries of Life*, Houghton-Mifflin and Company, 1978.

Napolean, Harold, *Yauyaraq: The Body Of The Human Being*, Center of Cross Cultural Studies, University of Alaska-Fairbanks, 1991.

Oates, Stephen B., *Let the Trumpet Sound, the Life of Martin Luther King Jr.*, Harper Row Publishers, 1982.

O'Brien, Coner Cruise, *Thomas Jefferson: Radical and Racist*, <u>Atlantic Monthly</u>, October 1996.

Orfield,Gary, *Growth of Segregation in American Schools*, a Harvard Graduate School of Education Study, 1993.

Rutstein, Nathan, *Healing Racism in America: A Prescription for the Disease*, Whitcomb Publishing, 1993.

Rutstein, Nathan and Michael Morgan, *Healing Racism: Education's Role*, Editors, Whitcomb Publishing, 1996.

Rutstein, Nathan, *To Be One: A Battle Against Racism*, George Ronald, 1988.

Sacker, Howard M., *A History of the Jews in America*, Alfred A. Knopf Inc., 1992.

Schafer, Udo, *Beyond The Clash Of Religions*, Zero Palm Press, 1992.

Smith, Charles D., *Palestine and the Arab-Israelis*, St. Martins Press, 1988.

Star, Rita, *Race: How Many Are There*, Healing Racism Inc., 1996.

Steele, Claude M., *Race and the Schooling of Black Americans*, <u>Atlantic Monthly</u>, April, 1992.

Stossell, John, *20/20*, ABC TV News, April 19, 1996.

Stroker, Philip, *American Jews: Community in Crisis*, Doubleday, 1974.

Takaki, Ronald, *A Different Mirror: A History of Multicultural America*, Little Brown and Company, 1993.

Tiger, Lionel, *Trump, The Race Card*, <u>Wall Street Journal</u>, February 23, 1996.

Washington, James M., Editor, *Selections from the Writings and Speeches of Martin Luther King Jr.*, Harper, 1986.

Weatherford, Jack, *Indian Givers*, Ballentine Books, 1988.

Weatherford, Jack, *Native Roots*, Crown Publishing, 1991.

Williams, James A. and Ted Jefferson, *The Black Men's Bahá'í Gathering : A Spiritual Transformation*, (self published), 1995.

Williamson, Joel, *A Rage for Order*, Oxford University Press, 1986.

Wilson, James A., Editor, *The Cabot Voyages And Bistol Discovery Under Henry VII*, Hakluyt Society Publications, 1962.

Zinn, Howard, *A People's History of the United States*, Harper Perennial, 1980.